FIRE IN THE OUTBACK

JOHN BLACKET

FIRE IN THE OUTBACK

The untold story of the Aboriginal revival movement
that began on Elcho Island in 1979

KHESED

A KHESED PUBLICATION

© John Blacket, 1997

Originally published in 1997 by Albatross Books Pty Ltd
PO Box 320, Sutherland, NSW 2232, Australia
ISBN 0 7324 1055 X

This second edition is published by Khesed Publishing
PO Box 448 Cannington, WA 6987, Australia
Phone: (08) 9451 7213/ +618 9451 7213
Email: admin@khesed.org.au
Website: khesed.org.au

Reprinted 2004, 2009

National Library of Australia
Cataloguing-in-Publication data

Blacket, John
Fire in the Outback: The untold story of the Aboriginal
revival movement that began on Elcho Island in 1979

ISBN 978-0-9581849-2-2

1. Revivals – Australia – History. 2. Revivals – Northern Territory –
Elcho Island – History. 3. Aborigines, Australian – Religion.
4. Aborigines, Australian – Northern Territory – Elcho Island –
Religion. 5. Christianity – Australia – History. 6. Christianity –
Northern Territory – Elcho Island – History. I. Title.

269.240899915

Front cover photograph: Ron Williams and Geoff Stokes erect a cross
in the desert near an Aboriginal site of spiritual significance
Printed by McPherson's Printing Group, Maryborough, Victoria

Contents

To:
Kevin Dhurrkay
Pastor Ben Mason
Galikali (Dianne Buchanan)
Rev. Dr Djiniyini and Gelung Gondarra
Rev. Ron and Diana Williams

Foreword

As a Christian Aboriginal, it's a great privilege for me to acknowledge in this book some of the great things that God has done in our time. In 1979, we had revival that began at Galiwin'ku, Elcho Island and it affected the whole of Arnhem Land. It spread south-west to Warburton Ranges, and then north-west to the Kimberleys. We also had teams going to north Queensland to minister and spread the revival.

This has set a course for the church at Galiwin'ku to become an outreach church. Ever since that revival, we have been going to places and sharing what God has done and what he is still doing. I am one of the products of that revival and I'm not the only one. There are a few of us still on fire for the Lord. Every year, on March 14, we celebrate that spiritual awakening and pray for a fresh touch from God through the power of his Holy Spirit. These are exciting times for the church in Australia. We must *repent* more and more so that times of refreshing will come to our churches.

Since 1977-1978, I have had the privilege of working as community worker with John Blacket. He is one of the *Balanda* (white man) staff who witnessed that revival from the very beginning. My perception is that John is a different man now since the revival. John is one of those people who can communicate to an Aboriginal person anywhere, because he has learned to listen and understand *Yolngu* (Aborigines), then takes the time to share with them. I admire him for this task and particularly for his endurance and patience with people. Now God has given him this important ministry of reconciliation and bridging of Christian *Balanda* and *Yolngu* in Australia. We want to see unity come to the church of God right across the land, then we will see revival come to the whole of this Great South Land of the Holy Spirit. This book is a milestone for that revival. I would like to commend John in his careful efforts in documenting and compiling these anointed stories. I'm sure you are going to enjoy reading this book and will be blessed by the Lord.

Alan Maratja Dhamarrandji
Galiwin'ku, Northern Territory, 1996

Preface

The Lord said, 'Ezekiel, son of man, turn towards the south and warn the forests that I, the Lord God, will start a fire that will burn up every tree, whether green and dry. Nothing will be able to put out the blaze of that fire as it spreads to the north and burns everything in its path. Everyone will know that I started it and that it cannot be stopped.'

But I complained, 'Lord God, I don't want to do that! People already say I confuse them with my messages.'

Ezekiel 20: 45-49

DURING A PRAYERTIME IN KHESED MINISTRIES' first council meeting on 10 August 1989, one of those present felt God was saying: 'There is a book that is to be written from what I show you to train others for this ministry, for many other labourers are needed in this work.' The idea had been raised a month earlier, but I didn't want to hear that!

I thought: 'There are plenty of books around that do that' and I deliberately pushed it right to the back of my mind, 'awaiting further enlightenment', which really meant, 'buried as deeply as possible'. But I knew God had spoken to me.

In January 1990, I was attending the Central Australian Christian Convention in Alice Springs. Some of the Elcho Island men told us what God had done in that powerful move of the Holy Spirit in their community around 1979.

After the meeting, a group of us were talking about it and Ben Mason, Aboriginal chairman of the convention, said: 'Someone needs to go around and collect all the stories and write them in a book.' I knew that this was the book which had been spoken about the previous August and that I was the person to write it.

I am greatly indebted to Ben Mason for that challenge and for his continued encouragement to me in this project. It really is a result of his vision and desire for reconciliation between black and white in this land, for the evangelisation of all people and for a mature discipleship.

This book has been written for:

* Aborigines — it is *their* story of God at work among them;
* those whose work among Aborigines involves receiving them and learning from them and letting them minister to them;
* those who may never meet an Australian Aborigine, but whose heart cry to God will help his great work to happen through them — for it is not finished: it has hardly started yet!
* All Australians who are looking for important clues for Australia and its people for the next ten years of development.

The book has taken me seven years of travelling around Australia, recording stories, asking questions, transcribing tapes, writing, editing, rewriting and sending letters to staff who were involved. I want to express my thanks to my family, who allowed me to be away from home for long periods during a time of heavy demands in our family life. I particularly want to thank my wife, June, who not only worked as a teacher to support the family so that I could work on this project, but also spent many hours encouraging me, praying for me, transcribing tapes, reading drafts and working with me on it.

My thanks also goes to all those who contributed to its production:

* with stories of their own personal lives and struggles, and what they know of God's work in the renewal movement;
* through hospitality to me;
* by giving funds for travel and other expenses;
* by transcribing tapes of interviews and manuscripts — spending many hours, sometimes on tapes of very poor sound quality, many of them being interviews with people who spoke limited English with very heavy Aboriginal accents, using many impossible-sounding names as well as words from their own language they believed I knew or they couldn't express in English; especially Alison Hill, whose contribution totalled hundreds of pages typed into the computer;
* in editing and commenting on the many editions of the manuscript, especially Ken Goodlet at Albatross Books. This also includes many hours of discussions with anthropologist Dr John Rudder. His advice and comments have been invaluable.
* in encouraging, advising, praying and contributing in any way: I believe you will hear the Master say to you, 'Thanks. Well done!'

Ultimately, all the credit for anything of value in this work belongs to God alone, and the failings are mine.

I have tried to let people tell their own stories in their own words as much as possible, but have taken the liberty to edit their words for clarity and flow of the story, sometimes without acknowledging the editing. In a few cases, I have changed names to save people from embarrassment, but this has not always been possible.

Some have sought to label this move of God with terms like 'charismatic'. Right from the beginning, I tried to stop such divisive and judgmental squeezing of God's work into human categories. Unfortunately, some of the story tells the sad results of this sort of thing, which at times is nothing short of what Jesus spoke about in Mark 3, verse 29 — blaspheming against the Holy Spirit.

The Apostle John wrote at the end of his Gospel:

> There are also many other things which Jesus did; were every one of them to be written, I suppose that the world itself could not contain the books that would be written. But these are written that you may believe that Jesus is the Christ, the Son of God.
>
> John 21: 25; 20: 30-31

I am very conscious that there are many gaps: untold stories, people I have not quoted, places and issues I have not touched upon. . . Many people have drifted away from the Lord and were too ashamed to talk to me about what God did. I was surprised to find that even many Aborigines with a very strong oral tradition have forgotten important details over the intervening fifteen years.

Some may be disappointed that I have not dealt with issues like social justice, Aboriginal land rights, organisations like the Aboriginal Evangelical Fellowship, United Aborigines Mission or Uniting Aboriginal and Islander Christian Congress, or what happened at Amata or Halls Creek, or. . . There are many issues that I would love to have dealt with in some detail.

I have deliberately concentrated on Elcho Island and Warburton Ranges. As far as I know, it was not until 1979 at Galiwin'ku that a powerful community-changing move of Holy Spirit power occurred among Aborigines. It seems to me that most of the powerful moves of the Holy Spirit amongst the Australian Aborigines have stemmed from this in some way. I am also quite aware that a lot happened in the communities around Galiwin'ku and in Central Australia [such as Milingimbi, Yirrkala, Ernabella and Amata]. There have also been significant moves of the Holy Spirit in the Kimberley, Pilbara, the south-west of Western Australia and other places which have been totally ignored in this story.

However, the scope of this book is quite large enough for one project. I believe it was defined by God as being the spiritual dimensions of a particular move of Holy Spirit power, and the things which I perceived to be directly involved in that. No doubt others will see it differently to me. I am very conscious that historians and others will criticise *my* efforts and those of my colleagues — God and time have already weighed some of our efforts! I have tried to write what God has been showing me *now*, with a deep sense of gratitude even to those whose actions I have criticised here who have persevered under incredible difficulties.

After studying the events involved in this revival, one thing stands out: it was *God* who prepared the way for this move of his Holy Spirit. . . in people like Harry Makarrwala. . . in visions and dreams. . . in sacrifices and teaching. . . in signs and wonders. . . in healings and struggles. . . in personal relationships. . . in meetings when God's power was clearly evident, and many people's lives were changed — some permanently.

I constantly thank God for the privilege of being involved in this story and of bringing it to you, and I pray you will be able to enjoy the challenges and thrills of God's purposes in renewing this land of Australia as its indigenous 'host' people and all its migrants pool their skills to work together in God's wisdom and power.

John Blacket
Perth, June 1997

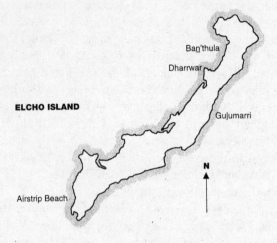

Ban'thula

Dharrwar

ELCHO ISLAND

Guḻumarri

N

Airstrip Beach

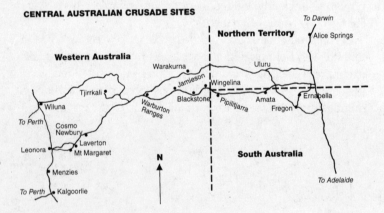

CENTRAL AUSTRALIAN CRUSADE SITES

To Darwin

Northern Territory

Alice Springs

Western Australia

Warakurna

Uluru

Jamieson

Tjirrkali

Wingelina

Blackstone

Warburton Ranges

Pipiliṯjarra

Amata

Ernabella

To Perth

Wiluna

Cosmo Newbury

Fregon

Leonora

Laverton

Mt Margaret

N

South Australia

Menzies

To Perth

Kalgoorlie

To Adelaide

KEY Crusade trips

———————— March – September 1982
– – – – – – – September – November 1982
–··–··–··– Eastern States
··········· Pitjantjatjara

1993

Cape York

Aurukun

Croker Is
Goulburn Is
Maningrida
Milingimbi
Elcho Is
Nhulunbuy
Yirrkala
Groote
Eylandt

Darwin
Oenpelli
Gapuwiyak
Katherine
Roper
River

Wyndham
Kununurra
Turkey Creek
Noonkanbah

Halls
Creek

Fitzroy Crossing

Strolley

Port Hedland

Jigalong

Meekatharra

Geraldton

Perth

Pinjarra
Gnowangerup

Esperance

Kalgoorlie

Leonora

Mt. Margaret

Wiluna

Warburton Ranges

Warakurna

Jameson

Blackstone

Amata

Ernabella
Fregon

Hermannsburg

Yuendumu

Rabbit Flat

Tennant Creek

Alice Springs

QLD

NSW

VIC

Canberra

Berri

SA

NT

WA

Introduction

An Overview

ON 13 MARCH 1979, WIRRIYI, a quietly-spoken Aboriginal man from Elcho Island, had this vision:

> A big fire came down at the other end of Galiwin'ku [Elcho] Island. The fire came down onto the land, set the dry grass ablaze on the sand dunes and immediately spread across to the north-east and north-west points of the island.

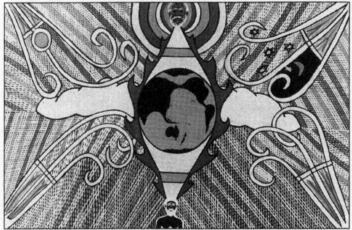

The painting by Gelung Gondarra shows the globe of the world (centre, with oceans in yellow ochre and land in black), God the Father (centre top) and the human race (centre bottom). In the corners are the four winds, top left is the sun and top right is the moon and stars, with the clouds across the centre.[1]

Then, it started coming this way like a bushfire, very slowly. It was burning up everything — all the trees and plants — and moving south through the grasslands, mangroves, open bushland and jungles.

Everything fell down and was destroyed. It totally destroyed all the trees, even the largest of trees from which the dugout canoes are made. It destroyed all the rubbish and buildings and steel girders and sheets of iron. Everything was burnt up, leaving nothing but very hot sand — like ashes — after it.

Nothing else was left at all.

At the same time, following straight after the fire, the grass was coming up green and, straightaway, the trees were grown up with flowers and fruit. They were really beautiful, like I've never seen before, like the Garden of Eden or Heaven.

The fire came right down here and over to the next island between here and the mainland and stopped there. When it arrived at my house, I was asleep. The fire touched me like an electric shock and threw me over the sand dunes to Wolmangur.

At the same time, I heard God's words coming from the tongues of the fire: his message in the fire. He said: 'That fire is the life of *Yolngu* [Aborigines]. That is for the end, for the future. If the *Yolngu* live like that fire — if your life is like the fire, burnt up — then, after it grows new life, it will be really good.'

In my spirit, I was there with the fire. It was like I was looking down at the fire and the island and I could see myself in there and I heard the voice. I wanted to run away from the fire back to the ocean, but I heard God's voice and I don't want to run away from God, so I stopped there.

The fire came and I fell down dead — my body was burnt to ashes. Inside, in the depths of my spirit, God was saying, 'That fire is my word! Anybody who believes my word will do that.'

As I stood there looking at myself burned to ashes, I saw the new life coming to me with the green grass and God's new life.[2]

✦ Fire as the essential symbol of the Elcho Island revival

The day following Wirriyi's vision, the church at Galiwin'ku on Elcho Island saw such a powerful expression of God's presence that they have celebrated 14 March every year since then as the day God brought revival.

Many others had dreams and visions around that time, some of which also included the image of fire. Buthimang, also from Elcho Island, told me of some of them and then he explained what he saw as its purpose: 'It was to encourage the people and give us excitement to keep singing praise to God, singing a new song in our own language to praise him.'[3]

I was one of those people who were encouraged in a similar way in a vision. I was a white missionary at Elcho Island in 1978, when the church asked me to move to Alice Springs to do a seemingly impossible task. I felt powerless and cried out to God. Then, God spoke to me in January 1979 and said:

> I will renew the land from the beginning![4] I have lit a fire at Elcho! That's what I did last year. . . the struggles. . . that night of prayer. . . I have lit a spark there that will light fires all over the land! It will go from black to black all over the land and from black to white. I will renew the whole land and it will go beyond Australia to other lands.

That vision gave me a sense of expectancy and direction for my new work in Central Australia. This helped prepare Aborigines, missionaries and others for the move of God's Holy Spirit which followed there as well.

Fire has an essential role in regeneration in Australia. It breaks open the seedpods, allowing the rain to generate new life. It is also an image used in the Bible for the Holy Spirit. Australia, and the South Pacific, has been called *Terra Australis Espiritu Santo* — the Great South Land of the Holy Spirit.

The fire and the Holy Spirit, then, are essentially linked with Australia.

This new move of the Holy Spirit began amongst Australia's Aboriginal people at Galiwin'ku, Elcho Island in 1979 and spread across the land. This book tells the story of how that happened and some of its results.

✦ The spread of revival from Elcho Island to Aboriginal communities throughout Australia

As a result of the events at Galiwin'ku in 1979, people suddenly became more aware of God's presence: they wanted to be with God and with each other like never before. Long-standing fights between families were healed. There was a concern for other families and a deep desire to be with them and with God. There were miracles and there were healings but, probably much more significantly, there were healings of relationships.

At the end of 1978, there had been less than fifty Aborigines who went to church at Galiwin'ku. After the events of 14 March 1979, there were over two hundred meeting together and worshipping God for three or four hours or more every night of the week — and there were only around eleven hundred people living in the town, half of whom were children!

During 1978, evangelist Dan Armstrong had been invited to come from Canberra to Galiwin'ku for a mission. He arrived at the beginning of May 1979 with a small group from New South Wales, just six weeks after the revival started. They found that they had come, as they put it, 'on the crest of a wave'. During the time they were there, the numbers grew to over five hundred and every family on the island was touched in some way by the revival.

News started to spread to nearby islands and communities. People came to visit their relatives and experienced for themselves the renewing life. They went back to their communities and shared what they had found, telling of a new dimension to their faith. Very soon the invitations began to pour in to the Galiwin'ku church: 'Come and share it with us!' As a result, groups of Elcho Christians moved out all over Arnhem Land and beyond to share their new understandings.

In August that year, the first Central Australian Christian Convention was to be held in Alice Springs and I had invited a group from Elcho Island to attend. About thirty of the Elcho Islanders joined hundreds of locals who began to discover from the Elcho Christians something of this new relationship with God. These desert people then went back to their communities and talked with others about what they had heard and experienced.

This was the beginning of the revival which had a transforming effect in a large number of Aboriginal communities spread over north Australia in 1979 and 1980.

Then, in 1981, a small group of Elcho Islanders went to Warburton Ranges community in the middle of the Western Australian Desert. That community had become known as one of the worst Aboriginal communities in Australia, but in one weekend it was radically transformed. The people from the Warburton Ranges began to share what they had received with others in Western Asutralia and, wherever they went, whole towns were transformed, leaving government officials puzzled and amazed. Teams travelled from Western Australia into South Australia, Victoria and New South Wales, visiting mostly Aboriginal communities and bringing hope, release and new life.

✦ The aftermath of the Aboriginal revival

After experiencing God's power and miracles came learning to hear God's whispers. Listening came through facing up to criticism and diversion which began to come from within the church. New Aboriginal Christians and their leaders began to feel intimidated, confused, overly cautious and distracted by temptations.

But Aboriginal Christians had to learn to listen to God in new ways. God's fire had begun doing a deeper work, dealing with lusts, distractions and demonic powers. The intimidation, confusion and temptation caused many to leave the church. Most of them, however, still believe in God and know that what they experienced at that time was real. Now, they are learning to hear and obey God's gentle whispers in the clamour of the world around them.

Today, there is a hunger for a greater understanding of God — for the spectacular and for things even greater than before, but also for a much deeper relationship with him than in the past.

In the years since the revival, most of the 'froth and bubble' and excitement has gone, replaced by a deepening of faith. They are seeing the gospel as something which affects the whole of life, requiring a new understanding of caring for the poor, of justice and of relationships. There has also been a struggle to work through the relationship between the gospel and Aboriginal culture.

They have struggled to see how they can use their own dance, music styles and instruments in Christian worship, wondering what changes *can* be made and what spiritual powers are involved. They have struggled over pastoring their churches effectively and consistently; over how to effectively evangelise their own people and the world; over finding their own authentic ways to worship God; and over reconciliation. Groups of Aborigines are now going to whites and asking forgiveness for their attitudes of resentment and hatred towards them — despite all the injustice, hatred and oppression they experienced from the whites.

A whole new Aboriginal church structure is also emerging out of the revival. The Uniting Church in Australia has responded to the vision and requests of Aboriginal leaders by establishing the Uniting Aboriginal and Islander Christian Congress, giving Aboriginal Christians the freedom and some of the resources needed to become the church of Jesus Christ in whatever way they feel God is leading them as Christians. Some other denominations are taking similar steps.

But there is something much deeper than structure that is emerging, something free of Western style and methods and world view.

There is a vibrant new Christian life in many of the 'outstations' or 'homelands', where family groups have moved away from the tensions of larger communities to their own clan land. At least one of these has been designated as a place of prayer and Christian renewal and many of them have a cleared area with a cross as a focal point in the community.

There is a vibrant new life among children and teenagers, especially in these outstations. The sense of the presence of God as they dance and worship is not found among many adults anywhere, but those who are present cannot help being drawn into God's joy and peace.

There is also a commitment to prayer for the whole nation among many, which is growing.

There have been many prophecies about Australia and about the Aborigines bringing revival. There have been prophecies about Aborigines having a key place in the revival — even that it would be tribal people from the desert who would bring such revival to Australia — that it cannot happen without them and will spread across the world from Australia. Similar words have been spoken in America, South Africa and other countries about Australian Aborigines.

There is an expectancy and excitement building. There is a developing unity and reconciliation across churches and races.

The story that follows is told to encourage you. I believe you will find that it is not just for people interested in

Australian Aborigines, revivals or church history, but is also important for you, whoever you are. It is told so that we can learn from the account of the way God prepared Aborigines for revival; learn from the stories of the quenching and inadequacies of the revival; and learn from the stories hope, expectancy and excitement as we discover more of God's nature and plans.

1

Gathering firewood

THE BACKGROUND TO
ABORIGINAL REVIVAL TO 1900

GOD WAS ALREADY IN AUSTRALIA BEFORE 1788. Before we hear
the stories of the revival amongst Aboriginal people, we need
to set the scene by looking at the traditional spirituality of
those who were here before Western settlement.

There are no written records or movies of the situation
before outside contact, but Aboriginal life stories — their
paintings, songs, dances and their meanings — are etched
into their spirits, minds and hearts. These stories tell about
how things came to be like they are — how the emu lost its
wings, how that hill or this waterhole came to be. They are
often called 'Aboriginal dreaming', but some Aborigines object to this non-Aboriginal word because it implies that the
stories are not true, but are only dreams and made-up stories.
One of Australia's leading Aboriginal theologians, Rev. Dr
Djiniyini Gondarra, underlines the importance of the stories
when he says: 'The stories deal with the law of the land.'[1]

Where did Aborigines get these stories from? That's a
whole world that Aborigines are starting to explore.

Did Aborigines worship God before Christianity came to
Australia? Some people claim that Aborigines were animists,
worshipping rocks, plants or animals. It is more appropriate

to suggest that they worshipped ancestral spirits, but they did not worship the rocks, plants or animals any more than Christians worship the cross of Jesus Christ. Precisely *what* they worshipped may be argued, but the first Christian missionaries to arrive in Australia did not come into a spiritual vacuum. They were coming to a people with a deep understanding of the Creator.

✦ The God of traditional Aboriginal spirituality

Djiniyini wrote in one of his booklets:

> God was already active in Aboriginal people and was already present with our ancestors long before the early missionaries came to our country.[2]

Aborigines are a spiritual people, very aware of spirits and spiritual powers around them, including the Creator Spirit. Djilipa, an Aboriginal Christian from Elcho Island, told me about God like this:

> God, his Spirit, has been moving in the beginning. And before missionaries came through to this island, our people, *Yolngu*, were living here. We didn't know God's name, but God was there. He has revealed himself already and God has spoken through our people, but they didn't know God's names and Jesus' name before the early missionary came here.[3]

Djilipa's brother, Rronang, a Uniting Church minister lecturing at Nungalinya College in Darwin, told me this:

> [Here is] a little bit of the story that I heard from the old people:
>
> There is a Creator Spirit, and that big Creator Spirit made the universe. There is another spirit that can make us enemies to each other, so we fight.
>
> The old people who've been given this law usually say, 'But we have to do a little part: we have to obey.' I don't know who gave that law! Somebody gave that law to the old people, but we don't want to go against it, otherwise

we put ourselves into trouble.

It's very hard to mention the Creator Spirit's name because he's so great! We shouldn't mention his name or search for him. It wasn't so much they didn't know the name of God, but it's too holy, too big. But they are not really sure what his name is.[4]

This Aboriginal expression of the significance of names sounds similar to the Jewish attitude, where they never spoke the name of their God, Yahweh [Jehovah]. Rronang told me how some of the old stories had helped his people to know about God as they looked and thought about the world he created. He put it this way:

People used to say, 'Don't hit that mountain! Don't destroy this tree!' As soon as they say that, there is something in their mind of respect for the Creator Spirit: *'The Creator made this!. . . Don't come closer to that hill: that is sacred!'*[5]

Ron Williams, an Aboriginal songwriter, storyteller and theologian who has travelled widely in Australia, told me about some other aspects of this Creator Spirit:

They are well aware of the evil spirits and they did know that there was a good spirit: that there was God providing and caring for them. A lot of them have dreams.

A number of tribes talked about this Person coming with a heavenly glow about him and healing the sick people maybe every second generation. They knew when he was coming. They used to call him the 'Big Boss'. Tim, an Aboriginal Christian leader in our church, still remembers his father talking about it when he was a boy. People got ready. They knew he was coming and all lined up crippled ones. . . and he touched them and gave them some teaching, some laws.

Another tribal person told me a blackfella came with a heavenly glow about him after people had been fighting. Some were dead and wounded and he came and growled at them, 'Don't do that!' He touched the ones that were wounded and sick and made them better.

A lot of tribal people have got stories of this Person coming and giving them laws to live by and healing them. They pass that story on to the younger generation. . . Ngaanyatjarra mob. . . Pitjantjatjara mob. . . around Kalgoorlie. . . down south. . . around Onslow, they told of a Person who came and gave them food.

There was a knowledge of a Supreme Being who spoke their language, provided food and helped them with their sick and provided laws.[6]

Ron talked about a story he heard from the Gugawaladgi tribe at Mossman in Queensland:

A bad spirit was killing people and eating them and God sent his Son to have a fight with the devil and beat him. He left a symbolic presence and said, 'I'll always look after you and won't let the devil hurt you any more.'[7]

Ron described the 'symbolic presence' as a carving in the rock next to a spring 'like a shepherd holding a little lamb':

There's spring water running down from the hills — down the bottom of the hill there's the spring water. Those who jump in there, they have sores healed. 'And as long as my image is here in the stone, you won't have to be afraid of the devil any more.'[8]

Ron says, 'Aborigines study the stars and follow the stories about the stars.'[9] He was told by one group that they act out a story of the Southern Cross in ceremonies. At initiation time, they say to the boys, 'One day you'll understand this cross — and that will save your people.' They have stories about the stars. The Southern Cross moved down from the northern hemisphere to the southern hemisphere at the time of the birth of a saviour. They see God's message to them in the stars.

Aborigines believe God was in this land of Australia before Christianity came, that he revealed himself to them through his creation and that he spoke to them as they meditated on the things he had made. Sometimes, he gave them dreams and visions and led them, not just in some of their traditional stories, but also in events that have happened throughout the generations for hundreds of years and are still happening today.

Another Aboriginal Christian from Elcho Island, Dangatanga, told me an old story his father had told him:

> The clan was fighting, making *mari* (trouble) between us at Wessel Island — maybe over a promised wife. They killed a man. His brother killed him dead and they buried him and covered him with bark and leaves. Next minute, they saw a light coming from somewhere. They didn't know about Jesus: they didn't know his name then. Those old people used to call a falling star *'larrpan'*. But this was a powerful light coming straight toward that person [in the grave], not like lightning, but like a searchlight.
>
> Next minute, that man just got up and started to walk! He walked over to his brother and showed himself to him, but didn't speak.
>
> The brother who killed him said, 'Hey, this man is alive!' and he told the family, but that man just disappeared! The light took him! He went up into the light![10]

They believed that God was speaking to them through this event about the sin of killing their brother.

There is a story from the Central Desert which also shows God meeting and teaching people:

> A long time ago, before the white man came, there was a family group — small children, uncles and aunts, cousins, grandparents. They lived in Central Australia, somewhere between Kalgoorlie and the Northern Territory border. There was a drought. They travelled from one dry water-hole to another until they came to the best one which *always* had good water in it, but it was *dry!*
>
> They had travelled a long way and they were so thirsty and dry that their tongues were sticking to the roofs of their mouths. They were very weary and weak. What could

they do? They didn't want to die. They called out in raspy voices to the Great Spirit in the sky for help.

Suddenly, a very bright light came down from the sky just near them and in the light was a man, 'a real proper man'. He was standing before them, but his feet weren't touching the ground!

He spoke to them and said, 'I will show you where the water is, but you must always remember that this must never be a sacred waterhole: it is always to be for everyone. . . and it must always be a place of peace. There must never be any fighting there. If you go in that direction, you will see the shiny thing where the water is.' He pointed out to the horizon in an area of their country where they never travelled because their people had *never* found water there.

Immediately, the man disappeared; their throats were moist and they were all strong again. They got up and walked — for a long time — in the direction the man had pointed. Late in the day, they were getting tired again, especially the old people and children. Finally, when they could go no further, they called out to the man in the light and he reappeared. Again, his feet were right up above the ground as he stood there in the light.

'Now I will show you where the water is, but you must always remember what I told you — this waterhole is for everyone and it is a place of peace!' He pointed and said, 'If you look over there now, you will see the bright, shining thing where the water is.'

They looked where the man pointed and saw a golden light shining. In a place where you don't find water, the sun was shining on water and reflecting onto all the rocks around it!

The man had again disappeared, but they were saved and very happy![11]

✦ The spirits of traditional Aboriginal spirituality

God was here before Westerners, but so were other spirits: those invited in or accepted by Aborigines over thousands of years.

Because Australia is a large island, isolated and protected

by huge oceans, the Aborigines have lived in this land for thousands of years with very little outside contact. In adjusting to this land, they have developed laws, customs and ceremonies which encouraged or discouraged various spirits.

Many regard Aboriginal ceremonies and law as evil and demonic. Rather than make a judgment on these ceremonies and laws, which is not central to our providing a description of Aboriginal spirituality, we will briefly show how Aboriginal people understand the demons and spirits.

A strong emphasis on personal relationships developed amongst the people, between individuals, between the clans and tribes, with the land itself and with the Creator Spirit and ancestor spirits. So the spirits of sharing and cooperation were strong in the land. This sharing was based on clear obligations and taboos within the clan. There were trade and ceremonial links covering thousands of kilometres across the boundaries of the hundreds of tribes. This honoured the good spirits in the land.

But there was fear and animosity towards Aborigines who belonged to other groups. Each group tended to refer to other people as aliens or even 'non-people' in their languages. We have no knowledge of any invasion by outsiders before the thirteenth century, but there were many battles as the Aboriginal tribes fought against each other. Sometimes, a whole tribe was wiped out and its territory taken over by others. George Dangumbu, tribal elder at

Harry Makarrwala, wearing the mindjalpi *showing his authority in the land*

Elcho Island, told me: 'Before I learned to throw a hunting spear, I learned to throw a fighting spear. We were always fighting. It is not true that we were a peaceful people.' There was a very violent, murderous spirit in the land. All of this gave power to some of the bad spirits in the land.

Something of the 'feel' of the spirits in the land is brought out in this statement by Ron Williams, when I asked him how Aborigines know there are spirits in the land:

> Sometimes there's willywillies, sometimes the wind blows, sometimes the fire crackles and sparks jump out, sometimes you can feel things, like something is looking at you: you can feel there is a spirit in the land. You see signs, you hear things and you feel it in your bones as well. They think of some as good spirits. If there's sparks jumping out, they're cheeky spirits.
>
> There are spirits around that they know are violent and murderous. The tiger snake — he's cheeky and his nose goes flat. We chuck sand at him and he stands up and his head flattens out like a cobra. They have a lot of dreamtime stories about how the snake went wild. They'll talk about a person who's got a bad snake-like spirit in him.
>
> Often, when someone sends a curse on them to kill them, they'll see a snake or some destruction like a wild bull has made. They have dreams and visions of these tormenting spirits coming at them. I find it difficult to express, but I know those things are there.
>
> In some of the areas where clans have been fighting, you can almost feel that in the atmosphere. We've been to places and prayed for places. I remember one place where a man killed a woman and you often saw a wild bull on the road — but it wasn't a bull, you know?
>
> They have to have respect for the spirits in the land.[12]

Ron talked about a place where he saw two possum eyes looking at him one night, but realised it was a barren place with no trees, so he felt it must have been a spirit. Then, he found out it was a place where no *Nyoongars* (Aborigines from the tribes of the south-west of Western Australia) from that area would travel at night time because it was a spirit place.

He said whites don't feel the spirits because they don't believe these things. His American wife was like that until she drove into a canyon near Exmouth and was so frightened by the spirits that she had to turn around and leave. She felt something like two big eyes looking at her and she couldn't get away quickly enough. He said: 'After it's happened a couple of times, you know there's something there.'[13]

✦ Non-British, outside influences on Aboriginal spirituality

There is some evidence that Chinese visited this land, possibly as early as the thirteenth century, and later there were Dutch, Malays, Macassans and other Asians.

From early in the seventeenth century, some of the Dutch and Portuguese sailors on their way to Indonesia were shipwrecked and, in 1623, some were put ashore after a mutiny. There is evidence that they lived with Aborigines, had a significant impact on their culture and probably also on the spiritual fabric of the land around the west coast.

In the nineteenth and twentieth centuries, there were Japanese pearl-divers in the north-west, Afghan camel drivers in Central Australia and Pacific Islanders in the north-east, all of whom related more closely with Aborigines than the British did. Each of them brought their own spiritual influences with them.

As Arnhem Land is the major focus in this story, we will now take a brief look at the Asian spiritual influences there.

Little is known about the influence of the Chinese and Malays in Arnhem Land, but some research has been done on the Macassan influence. For 300 years (from around AD1600), Macassan sailors used to visit the coastal areas of north Australia every year, including Elcho Island. In cooperation with the local Aborigines, they established Australia's first export industry — collecting and processing trepang, a sea slug, which was smoked and taken back to Indonesia and then traded as far away as China.

They brought with them metal axes, knives, cloth, tobacco, alcohol and other goods to exchange for pearl shell, turtle shells, ochres, cypress pine and trepang. Language, ceremonies, sacred objects, beliefs and social life were also exchanged and children of mixed race were born.

The Asians also warned the Aborigines of white men and their guns and ways. Aborigines say Captain Cook saw only animals and nomads, but the Macassans saw the people and their culture.[14]

The exchange was not all of advantage to the Arnhem Landers. They acquired smallpox from these visits, which probably killed huge numbers of them in the nineteenth century. Malaria, tuberculosis and leprosy probably also came in from the same source, as well as alcohol, causing social breakdown and even murders. At Elcho Island, a misunderstanding over an Aboriginal sacred rope led to the deaths of large numbers of Macassans and Aborigines in a war that lasted several years.[15]

What spiritual impact did these contacts have on the people and the land? It appears to have increased the influence of spirits, such as violence and murder, and introduced or changed the power of others, such as the desire to escape to unreality through alcohol.

The Aborigines adopted some of the ceremonies associated with the Macassan Muslim folk religion — including one where they chant 'Allah'. But somehow in it all, it seems that the Aborigines did not adopt the Macassan Muslim folk religion.

One dreamtime story tells of a dog (symbolising Aboriginal people) who meets the first Macassans and rejects their offer to share everything, saying, 'If I take all these things, I will be just like you and I want to be like me.'[16]

Traditional Aboriginal water transport was by bark canoe in crocodile-infested waters

Macassans taught Aborigines to make dug-out canoes from trees, some even having sails

Ron Williams states:

We've been preserved from Hinduism, or Islam, or Buddhism [by God's actions and messages preparing Aborigines] for a revelation of who Jesus Christ is. I think Aboriginal people are waking up to that now, but God did speak from time to time. It was the God of glory speaking to the Aboriginal people down through their dreamtime, but they didn't realise who he was, because Satan wanted to keep that revelation. They were well aware of the spirits.[17]

While the influence of such Asian spirituality was limited, it was, however, another element in the preparation for Aboriginal revival.

2

Lighting the fire

THE ARNHEM LAND ABORIGINES AND CHRISTIANITY TO 1970

ABORIGINES TRADITIONALLY MADE FIRE by rubbing sticks together in contact with dry leaves and then blowing on the red-hot sticks to bring a flame. Revival came to Arnhem Land through the friction and heat of the gospel rubbing against Aboriginal traditions and culture.

✦ The clash between Western and Aboriginal world views

The impact of predominantly British settlers on the land and its people has been much greater and more disruptive than that of the Asians and earlier European intrusions. The first 150 years or more of British settlement, from 1788 onwards, were marked by a very deep clash of world views and cultures that few people seemed to understand at all. A few examples of this should clearly illustrate the point.

1. *Differing attitudes to fire*
Aborigines are firelighters, using bushfires as a means of hunting, by smoking animals out to a place where they can be caught more easily. Fire also removes dead timber and grass and cracks open seedpods, causing new plants to grow.

Making fire by rotating the point of a stick against another stick. This is
a competition at the annual sports day at Galiwin'ku around 1950.

But Westerners see bushfires as a threat to their livestock,
crops, possessions and lives and are firefighters. This difference is very significant in our story.

Rev. Kerry Medway was an Anglican minister in the north
of South Australia in the 1980s, who often visited the
Aboriginal community at Ernabella. He was there one time
when a bushfire was threatening the community. Only a
year earlier, a bushfire had destroyed a lot of property there,
so some people were anxious about this fire. He was just
getting into bed when he was asked to help about thirty
whitefellas (a local name for whites) to fight it. Someone
suggested getting some of the Aborigines to help.

Kerry takes up the story:

So we drove down into the camp, going 'beep, beep beep'. . .
'Come out and fight the bushfire!'. . . Not a soul to be seen.
Finally, an old Aboriginal man came out of his humpy and
wandered up to the car. He leant in the window and said,
'Oh, g'day, Tjilpi' (that means 'wise old man'). 'What's the

trouble?' I said, 'Bushfire, bushfire! We're all going to be killed! Come and help us fight the bushfire!'

Well, he chewed his tobacco for a couple or more seconds — seemed like hours — and he said, 'No worries, Tjilpi — bushfire come, burn the house down. Tomorrow build another one.' And then he went back to bed![1]

2. *Differing attitudes to the land*

Aborigines are land keepers, seeking to take care of the land in its original state. Westerners are land users and controllers, seeking to make it produce as much as possible, exploiting it through farming and mining. The point here is not to argue that one attitude is right and one is wrong, but rather to indicate the marked difference in attitude. I believe each should be evaluated in terms of our God-given responsibility to the land, especially in the light of Genesis 1 to 3.

3. *Differing attitudes to society*

Aborigines greatly value and build life on social relationships, but Westerners tend to use those relationships for satisfaction of individual needs and then discard them. Westerners value and hoard possessions and build life around them more than on personal relationships, but Aborigines use and discard possessions, seeing them as of little importance in building community.

4. *Differing attitudes to time*

Westerners live by the clock but, for Aborigines, the time for an event is when everyone is ready for it.

These are all outward expressions of fundamental differences in world view which have very deep roots.

In a Western world view, understandings are filtered through the physical senses of sight, sound, smell, touch and taste, and by cultural factors. Most Westerners have been conditioned not to use spiritual senses, but to filter their perceptions by reason, tempered by emotions. Aboriginal perception of the world, on the other hand, is filtered by spiritual understandings, experiences and sensations: Aborigines hear the inner voices of the spirit world through such means as singing and dancing, through ceremonies and through dreams.

Christianity was brought to Aborigines by Westerners, along with Western economics, law, government, literacy and materialism. Naturally, Westerners have taught these by reason rather than by spirit and experience, without realising how differently Aborigines learn and view the world. The result has been that Aborigines have not been able to understand these things.

Ron Williams comments:

> I get more excited looking at it [life] from an Aboriginal culture than the European culture I've grown up with. The European doesn't have as much bite in it. When I see it from an Aboriginal point of view, I can easily go back into the dreamtime and eternity much more quickly than having to question God [through an abstract rational Greek world view].
>
> 'The Word became flesh and dwelt among us' is already there. Aborigines are more like Hebrew people in their thinking than Greek. The 'fall of man' is Greek thought, but Hebrew thought is the 'desecration of a sacred site'. 'Falling short' or 'missing the mark' as an explanation of sin is difficult for Aboriginals, but when you desecrate a sacred site it's much more horrible to them.[2]

World view differences have been at the heart of a clash of cultures that has caused many misunderstandings from the first settlement in Sydney in 1788, right across the land up to today. British arrogance has made little effort to understand, judging Aborigines from its own world view. Explorer William Dampier's description of Aborigines as 'the miserablest people on earth' showed no awareness of the richness of their culture and lifestyle.

Traditional Aboriginal shelters at Milingimbi

This lack of awareness resulted in many massacres and deaths. Within ten years of their arrival, an unofficial war developed between the military in Sydney and Aborigines. Westerners even had arguments over whether Aborigines were really human or just monkeys, and some made a sport of shooting blacks.

Aborigines not only used their traditional weapons such as spears to retaliate. They have also used spiritual forces and powers that the Westerners did not understand, powers that are still used today. Aborigines talk about men who have power to put a person to sleep and remove an organ from their body before allowing them to wake and return to their people, where they die suddenly shortly afterwards.

Men with special powers are said to 'sing' a person to death hundreds of kilometres away by pointing a bone at them. These men also use other spiritual powers such as 'astral travel' to travel out of their bodies in the spirit.

When someone dies, Aborigines believe that someone has caused it and so there must be payback, except in the case of very old people. Even if Western medicine attributes the death to an illness, sorcery is blamed for the illness and the death. Payback is generally by spearing, but curses are also still used. Some of the land and some Westerners have been placed under traditional Aboriginal curses, resulting in land being unproductive, in accidents and in sickness.

These spiritual powers are not only used for fighting. When someone becomes sick, Aboriginal 'medicine men' often use remedies with herbal and animal products, some of which are now being marketed in pharmacies and stores across the world. But they have also used spiritual powers. Sometimes, they suck a stone or object out of the patient's body through the skin so that the person will recover.

Westerners often consider these spiritual powers to be pure superstition and have tried to explain them by saying they were the results of cultural expectations and auto-suggestion. Many Christian missionaries have had difficulty accepting the reality of spiritual powers because of the influence of their own culture.

✦ The clash of cultures in Arnhem Land

The clash of world views has not been as intense in Arnhem Land as in many other places. Arnhem Land covers 80 000 square kilometres in the north-eastern corner of the Northern Territory. It was made an Aboriginal reserve in 1931, which restricted access by *Balanda*, the local name for non-Aborigines. Very few *Balanda* had ever lived there before that.

The Anglican and Methodist churches began to establish mission settlements there in the early 1920s. Today, these settlements are no longer missions, but are communities governed by Aboriginal councils, generally with representatives elected from each tribe or clan living there.

Galiwin'ku, on Elcho Island, is one of the largest communities with over 1 000 people. Other communities are as small as 150, but there are also many outstations or homelands where family groups of ten to one hundred people live. There are now also several mining towns with *Balanda* populations who are given restricted access to the area.

There was very little contact with Westerners until the early 1900s and then it was mainly contact with missionaries, most of whom tried to understand and love them. But the missionaries had to work through many issues of world view and culture to bring Aborigines the message of Jesus Christ.

But however hard the missionaries were to try, the very message they brought contained difficulties for Aborigines. They have no concept of a single chief or of the authority base of a kingdom that lies at the heart of Christianity. Aboriginal leadership is *shared* by elders, where each one has a different role in their ceremonies and other aspects of life.

Aborigines didn't have sheep or bread, so couldn't understand Jesus' word, 'I am the bread of life', or John the Baptist's statement about him, 'Behold, the Lamb of God.' These concepts needed to be explained through cultural equivalents like a yam or kangaroo's joey.

Aborigines build traditional bark shelters tied to bushes or saplings. The best place is on sand, where they can be comfortable when they sit or lie down. So to them, Jesus' story about building a house on firm rock rather than sand so that it can withstand the wind, rain and floods is laughable and stupid.

Sixteen years after the Methodist church began work in Arnhem Land, a retiring missionary addressed the mission board on the 'apparent poverty of results', especially in terms of church members and Christian converts. He tried to help the board to understand a little of what it meant to preach the gospel to Aborigines who were nomadic, asking:

How are the parables of the sower or of the vineyard to be understood by people who do not possess even a rudimentary knowledge of agriculture? What can the parable of the good shepherd mean to people who know nothing of the domestication of animals? How much of the real meaning of even the prodigal son can be readily grasped by those who know nothing of 'inheritance' or economics at all akin to our own and in whose lives conceptions of industry and thrift have no place?

To an Aboriginal, the injunction to select for his camping place a piece of hard, rocky ground rather than the soft warm sand would be obviously absurd.[3]

The missionaries may have had better results if they had begun with creation and the stories of the Old Testament. Traditional Aboriginal culture is similar to the Hebrew culture of the Old Testament in some ways. One man seeking revenge after an accident said to me, 'I was only doing what the law says — blood needs blood.' The principle of 'an eye for an eye and a tooth for a tooth' applies without any consideration of motive and intent.

It was into this world view that Christian missionaries entered early in the twentieth century in Arnhem Land.

✦ How Christianity came to Arnhem Land

In 1912, a national committee of all the Christian churches met and divided up the whole of Australia so that they didn't compete with each other in working with Aborigines. The northern coast of Arnhem Land was allocated to the Methodist church.

Work with Australian Aborigines by all the denominations before this had ended in failure. But around 1900, the Methodists came to believe that Aborigines could not be Westernised or 'Anglicised', but they could be 'Christianised' and that the church had a responsibility to take the Christian message to them.

Christianity reached Arnhem Land in 1916, when Rev. James Watson arrived at Goulburn Island. Then in 1923, a second Methodist mission was established further east, at Milingimbi Island. The missionaries found Milingimbi a very difficult place with frequent tribal wars.

Rev. Dr Djiniyini Gondarra says:

> The gospel of Jesus Christ was so powerful, bringing the Spirit of reconciliation and restoration, and many enemies were won by the power of the gospel. . . We are thankful to God for the pioneering, faithful Christian witness given to the Aboriginal people in this community by our loved pastor and his wife, Rev. and Mrs Webb, who began their ministry in Milingimbi mission field in 1926.[4]

Rev. T. Theodor Webb was an exceptional missionary, way ahead of his time and highly regarded by the Aboriginal people and also anthropologists. He realised that he needed a lot of help, not just for the enormous amount of physical work to be done, but also in learning the language and customs.

In many ways, Webb had been God's gift to preserve the Arnhem Land Aborigines from destruction by the outside world, and even from those in the church whose views were mistaken. He often spoke out boldly to the mission board and the government, pointing out the need for justice and reality.

When the government planned punitive measures following the Caledon Bay

Rev. T.T. Webb, dwarfed by an anthill

massacre of Japanese fishermen by Aborigines, Webb objected strongly to the government.

He fought to have a new mission established in the area. Webb also closed children's homes so the children were raised by their own families rather than by Western missionaries in dormitories.

He struggled to introduce Christianity to Aborigines without causing them to lose their culture. He believed Christ could liberate and free them from fears, especially of evil spirits and sorcery, but was convinced it had to be done within the context of their own culture.

In 1927, a young missionary couple arrived to help at Milingimbi: engineer Harold Shepherdson and his new wife, Ella. The Sheppies, as they became known, lived and worked for fifty years at Milingimbi and Elcho Islands. They also had a major impact on the people, particularly through their stability and gentle strength. Sheppie came to realise the importance of the people being able to stay in the bush rather

Mr and Mrs Sheppie leaving Milingimbi to establish Elcho Island mission in August 1942, with their Fijian boat captain, Aminiasi

than congregating in mission settlements, so he built his own aeroplane to take the gospel and medical help to them.

Sheppie was a man of few but very effective words and positive actions. He consulted fully with the people and had a deep compassion and sense of justice, especially for the children.

He hated seeing a girl of twelve or even younger being given as wife to an old man who already had several wives. One day, two Aborigines were having an argument, one waving a spear at the other. Sheppie walked up behind him and snapped off the head of the spear and walked off while the crowd laughed and the angry man continued to wave the spear around, unaware of what had happened.[5]

In 1954, the value of Sheppie's work was recognised by the government which awarded him an MBE[6] and by the church, which ordained him without formal training.

Mrs Sheppie's work among the women and children was also very significant. She started a school, gave medical attention to many Aborigines and was greatly loved by all.

✦ The first Aborigines to accept Christianity in Arnhem Land

The first Aborigines in the area to accept Christianity were Birrinydjawuy ('Andrew') and Makarrwala ('Harry'). Without them, the work of Webb and Sheppie would have been severely hampered. Both of them had lived in Darwin and learned a lot of Western ways, so they were important bridges between the missionaries and the people.

Birrinydjawuy was from the Milingimbi area of the Gupapuyngu tribe. He was the first person, not only to become a Christian, but to start to discover the relationship between Christianity and their culture. On one occasion, some of his own clan got very angry and nearly speared him because he pointed out that the totem of a snake they were making was not alive. It could not hear or speak. It was just wood!

Arnhem Land pioneers Birrindjawuy (extreme left) and Wili, Batangga and
Makarrwala (last three on right) after a wedding at Milingimbi

Djiniyini points out that they were learning the difference
between a totem and an idol. He says that Aborigines do not
worship their totems any more than the Jews worshipped the
'covenant box' (ark) in the Temple.[7]

Makarrwala was from the Wangurri tribe, from east of
Milingimbi. He had a profound Christian influence on his
wider family, the community and the whole region. Members of his younger brother's family became key leaders in
the early stages of the revival.

After he became a Christian, he felt that he had to make
some changes in his life. Probably, the most significant of
these was his decision in 1942 that he should only keep one
wife, sending the others back to their families or giving them
to relatives as wives. This was a decision he made without
pressure or even suggestions from the missionaries, but because he felt God wanted him to do so.

Makarrwala has told his story this way:

The old life was bad; the new is very good. . . I have got the new law; because Jesus belongs to me and made my spirit new and has made my mind to understand and made my ears to hear. . . I had kept to the old law at first, but now the new law which is good and full of light; and I trust in the one and only God. . .

In the early days I did not want this law; but the old law is like darkness, the new law is like light. . . .this way is very good and I feel light. The old way was heavy, like a stone; my body was sorrowful, my mind heavy, my heart depressed and my flesh weary. But the new way is very good and light. Now I am new, I stand on new ground. By the hand of Jesus, God cares for me and Jesus is my way, leading me by the hand; wherever I go, Jesus is beside me, all the time, close to me.[8]

Birrindjawuy and Makarrwala were involved in an amazing incident in 1931 which showed some of the impact of Christianity. Webb reported the story in *The Missionary Review*,[9] just as the men told it to him.

At the time, there were very few Christians in the whole of Arnhem Land. There had been a lot of tension between Milingimbi Mission Aborigines and the Burarra and Kukuriya tribes who lived on the mainland further west. In 1930, three Milingimbi men had killed an old Kukuriya man on a beach on Milingimbi. The Milingimbi people buried the man, found the culprits and banished them from the island. The old man's tribe waited for the opportunity for the revenge that their law required. About fifteen months later, the Burarra and the Milingimbi people wanted to end the fighting and hoped it would happen at an important ceremonial gathering on the mainland nearby.

A group of twelve Milingimbi Aborigines set out to attend. On their way, they were told several times that the Kukuriya men were planning to kill them when they arrived. Before they camped that night, Makarrwala and Birrindjawuy asked them if any of them intended to make trouble and a few

confessed they would retaliate if the enemy were too harsh
with them. They were reminded of things Webb had said on
Sunday morning at the church service and they knelt while
Birrindjawuy prayed:

> Our Father in heaven, please look after us tonight and send
> your angels to help us. Make our hearts good and don't
> let them become *mari* [= hot with anger], so that we shall
> not want to make trouble. Please do this for each one of
> us. When we come to meet all those *miringu* [= enemy or
> hostile party], close their eyes so that we, who are few, may
> appear to them as many and open our eyes so that they,
> who are many, may appear to us as few.[10]

Next morning, they prayed for guidance and protection
before leaving. When they arrived on the mainland, they
again knelt to pray, but looked up to see their enemy appear-
ing out of the scrub.

They ran towards their enemy, stopping on a mound
where they were quickly surrounded. Makarrwala stuck his
spear into the ground and hung a small scriptural picture roll
on it which Webb had given them and they knelt and prayed
again. Showers of spears were thrown at them but, to their
astonishment, all passed harmlessly over their heads. Their
enemies tried various tricks to frighten them or get them to
run so they could spear them in the back. For two hours,
they stood facing an almost continuous barrage of spears.

Birrinydjawuy spoke with the murdered man's brother
and gave him a gift of tobacco which he accepted. The
spear-throwing eventually stopped and other leaders were
given tobacco. As the sun set, food was produced. While
they were eating, they were told that their enemies were
planning to attack them and kill them during the night.

After eating, Makarrwala and Birrinydjawuy visited the
enemy camps. The rest of their group were frightened they
would all be killed and pleaded with them not to go. However, Makarrwala and Birrindjawuy assured them that Jesus

would look after them. They took their picture roll and visited all the camps, telling them about Jesus and his ways and of his presence during the fight that day.

When they returned, their men said, 'Why are our hearts like this? We haven't felt angry and we haven't felt frightened. All day our hearts have been quiet and happy. This is a new thing for us.' Webb wrote:

> Suddenly, as they sat there in the darkness, five vivid lines of dazzling light streamed overhead, just above the tops of the trees. After a few seconds, there were a dozen more and then another twelve — dazzling, arresting, awesome, so that all the people gathered there were suddenly silenced.
>
> Then one asked, 'What was it?'
>
> Birrinydjawuy replied, 'I think Jesus has shown himself to us.' And they said among themselves, '*Yuwalk muka. Djesu muka.*' [= 'It is true. It is Jesus.'] Then they asked, 'Is Jesus letting us know it is true that our enemies will try to kill us tonight?'
>
> Birrinydjawuy thought for a moment and replied, 'I think that news is true and they want to kill us; but I believe that Jesus is doing this to stop them. They won't do anything now.'[11]

So they all danced and sang for hours. Next morning, they woke after a good sleep to find that the enemy had left, totally puzzled by what had happened.

After they returned to Milingimbi, they decided to do away with their fighting spears, to quit stealing and immorality and to live as Christians. They asked Webb to help them see what that really meant in their daily lives. Makarrwaḻa said to Webb:

> For a long, long time I have talked to those boys, but it seemed like trying to cut a great rock with a crowbar; now, at last, it has split open and my heart is very glad.[12]

A few months later, Webb reported a great reduction in

stealing, fighting and immorality, plus the establishing of a mid-week devotional meeting and Sunday school classes for men and women, in addition to those for children.[13]

✦ Changes in Arnhem Land during World War II

World War II brought massive changes to the area. For the first time, Aborigines in the area were exposed to large numbers of Westerners who were not Christians. They saw the massive technology of the war first hand as the Air Force established a base at Milingimbi. They experienced bombings and machine-gunnings from the Japanese in the later part of the war. Servicemen introduced them to alcohol on a large scale, petrol sniffing when alcohol supplies ran out — and probably also gambling. These all became major problems for Aborigines in later years.

The war brought a major change in Aboriginal attitudes to the *Balanda*. Just after the war, some of the tribal leaders of the area gathered together and were talking about the war and the power of the *Balanda*. They vowed they would never say, 'No!' to them over anything they wanted, because they were too powerful for *Yolngu*. But it was many years before they told this to any *Balanda*.[14]

The war also brought another important change for Aborigines: the establishment of a new mission settlement which became the centre of the revival.

Both the Sheppies and the Webbs had preferred Elcho Island as a location for the mission for many years. Milingimbi was a small, flat island with a poor water supply and a poor anchorage; it also swarmed with sandflies and mosquitoes. It was a place of constant tribal hostility, being located on the edge of tribal boundaries. Elcho had inspiring hills, good anchorages, good milling timber, better soil for cultivation, fresh water springs and creeks, and a degree of unity.

Sheppie asked the church to move the mission's sawmilling equipment to Elcho Island to protect it from Japanese attacks and this was done in 1942. Makarrwala and many of the Aborigines stayed on at Milingimbi or nearby on the mainland, but some key families moved to assist the Sheppies at Elcho Island. Their main leaders were Wili and Makarrwala's younger brother, Batangga, who were both clan group leaders.

All of Aboriginal life, including plants and animals, is divided into two groups or moieties: *Yolngu* call these '*dhuwa*' and '*yirritja*'. The two complement each other so a man must marry a woman from the opposite moiety. Wili was a tribal leader for the *dhuwa* clans and Batangga was a ceremonial leader for the other half, the *yirritja* clans. God raised these two tribal leaders up as the Christian leaders in the mission, one from each moiety to complement the other.

✦ Cultural changes that Christianity brought to Arnhem Land

As the missionaries taught the Christian faith and it began to be grasped by the new Christians, the struggles with cultural traditions began. One of these was in the marriage system. In 1981, Mrs Sheppie wrote:

> Polygamy was quite common and is still practised today. . . While this system had some advantages in the Aboriginal way of life, it was also the cause of a great deal of strife. Many fights have occurred because of the jealousy between the older women and the younger ones. Among the men, it also created bad feelings between the 'haves' and the 'have nots' and these feelings led to wife stealing.
>
> When strife occurred the women were always blamed and some were even killed. The men frequently got off with just a talking to and this seemed unfair. One man I knew stole a wife and went with her to the mainland where he stayed for ten years. When he thought his relatives had forgotten the incident, he returned only to find that his wife was given a rough time at the mission.[15]

Makarrwala's decision in 1942 to keep only one of his wives caused quite a stir, as marriages were often the result of very intense family and political pressures. It affected the whole area, including Elcho Island. When Makarrwala died in 1951, the matter was still not resolved and tribal law required his younger brother, Batangga, to take all six of his widows. Not long after that Batangga's wife died and he eventually took one of his brother's wives, but left the rest remaining as widows.

Shortly after this, Mrs Sheppie reported a Christian revival at Elcho Island with many baptisms, but also wrote that another leader 'brought in some reforms, such as the termination of the system of promising daughters, so that they were free to choose their own partners. The reform did not last long, because it met with too much opposition from the older men.'[16] Struggles continue even today, but the marriage system is changing slowly with Western and Christian influences.

Another change has been in the area of treachery and violence. Many people believe tribal Aborigines are peaceful people. George Dayngumbu, Batangga's son, strongly denies this. He told me:

> We always fight! Small problems — fighting, straight away!. . . But now, because of the missionary, there is less fighting now. The ceremonies were held to get people there [at the ceremony] to pay back someone — to trick them. . . to get that person to come here so we can kill him. That's the real reason!
>
> But if he has come and apologised and we make *makarrata* [a peacemaking covenant or treaty] then, instead of killing that man, we just spear him in the leg. Then, we make agreement — everybody, clan to clan. The proper way, everybody who kills somebody, must go through *makarrata*.[17]

If a man considered to be guilty goes away and hides, they often kill his brother as a substitute, so his clan may ask for a *makarrata* for him. Dayngumbu said that after the ceremony:

Batangga, Mrs Sheppie and their Sunday school class at Elcho Island

. . .his brother is free, and the clans can be friendly. But if the murderer comes back, he still has to face it.

It's very, very hard and tricky. *Yolngu* trick other tribes many times — trick to trick. In *Yolngu* ways, we are not honest people. Sometimes, we say we are honest people, but we are not.

But I want to get free, so I can be honest with other clans and go and apologise to other clans where I have bad feelings to them. Before, I would have said to my sons: 'You go and fight them. Take him hunting and kill him there!'

Now, because of Christianity, we stand in the light. Before, we used to stand in the darkness![18]

✦ The 1957 *Yolngu* covenant

But the changes were not just cultural. In 1957, Batangga, with the help of Wili and a younger elder, Burrumarra, led the people in a very significant action. Dayngumbu told me how the men went out into the bush where Batangga talked about

Makarraṯa (peacemaking) ceremony in which one of the offending group would be speared in the leg.

God's ways and led them in prayer. Then they made some of their tribal *rangga*. *Rangga* are poles with sacred designs carved and painted on them. These designs represent their personal and clan identities and their affiliation with particular sites. As the men and boys made these, they sang the songs of the totems and ancestors. Batangga said to them:

> If you're going to bring them into the open, the Lord will bless us. All the good things that we have in our life is the Lord blessing us. Your life, my life is what is important in Christ, not our totems! He wants us, not our totems.[19]

They normally put feathers on the *rangga* and wind string made from plants around the poles to cover the secret designs before bringing them before women and children for their ceremonies and dances. But this time, Batangga asked them to leave the secret designs visible. He told the women and children to prepare a place for something special alongside the church.

Batangga said to the men, 'This is something different

happening in our life, that we're going to bring the *rangga* outside. '

Dayngumbu described it this way:

In the middle of the night, they all brought them out — quietly. So next morning, everybody was very surprised: the totems were all there and everybody had a special service there — in a Christian way, not any *bungul djama* [= traditional ceremonial dancing]. They offered themselves and these *rangga* back to God.[20]

They made a large sign with fifteen-centimetre-high letters in their own language which said:

Duwalinya wurungu walala liya go bunggawa Badangga
[This one — old one — their head and leader: Batangga]
Duwala bala naburu yuru marngal'yun djiwarlili Godgala.
[This — now — we will worship — to heaven — to God][21]

At the time, very few people understood what was being done; but undoubtedly they were making a decision to follow God, in such a way that it showed that they believed that everything in life must come under his leadership. The poles and their designs represented the most powerful things in their life — even they were to be subject to the one true God in heaven whom the people would now worship.

Aboriginal Christian leaders have recently called this their 'covenant with God'.

Change brings reaction and this step towards God was soon challenged. A traditional ceremony from another area had suddenly spread over much of Australia. It became a very strong force around this time among the *Yolngu*. The Aboriginal leaders banned it from Elcho Island, because of some of the things they could see in it. However, many of the people joined in its ceremonies on the mainland nearby. After the revival, some of the Christian Aborigines came to the point of saying that this ceremony stole their covenant with God.

Rangga poles near the Elcho Island church, 1957

Batangga with the rangga poles: 1957   The cross atop the rangga poles: 1957

✦ The 1972 challenge to the power of the sacred stones

In 1972, there was a challenge in which it was understood by the people that the power of God was being pitted against the power of sacred stones from a *mindjalpi* [sacred dilly bag]. Aboriginal life stories tell how Aboriginal men stole a *mindjalpi* from the Djang'kawu sisters a long time ago. The Djang'kawu were two sisters who were spirit beings. They helped people relate to the land after its creation. One old man explained:

> The dilly bag which belongs to the men in each *mala* [clan] is the proof that the *mala* has the authority over that land — because the dilly bag came from Djang'kawu.[22]

The issue of power and authority is very important, especially in how it is used. The *mindjalpi* is the basis for all their authority: for their discipline over young people and every member of the clan, so that their rules and customs are observed. But it can be used for all sorts of other things, such as to manipulate for personal gain.

In 1972, the whole community was gathered at Galiwin'ku for a concert at the school. During a traditional dance, one of the men dancing suddenly collapsed and died. Accusations and rumours spread quickly. *Galiwin'ku Church News* reported, 'Claims had been made that a certain small stone in one man's possession had the power to kill any person who touched it.'[23]

Wili's son, Djiniyini, and Batangga's son, Kevin Dhurrkay, were Christian leaders at the time and were present at a fiery meeting on the oval on Sunday morning:

> Djiniyini asked for the stone and, amidst protests from the crowd who feared for his safety, he held it and proceeded to witness to the power of Jesus Christ. He said that such objects have no power in themselves and that, if a person who touches it should become sick or even die, it is the great fear he had that is the cause. When asked if he had anything in his possession that possessed power, Djiniyini replied, 'Yes, I have the Bible!' After bearing his testimony, Kevin fearlessly picked up all the much feared objects which people had fearfully tipped out of their 'medicine bags' and he put them all back into their bags.[24]

All this can be seen as preparation for the coming revival: as God rubbing the sticks together to produce heat. He was blowing his breath on the dry twigs and leaves and a spark was lit that soon became a refining fire.

3

A strong wind fans the flame

THE PREPARATION FOR REVIVAL DURING THE 1970s

IN THE 1970s IN ARNHEM LAND, the people's actions and motives were being purified along the lines indicated in the book of Zechariah, in preparation for the coming revival:

> Then I will purify them and put them to the test,
>   just as gold and silver are purified and tested.
> They will pray in my name, and I will answer them.
> I will say, 'You are my people,'
>   and they will reply, 'You, Lord, are our God!'[1]

Ron Williams explained the process involved in this purification this way:

> The Lord through his Spirit exorcises the demonic in the culture and makes them [the people] free. There needs to be exorcism of the culture, purifying: a fire burning so the gold will come out.[2]

As the sticks of Christianity and culture were rubbed together in Arnhem Land in the 1970s, a fire was produced. But it seemed in the early 1970s that it was actually *two* fires that God lit: one amongst the *Yolngu*, the Aboriginal people, and the other amongst the *Balanda*, the non-Aboriginal people.

✦ Fanning the *Balanda* fire

In a paper written about the revival Galikali, the Galiwin'ku Bible translator, wrote of the situation before the revival:

> Over the years, [*Balanda* staff] tended to be relatively 'short-termers' and very few ever acquired a working knowledge of the Aboriginal language. As the Aboriginal Christians' English was also drastically limited when it came to communicating 'heart matters', the custom over the years was for Aboriginal and non-Aboriginal Christians to meet in separate groups for the less formal mid-week sharing/Bible study/fellowship.
>
> Sunday and special services were, of course, shared, and there was rich one-to-one sharing across the language barrier as individual relationships developed. But it would appear in retrospect that God dealt with us as two separate groups, in preparing for the outpouring of his Spirit experienced especially in 1979.[3]

Galikali (Dianne Buchanan) with Margaret Miller (on right), members of the Bible translation team at Elcho Island

A number of *Balanda* played a significant role in bringing about revival. The Sheppies continued to live in retirement at Galiwin'ku until 1977, continuing their important work. They were, however, not the only significant *Balanda* influences during the 1970s.

In the 1960s and 1970s, Jim Kraak was engineer in charge of the Elcho workshop. This had a dirt floor, but Jim had every piece of machinery sparkling clean and Aboriginal workers and trainees in spotless white overalls.

Jim really lived as a Christian and spoke about his relationship with God openly. His faith was exciting and infectious. He was keen on music and the dramatic presentation of the scriptures, using devices like a winch in the roof of the church to lower angels down during a presentation of the Christmas story. His God was real and exciting and he wanted others to experience him like that, rather than just to hear about him with their ears and know about him in their minds.

Another very important *Balanda* missionary was Dianne Buchanan or Galikali (her *Yolngu* name), who went to Elcho Island as a young teacher in 1969 and was appointed as Djambarrpuyngu Bible translator in 1977. She was one of the few really long-term missionaries, remaining there until her death through cancer in 1993 when she was still only forty-seven years old.

Like the Sheppies, Galikali had a quiet, steady influence and she encouraged Christian growth in many of the people without seeking to be in the public eye at all.

John and Trixie Rudder were also significant. They were missionary schoolteachers who arrived in Arnhem Land in 1966. In 1968, John started to hear stories of unusual things happening in groups in Darwin, which were explained as the presence of the Holy Spirit. Several friends in New South Wales also sent him a magazine describing some of the same things. John told me some of the story:

> I went in to Darwin when our son was born [January, 1969] and searched out a group where people were being baptised in the Spirit. I went to the funny little meeting. . . discordant singing — worst I've ever seen! But there was love amongst them. . . I spent all my time with them — asked them to pray for me for baptism of the Holy Spirit, and the deep peace of the Lord I first experienced in 1962 came back. [4]

John and Trixie Rudder

Galikali continues the story of the way this experience spread amongst *Balanda*:

> John Rudder was the first mission staff member to be baptised in the Holy Spirit in January 1969. Minister Ken Higgins followed in April 1970 and a steady stream of others for the period 1969 to 1970. Some staff came already Spirit-filled but, for most, the openness to the Holy Spirit grew with sharing in the fellowship here.
>
> Running parallel was the impact passed from one to the other as staff left and new folk came with tapes and books by evangelical teachers like Watchman Nee (especially *The Normal Christian Life*) and Major Ian Thomas, Derek Prince and other charismatic leaders.[5]

News quickly spread of what was happening. Within days of his experience, John Rudder was called into the mission superintendent's office in Darwin and told that they didn't want any of what was seen as excesses at Elcho Island and he was not to teach or carry on with any charismatic teaching or practice out there.

But when John returned to Elcho Island, he felt that God had shown him the power that met so many of the needs of people in their daily lives. He was also aware that others were searching for this answer and he wrote later:

> From the beginning of the 1970s, there was an awareness amongst the whole staff that there was something missing. We weren't seeing the breakthroughs that we wanted to see.[6]

After the *Balanda* minister of the Elcho church, Ken Higgins, came back from leave filled with the Holy Spirit, a group started to meet together to explore this experience further. They started to feel that events they read about in the Bible like supernatural healings should also happen today, so they began to pray for healing for people and saw them healed. The *Yolngu* needing healing often had real faith that God would heal them, but it was the *Balanda* who took the lead in this prayer most of the time in the first half of the 1970s. A prayer chain was set up, so that word could be passed on quickly whenever there was a need.

The Galiwin'ku Health Centre was nearly always short-staffed. It was often called a hospital, but a doctor only visited around every six weeks for about six hours if the weather permitted the plane to get there. The sisters frequently dealt with situations that took them way beyond their training and experience. They would start their in-patient rounds at 6.00 a.m. and do the last one at 11.00 p.m. or midnight and invariably had several calls during the night.

Rhonda Loechel, one of the nursing sisters during the 1970s, reported some of the situations where miraculous healing took place. One night, during a 'flu epidemic and chickenpox outbreak, they had just sat down to tea when there was a scream from downstairs that a baby had stopped breathing. The baby, only six weeks old and tiny, had developed pneumonia. Somehow in the middle of trying to revive her, they managed to let the group know they needed prayer:

> We sucked out this child, breathed it. . . it started breathing again. The little chest was going. . . grunting breaths, then people came into the room and just started praying around this baby. The mother sat down on the floor in the corner, totally secure that the baby would be quite all right. . . those little breaths, they grunted and grunted and became more frequent and turned into a cry and, within just five minutes, the cry was so loud that we had to give it to the mother to breastfeed. . . to shut her up because she was screaming so much.
>
> We had a woman with obstructed labour. We tried to do a forceps delivery because we were getting desperate, but. . . we just couldn't get the forceps on. It was totally obstructed. There was no room for the forceps. . . [there was] crying and praying and I tried again and I felt those forceps pulled around from out of my hand. . . from inside into position and I was able to deliver the baby!. . .
>
> Sometimes, you can call for a doctor's help. When we couldn't do that, we called out to God sooner and deeper and more urgently — with no alternatives, totally submitted to him. That was all we had. . . and in our weakness, he is able to flood in with his power. . .
>
> There was a woman whose heart stopped one night, so we prayed and spoke to the heart and asked God to start it and it started. After a few minutes, there was no pulse again, so we prayed. . . That happened three times. . . She walked onto the medical plane. When they got her to Darwin, they couldn't find a thing wrong with her.[7]

The *Balanda* Christians involved in this prayer for healing also started to discover other aspects of the spirit world. They would pray or sing and perhaps someone would start to confess something. They shared things that were on their minds or hearts and began to realise that they were hearing things that the Holy Spirit was showing them. They didn't know that they were experiencing things described in the Bible. John Rudder said:

> We just praised the Lord and sang choruses and sat around and listened to the [Holy] Spirit. . . that's where I started to learn what it was to function as one who could see in the Spirit.[8]

They also came to realise that demonic powers were real and that the Spirit of the Lord Jesus Christ was stronger than all those forces. They saw the results of deliverance in people's lives as they took authority over demons.

As they prayed for, cared for and loved those who were not Christians — especially some of the *Balanda*— they started to see some of them become Christians, sometimes with dramatic release from occult powers and practices in which they had been involved. John Rudder's report continues:

> At times when we prayed, God set people free [of the occult]. . . Using Jesus' authority, we were telling things to go. This went on for months. People were getting healed and made whole and getting a lot of help. We really were depending on the Spirit in the early days. There was nothing else to depend on: just the scriptures and the Spirit![9]

It was around this time that books on deliverance from evil spirits began to appear in some bookshops. They read some of them and started to copy the methods in them and their effectiveness ceased for about two years as a result: they came to realise that the Holy Spirit would not be tied to any methods!

Jovilisi Ragata was a Fijian missionary who had worked in Arnhem Land for many years. While he was at Milingimbi in the mid-1970s, he came to realise that some *Balanda* were making problems rather than solving them and he started to pray, 'Lord, please change them or move them.' After he moved to Elcho Island in 1978, this praying proved so effective there that someone asked him to stop that prayer because of staff shortages!

Then, late in 1978, teacher Derek Prince's tape on fasting arrived. Galikali reported:

> [It] made a strong impact on quite a number of staff members. From then on, fasting was regularly practised individually and corporately, mostly for one to three days and even sceptics were convinced. There were especially significant corporate prayer times as the group agreed together and fasted over Christmas and New Year weekends.[10]

✦ Fanning the *Yolngu* fire

At the same time, God's Spirit was at work among the *Yolngu*. There were many factors involved in this fire. In 1969, Billy Graham brought a team to Australia which included Negro evangelist, Ralph Bell, who visited Elcho Island for one weekend. John Rudder had this to say about the visit:

> We saw a cyclone turned aside during the crusade when we prayed. We spoke to a ferocious storm and told it not to rain until after the last meeting and, as I filled in the last of the 250 commitment cards, it got wet! A good half of the adult population responded, including a lot of ceremonial leaders. . .[11]

However, there was still a long way to go before there was a lasting effect. After that crusade, a lot of work was done on teaching material for new Christians, some of which was used in the early 1980s.

During the early and mid-seventies, there was massive social change for Aborigines in Arnhem Land. There was the first talk about land rights. And the Methodist Church in the area united with the Presbyterian and Congregational Churches (five years ahead of the national formation of the Uniting Church in Australia in 1977). The church then spent months of work listening to Aborigines in 1973, producing a document called *Free to Decide*. This pioneered a new policy of self-determination. Djiniyini Gondarra has made this comment on it:

> The church had to take a very slow step in this change and not rush in quickly. There was very strong pressure from the government. . . [which] felt sorry for Aboriginal people and felt they should have more money. All the workers were put on a training allowance and later onto Award wages. They received this money too quickly and did not know how to use it wisely. The Christian church knew that change must come and that equality of opportunity must apply to all Australians, both black and white.[12]

Uniting Church training officer, Richard Trudgen, adds:

> The training allowance and Award wages meant they could get two days work and then sit down and stop working, acting like millionaires.
>
> One man I was working with got his new house, Award wages and electric light. They started to stay up all night playing cards because they didn't have electric light before. Then, he tried to go to work and was absolutely exhausted, wondering why it was all different and saying: 'We should be happy — we've got everything. We can go to a pub and do everything a person is supposed to be able to do, but we're less happy than ever!'[13]

Richard added that he felt this was one of the things that led people to a spiritual search.

Djiniyini feels a slower rate of change would have been better for the Aborigines and some of these changes were not for the best. He continues:

> Many of those changes took place in Arnhem Land, destroying the Christian community spirit — and there was no longer respect for each other in the community. The people were travelling backwards and forwards by charter aeroplanes, bringing things for their children and for their wives, as well as bringing liquor which destroyed the life of family and community. . .

It was like the early days when the missionaries went to stop the tribal fights. The churches and missionaries tried very hard to stop drinking and fighting and helped the communities in Arnhem Land to see and understand that many white-man values are bad and make you spoiled. . .

The Aboriginal people were listening to many voices; the government was saying you are free people and you must have everything you want, just like the other Australians. . . Many of the people were already saying things like: 'Don't believe what the church and missionaries are telling you. You must accept all the white-man's values because they are better than our own; leave your old ways of living and live like the rest of the Australians.'[14]

With the help of the government policy of assimilation, the scene was being set for renewal: people desperately needed to find firm foundations for life. It was within this context that some extraordinary events began to take place in the *Yolngu* community. It was a time of struggle that prepared some of the young *Yolngu* for greater leadership.

One such early event concerns George Dayngumbu. During the time the *Balanda* were discovering the healing power of the Holy Spirit, Batangga's son George Dayngumbu was very ill. There seemed to be some sort of curse on his family. Around October 1974, Ken Higgins had been talking to one of George's brothers and discovered that four of these brothers had received power from a sacred object in a ceremony. All of them developed chest problems. One was the man mentioned in the last chapter who died dramatically on the stage at the school concert, probably from a heart attack. Another died from lung cancer in 1981, a third had constant asthma and died from it in 1990, and George was the fourth one. At the time of this revelation to Ken, George was very sick.

One of the sisters at the health centre at the time later told the story, with some details added by John Rudder:

George was sent home to die of emphysema. We got this call for prayer in the early evening. When I got to the hospital, I can remember him lying back on the bed, not moving anything except breathing, with an oxygen mask on his face.[15]

They ended up with an unusual deliverance prayer meeting around the bed, with messages being translated and people telling George that he had to renounce these things that were killing him. The relatives (including some of the brothers) who were there agreed that this was right. While they were praying, there was a group of old men outside singing 'death songs'. By the time we got halfway through, there were no old men left. They just disappeared.'

Some had gone into the labour ward to pray and sing, because there were too many people around the bed. George started confessing his sins in broken English, still gasping for

Sheppie and George Dayngumbu, 1992

George and Guymun Dayngumbu
and family

breath: 'I made god for the bush, I made god for the beach. . .
I confess my sins.' As he spoke these words, he started to
get stronger, sitting up and taking off his oxygen mask.

They copied a method of deliverance they had read about
and gave George a kidney bowl, telling him to spit out the
rubbish as these things were confessed and renounced. God
answered their prayers and George was breathing normally
before the prayer time finished.

Within a few weeks, he began to realise that the power of
his healing was taken away from him when he went to the
ceremonies and sang the old traditional songs. That took him
away from God and he found it difficult to breathe again. He
came to believe that God did not want him involved in the
secret ceremonies.

Another event of some importance took place in 1976,
when a confrontation began with one of the spirits in these
ceremonies. The Bible Society held a workshop for translators

and their assistants at Elcho Island. One *Balanda* translator raised a concern that the name of a particular spirit was being used for God by some people when they were preaching and praying.

This was discussed by a group of *Yolngu* who listed off aspects of the character of God as revealed in the Bible, comparing them with the character of this dominant spirit of the area. They saw very clearly that *Motj* was not God and banned the use of that name for the Christian God. One old tribal elder who was not a Christian said to me one day, 'That one is the same one as the serpent in the Garden of Eden.'

It was a very important decision, although some Christian *Yolngu* leaders don't see its significance yet. It seems to some *Balanda* and a few *Yolngu* that the character of *Motj* is actually more like Satan than God.

Another important development at this time was the ministry of Djiniyini Gondarra and his wife Gelung. Djiniyini was Wili's son and a key leader in the Christian church, in the Golumala clan and among all the *dhuwa* clans at Galiwin'ku. He was thoroughly trained by the old men, in Western schools and by the Methodist Church, before being ordained as a Christian minister at the end of 1976.

He and Gelung had come to trust God for their daily needs and food during their training in Papua New Guinea from 1973 to 1975. During 1976, he and parish minister, Ken Higgins, shared deeply in prayer as they worked together, experiencing a new awareness of God's presence in his life. Then, Ken handed over to Djiniyini as parish minister and moved to Brisbane.

Serving both the *Yolngu* and *Balanda* in the community was a tough job for Djiniyini. About ten per cent of the total population were *Balanda* and most of them were still missionaries employed by the church.

There were two or three times more *Balanda* attending church than *Yolngu*. However, Djiniyini ministered very ef-

Djiniyini and Gelung Gondarra. Djiniyini was the pastor and teacher of the
Galiwin'ku church during the revival.

fectively to both the *Balanda* and the *Yolngu*. Djiniyini was
keen to see the church become biblically-based. Galikali
commented:

> For the first time, people were hearing consistent, solid
> teaching in their own language. White staff had often used
> interpreters, but that surely wasn't the same. Who can tell
> how significant also was the increase in general self-esteem
> and easing of feelings of oppression and dependency that
> came with one of their own number coping competently
> and with great spiritual sensitivity with the role of pastor
> to a mixed congregation?[17]

During 1978, God's messages came forth more and more
clearly and strongly in Djiniyini's preaching as he spoke on
issues like sorcery and monogamy.[18] Sometimes, as he
preached in the church, a person walking past outside would
be drawn into the church to listen just by the sound of his
voice and was touched by God's presence.[19]

There was still very little interest in the Bible among the *Yolngu*. Aborigines are a people of the spoken word more than the written word, so cassettes were beginning to be an effective means of bringing them in touch with God's words from the Bible.

There were few Aborigines able to read the Bible well enough to teach others from it, even in Djambarrpuyngu, their own language. Djiniyini was one of the most capable and God used his gift as a teacher effectively.

In June 1978, a murder took place and Djiniyini began to go through the refining fire. A member of Djiniyini's clan was accused of murdering a young man from another clan. Four young men had been in a broken-down boat that was drifting out to sea. When they were rescued two days later, many miles out to sea, one of them was reported to have jumped overboard and to have tried to reach land, but was never seen again. Some Aborigines felt there was a spiritual cause and a young man from Djiniyini's clan who was in the boat at the time was considered responsible. (About four years later, he confessed that, indeed, there had been a fight and he had actually killed the other man.)

In the process of working all this through at the time of the death, Djiniyini called out to God and felt they should use a dangerous ceremony: the peacemaking ceremony called *makarrata*, mentioned in the last chapter. It is dangerous because sometimes the person being speared in the ceremony dies from loss of blood. But Djiniyini felt something had to be done to bring reconciliation, even though his clan believed their young man was innocent. The *makarrata* seemed the only way to avoid the other clan's judgment of payback and death.

The church prayed about the matter and God's peace became very real to them all as they went through the *makarrata*, the young man being speared in the leg. Djiniyini said it was a real test that his clan shouldn't get involved in accusations and paybacks. It was, Djiniyini said, 'one of the biggest events for me and my clan. If we were to get involved in that, the birth of the Spirit wouldn't have come. But we were patient to wait to see that the pain was to reconcile people in that birth.'[20]

In the next few months, Djiniyini and Gelung went through intense refining. Gelung was in Darwin Hospital for over six weeks with complications in the pregnancy of their fourth child and found it very lonely away from her people. She was amazed at how people came to see her whom she had never met, but who were praying for her. Nangalawuy, the baby, was induced in August three weeks early and all seemed well.

They stayed in a hostel in Darwin for a short time before returning to Galiwin'ku. While they were there, Gelung seemed to be suffering some sort of post-natal depression. She thought she was going out of her mind and was going to die. She pleaded with Djiniyini to take her back to the hospital and make arrangements for someone to look after their baby. They prayed with her and, when everyone else was asleep, she became aware of the Holy Spirit descending on her in a way that none of them had ever experienced before:

> *Gelung*:The others finally went to sleep and I was there by myself — sitting there praying, praying, praying. . . all night praying, and around about two o'clock in the morning, I could feel God's presence was there. I put my hands up. . . It was like streams. . . snow. . . I could see it snowing upon heaven. . . It opened up. . . Healing. . .
>
> *Djiniyini*: She called us and woke us up.
>
> *G*: I said: 'Can't you feel God's presence, it's so exciting!'
>
> *Dj*: It's two o'clock in the morning! [You're] outside here praising the Lord at two o'clock in the morning, when you're really tired out!
>
> *G*: The others came out, they started praying with me, praying and praying. Then, I asked the Lord, '*Bäpa*

[Father], come! Everybody should have this gift.'. . . They're all sitting there and feeling very tired, but they didn't feel it yet. . . But after that something happened.

Dj: We start to pray — the first time we were given the gift of tongues.

G: First time we experienced God in that way. . .

Dj: And the healing took place just like that [snap]. . . the first time for us to put our hands up in the air. . . From there, we came back to Galiwin'ku. We were really filled with God's Spirit, but she was moved and sharing with all the people about all the things that were happening. And they just laughed at us.

G: They couldn't believe it. 'Miracle? miracle?. . . crazy!. . . ' 'I'm not crazy, but I'm crazy with God!'[21]

Yolngu were amazed and couldn't understand but, for Djiniyini and Gelung, it was more than the birth of their child: it was a spiritual birth for their people of something of the Holy Spirit's life among them in a vibrant new reality. Djiniyini commented that he saw the struggles of that birth as a parallel and a symbol of the birth of the revival:

I see Gelung's suffering — this is the first time I've talked about it — always I see it as a picture: she was a symbol of a mother, a symbol of a church and the birth of a child. What I'm saying is you've got a church here which is really longing to see the revival. But also with that is her suffering. . . her cry of frustration.

The church is always seen as a mother figure — mother nurturer of these people, but at the same time going through all the pain. And we were praying for this revival and for the Bridegroom to come. . . I'd been praying for three years for that revival. But God said, 'First, I must show you the pain. I must show you a real experience![22]

Another important development in this period was the evangelistic work of Kevin Dhurrkay, one of Batangga's sons. He was well-trained tribally and in the Western world and the church. He was a trained school teacher and deputy principal of Shepherdson College, the Galiwin'ku school. Around 1970, his gift in evangelism had been noticed as he preached with his own style, rather like Billy Graham or Ralph Bell, for whom he had been the interpreter.

He and his wife, Nyiwula, and their family also went through the refining fire in the 1970s. Two of their children died, one in 1977 and the other early in 1978. Funeral arrangements are not made traditionally by the parents, but by other members of the extended family.

The family arranged a traditional ceremony in the camp, but Kevin and Nyiwula wanted a Christian funeral, so they made a large banner with a text on it which they placed above the coffin during the ceremonies. They also insisted that the funeral procession should take the coffin to the church for a service of thanksgiving to God. The sense of God's presence in their thanksgiving service was noticed by non-Christian *Balanda* present. It was another time of affirming that he and Nyiwula would worship the true God.

From that time on, their marriage, their relationship with God and their ministry changed dramatically. Kevin was invited to nearby communities to conduct crusades and they saw a release of the power of the Holy Spirit.

He was invited to Milingimbi in November, 1978. For months, there had been a hunger for God there, with a sense of expectancy that God was about to do something that was even stronger than at Elcho Island.

The church leaders had decided to show a Billy Graham film. They wanted Kevin to speak briefly after it and make an appeal for commitment to Jesus. He took a group from Galiwin'ku with him as a choir, who found themselves weeping as the appeal was made. Some of them were not Christians, but they and around a hundred others responded to the appeal.

The following Sunday over 300 tried to cram into the church.

Kevin and Nyiwula Dhurrkay at the time of the revival

Kevin and Nyiwula were also invited to Yirrkala that month for the church anniversary. At the end of the weekend, they talked and prayed most of the night with the people who pleaded with them not to return to Galiwin'ku because they needed them at Yirrkala.

Other communities pleaded with them to visit them. They were away in ministry almost every weekend at the end of 1978. Many people made commitments to Jesus, some just from hearing tapes of Kevin's messages. Some were amazed that God could speak to them just through hearing this man's voice and wanted to meet him face to face.[23] In her Christmas letter that year, Galikali wrote:

> Elcho folk coming home after a visit to Milingimbi insist that *everyone* at Milingimbi has turned to the Lord. Not exactly true, but the difference since twelve months ago is certainly dramatic. Elcho has not seen such a dramatic change, but there have been many conversions. . . We are praying for a deepening work of the Holy Spirit, that these

many 'baby Christians' will be established and grow quickly with a hunger for God's word, and that leadership will
emerge quickly in each centre.[24]

There were many other important developments that were
not visible to most people, like the Sunday school for old
ladies. These women were a rather 'outcast' group — mostly
widows and discarded older wives. As most of them were
illiterate and understood very little English, they were
diligently taught by Mrs Sheppie. Galikali had reluctantly
taken over from her and soon found they were a real power-
house of believing prayer. They helped her own faith to
develop rapidly through their belief in God's love and power.

✦ The *Yolngu* and *Balanda* fires become one

Towards the end of 1978, the *Balanda* and *Yolngu* fires came
together. There had been fairly strong divisions in the community in the mid-1970s. Both in the community and in the
church, the Christians had a new desire to work together with
non-Christians and to heal relationships with them. An excitement and expectancy started to build in the preaching and
in the church in 1978.

I remember preaching on Pentecost Sunday and challenged Christians whether they believed that the things that
happened at Pentecost in the Bible could really happen today
at Galiwin'ku. We came to believe that God was not just God
of the Jews two thousand years ago, but that the sort of
activity recorded of the Holy Spirit in the book of Acts was
actually going to happen amongst us at Galiwin'ku.

In August, after Djiniyini and Gelung returned from Darwin after the birth of their baby, he started asking what new
life was happening in the church around Australia. As a
result, the parish invited an evangelist named Dan Armstrong
to conduct a mission at Galiwin'ku in 1979. Galikali, the Bible
translator, suggested regular neighbourhood prayer times in

preparation for this mission. Keen groups began to meet to pray for their clan members, neighbours and workmates — and saw answers to their prayers.

But there was also a feeling that united prayer for the whole community was needed. Morning prayers had been held in the church before work every morning since the Mission settlement had begun. By 1978, only a handful of people gathered each day for the half-hour ritual of songs, Bible reading and prayer. An urgent prayer request for healing for Ken Higgins brought action. Church elders decided to invite people to a time of prayer for an hour twice a week in the church before morning prayers. Between ten and twenty people gathered in groups of up to four. It was agreed that this was not to be a time for talking with each other: it was only for prayer, in whatever language people wanted to use — Djambarrpuyngu, Fijian, English. . .

Within twenty-four hours of these prayer times beginning, there were two clear indications of God's answers. One of the *Yolngu* Christians became wildly excited when one of her family became a Christian that day. She was sure this was an answer to her prayer. Then a *Yolngu* man who hadn't been near the church for several years told Christians he didn't know what was going on, but he could feel that Christians were praying.

At the beginning of December that year, John Rudder returned for a week. He had moved to Canberra a year earlier and came back to discuss some fieldwork he wanted to do at Galiwin'ku as part of his post-graduate studies. Before he left Canberra, he was told that God had other plans for his trip, but he didn't have any idea what that meant. At a fellowship meeting the night he arrived, a young *Balanda* man was released from spirits of fear when John commanded them to leave in Jesus' name. They had entered his life when he was a child growing up at Elcho Island and he had attended a ceremony and seen ritual objects.

During that week, Djiniyini had a sense of release when John prayed for him over some personal issues that had affected him for many years. Many other *Yolngu* and *Balanda* came to John for prayer — something most of them would not have done when he was living there. I spent some time discussing with him a number of questions and problems I had and God answered my cry for help.

One of the *Balanda* women had been to Gove on a plane and had returned with a very painful earache. She asked for prayer and God brought a group of fifteen *Balanda* together that night for an unexpected time of fellowship and prayer that went through to three o'clock in the morning. At the beginning of the evening, John asked everyone to be quiet and let God speak to them, after which he asked what God was saying and what was going through their minds. A strong sense of inadequacy emerged in a number of people, and this was dealt with in prayer.

When it came to praying for Mary's earache, John remembered the words in the Bible about calling the elders to anoint with oil and pray for healing.[25] A bottle of cooking oil was produced and John handed it to me, saying, 'You're the priest: pray for her.' I had never experienced anything like this before and didn't know what to do, so I poured it over her head as I prayed for her and began speaking in tongues, which I had never done before. As Mary was healed, she was also given this gift by the Holy Spirit.

A few minutes later, John asked me to pray for Mary's husband, Wendell, one of the church elders. I had thoughts going through my mind which I spoke out as I found myself praying prophetically for the first time. Wendell received the gift of the Holy Spirit in the same way as it happened in Acts 2. Others were similarly blessed that night in an incredible outpouring of God's love and mercy.

Around 2.00 am, as we were worshipping God, John felt

God showed him that there was a dark black spiritual cloud hanging low over that area of Arnhem Land and its name was *Motj*, the dominant spirit of the area whose name had been used for God. He felt God was saying that we were to take authority over it in the name of Jesus Christ and cast it out of Arnhem Land. As we did so, John felt like he was standing, to use his words, 'two hundred miles tall', looking south over Arnhem Land. He saw the spirit like a dark shadow, flowing south through the desert and out to sea through the south-east and south-west corners of Australia. There was a sense of God having done something momentous and awesome.

Next day, John felt God confirmed to him what had happened through a promise he read in the Bible which he had never seen before:

I will remove the northerner far from you and drive him into a parched and desolate land, his front into the eastern sea and his rear into the western sea; the stench and foul smell of him will rise, for he has done great things.[26]

Within a few days, *Yolngu*, who had never been near the church, started to come to Djiniyini and ask about God; he was quite amazed at what was happening. He said to me, 'I am so thankful for our family looking after our children, because so many people are wanting our time.' A few *Balanda* also began to realise that God had really started to do something in the community which was totally beyond their experience.

Then John returned to Canberra, I moved to Alice Springs and Djiniyini went on two months' leave. Others who could be blamed for what God was doing or who might get in the way were also absent from Galiwin'ku for the next few months.

Then, in January 1979, a small group of *Yolngu* sensed God's presence on the Galiwin'ku beach in a unity they had never experienced before. Djilipa tells the story:

I was there — the elders, all the leaders, Kevin Dhurrkay — and maybe a few *Balanda* were there. We always used to have fellowship and Bible study at the church, but after Djiniyini went on holidays, we went to Mission Bay.

Someone said, 'How about we go down to the beach, have a barbecue and fellowship?'. . . Straight after the barbecue. . . [we were] singing and praising. After that, Kevin spoke to us. I was playing guitar and Kevin was praising God.

We were singing maybe four or five choruses and the power of the Holy Spirit came into our hearts; we were feeling something — it's different. That was the first time we had fellowship like that.

We were sitting down in a small circle holding hands and we were singing and, at the same time, we were filled with the Holy Spirit — everyone, at the same time. We felt his glory and power and we were excited because we felt the power. Each one felt the power of the Holy Spirit — it came into our heart and there was a joy. But nobody came and laid hands on us.[27]

Bibuka told me of a vision she had in 1975, some of which was fulfilled at this gathering on the beach:

I was sleeping and saw the old church and lots of *Yolngu* standing and praising God, saying 'Alleluya!'. . . and there was a loud noise, shaking the church like Pentecost — rain or wind or something — and everyone stood up shouting and singing, 'Praise the Lord! Praise the Lord!'

That was the first time I saw a vision. . . and it really happened — lots of people praising God like that!

When Djiniyini was away on holidays after we had that fellowship down on the beach; that time, Djaymila was playing guitar and he nearly fell in the fire and got burnt. He fell over, excited in the Spirit! And everybody was praying in tongues — all the ladies. There was a real unity, then — and it really happened.[28]

It was at this time that the Christians started to long to be together with each other and with God.

Nyiwila tells of the first two weeks of March:

Lorru was sitting one night at her house and wondering which elders of the church she would visit. That night, she needed prayer desperately. The word of the Lord came to her and said that she should come and see me and my husband Kevin. Instead of hesitating, she responded to God and came to our house. . . She came in and asked if we could pray for her.

As we were praying, the anointing of the Spirit filled the lounge room and Lorru began shaking, because she also was filled with the Spirit. Halfway through praying, Lorru opened her eyes and saw two feet with sandals standing in the midst of us all and she saw the nail marks on the Lord's hands. . . After she told us what happened during the prayer, we read Acts 2 — how the Bible tells us plainly that in the last days, God will pour out his Spirit among all flesh.

Another time, Galang'kalwuy came to us. He was mentally ill. . . Galang'kalwuy said: 'Will you pray for me, please, because I know and can see Jesus living in you.' So we asked him to come inside and we spread a blanket for him.

We sat down beside Galang'kalwuy and Kevin asked him, 'What is wrong with you?' He replied, 'I feel like I am having mental problems. I want you to pray for me.' We prayed for him. As we prayed, the Spirit of the Lord filled the room and for the first time we saw unusual things happening at that moment. We told him that by Jesus' blood and by his power he would be set free from this spirit inside him. There seemed to come out of his mouth foam that looked like white cotton balls. We kept on praying until the last of the foam was out. After that, he felt much better and free inside.

We knew straight away that it was the power of the Almighty and that by his blood he had been set free from the unclean spirit. We praised and thanked God for setting Galangkalwuy free that afternoon. What a wonderful and miraculous God we have that cares and loves us and is always with us in times of trouble! As he has said, 'Lo, I am with you always till the end of the age!'[29]

Nyiwula then went on to tell of another event that took place just one week before the momentous events of 14 March, 1979:

We came back one night [about 9.30 pm] from our usual prayer meeting and decided to stay outside instead of going straight to bed, because Mändi came with us. . . While we sat under the moon and stars, Kevin started playing his twelve string guitar and Mändi joined in with his six string guitar. We felt deeply inside that we needed to make a new song. . . Therefore, we tried different tunes with our voices to. . . the rhythm of the guitars. We started to write the words for the song [until midnight and] till 2.00 am we started fitting the words with the tune. [It seemed] as if the Holy Spirit himself had led us through the hours. We finally came up with the song 'God Bäpa' [God the Father].

As we finished the song about 4.00 am, we all saw a white cloud coming from the east and it rested above the roof of our house. We then found ourselves in the mist of God's presence. We felt as if we were cold, but we were not sure why we felt cold and why we were in the mist. [NOTE: *In a hot climate, it is beautiful to feel cold, so Aborigines in North Australia feel the Holy Spirit's presence as cool rather than hot.*] At that time we felt peace and joy within us, something we had never felt before in our lives.

It was something new, wonderful and pure. It felt like something great happened that night that I can't even put in words.

Six o'clock in the morning, Mändi went home. Kevin, Dhängal and I went into the house and we started to get ready for work. I started making breakfast and Dhängal woke the children up and had them ready for school. . . At that time, we all worked at Shepherdson College as teachers. Even though we had been up all night, we never felt tired the following morning. All we felt was God's happiness.

During the recess at Shepherdson College, we told the other teachers about our experience and about the new song and how it began. We invited women to our house after work and had a prayer meeting. We taught them the song. At that time, only a handful of men were interested in God's work.

At the closing of the prayer meeting, we sang four songs. . . the final song was '*God Bäpa*'. The women were moved by the Holy Spirit as they sang the songs and experienced the tears of joy. . . they were speaking in tongues. The women were experiencing the same Spirit of God that was experienced by the disciples in the coming of the Holy Spirit at Pentecost.[30]

'*God Bäpa*' is a slow, quiet, worshipful song which has had a great impact on many people since then, drawing both black and white right into God's presence. During the investiture of Wili (Djinini Gondarra's father) as an MBE in the middle of 1979, the community sang that song in worship and thanks to God, bringing tears to official government visitors' eyes. It has been translated into other Aboriginal languages and into English:

God Bäpa, God Bäpa
    (God the Father, God the Father),
Garray Djesu, Garray Djesu [= Lord Jesus],
    (God the Son, God the Son)
Dhuyu Birrimbir, Dhuyu Birrimbir[= Holy Spirit],
    (God the Spirit, God the Spirit)
Nhuma lurrkun, wanganyngur
    (You in all, three in one).

Reflecting on these events later, some could see that God was building up one big fire, ready to throw on huge trees and logs and to blast it with his wind to bring revival.

4

Creating a hot fire

THE ARNHEM LAND REVIVAL, 1979

*What the world thinks is worthless, useless and nothing at all is
what God has used to destroy what the world considers important.*
1 Corinthians 1: 28

BEFORE DJINIYINI GONDARRA WENT ON HOLIDAYS in January
1979, he was feeling very heavy about the Galiwin'ku community. Later, he wrote:

> There was suffering, hardship and even persecution. Many
> people left the church and no longer the Christian gospel
> had interest and value in their lives. Many began to speak
> against Christianity or even wanted to get rid of the
> church. . . The people became rich and were handling lots
> of things, such as motor cars, motor boats, good houses,
> etc. . . The earthly values became the centre of Aboriginal
> life.
>
> There was more liquor coming into the communities
> every day and more fighting was going on. There were
> more families hurt and more deaths and incidents happen-
> ing which were caused by drinking. Whole communities in
> Arnhem Land were in great chaos. The people were in
> confusion and without direction.
>
> As I went on my daily pastoral visitation around the
> camp, I would hear the drunks swearing and bashing up
> their wives and throwing stones on the houses and glass

being broken in the houses. . . The whole of Arnhem Land was being held in the hands of Satan.

I remember I woke up early one morning and went for a walk down the beach and started talking to myself. I said, 'Lord, why have you called me to the ministry? Why have you called me back to my own people? Why not to somewhere else, because there is so much suffering and hardship?'

I then returned to the manse. It was 6.30 am and it was my turn to lead the morning devotion. The bell had already rung and I had rushed into the church. There were only four people inside the church. God had given me the word to read and share with those four people. . . Ezekiel 37: 1–14: the valley of the dry bones. . .

God Yahweh commanded the prophet Ezekiel to prophesy to the dry bones, how that the dry bones represent the house of Israel, and how they were just like bones dried up and their hope had perished. They were completely cut off. After the morning prayers, Gelung, the children and I were ready to leave for our holidays.[1]

Looking back on all this later, Djiniyini saw God's response to the cry of his heart for new life for the dry bones of the Galiwin'ku church and community in this way:

In Acts 1, verses 6 to 8, Jesus and his disciples met together before the Ascension took place. The disciples asked whether God's reign was now to come in full. Jesus told them it was not their business to worry about that, but said, 'You will receive power when the Holy Spirit comes upon you'. . .

There is something quite unpredictable, unexpected and mysterious about the way that God's rule is realised in communities and in the lives of individuals. So the disciples were told to wait for the Holy Spirit and then they would be witnesses when Pentecost came. Something quite unplanned and unexpected happened. They began to babble in other strange languages and people asked, 'What is this that is happening? What is going on?'[2]

✦ The Pentecost experience on Elcho Island

By the middle of March 1979, the fire of God was burning strongly at Galiwin'ku and there were many new Christians.

On 13 March, Wirriyi had travelled down from his outstation on the northern end of Elcho and was asleep at Galiwin'ku. That was when he had the vision of the island on fire described earlier.

The following day, Djiniyini returned with his family from their holidays. They had been away for two months and had travelled a long way on the plane that day. They were very tired as the plane came in to land and were rather surprised to see a lot of excited children and adults there, welcoming them home. Kevin welcomed Djiniyini and told him that some things had been happening while he was away and they wanted to meet at the manse that night to tell him about them.

They were tired and so were a bit disappointed at that request, but they were amazed at some of the people that arrived at the house that night. People began to share some of the things that had been happening, things that they did not understand. It was clear that the Holy Spirit had been working in their lives.

Djiniyini began to teach them about the Holy Spirit. He and Gelung shared some of their own experience of the Holy Spirit and what happened after their baby was born six months earlier. He told them he and Gelung had felt so discouraged before they went on holidays with all the drunkenness and things going wrong in the community that they had been really calling out to God and praying for revival.

As they sat there that night in the manse, Djiniyini asked them to hold hands and he began to pray, asking God to pour out his Holy Spirit to bring healing and renewal. Djiniyini described what happened:

Suddenly, we began to feel God's Spirit moving in our hearts and the whole form of prayer life suddenly changed and everybody began to pray in spirit and in harmony. There was a great noise going on in the room and we began to ask one another what was going on. Some of us said that God had now visited us and once again established his kingdom among his people, who have been so bound for so long by the power of evil. Now, the Lord is setting his church free and bringing them into the freedom and happiness and into reconciliation and to restoration.[3]

One man said later: 'That was the first time I felt I was floating.'[4] They were absolutely stunned by what they were experiencing. Djiniyini and Gelung looked at each other and the tears were streaming down Gelung's face. While they had been away on holidays, they had prayed and asked God for directions for the church for 1979. Djiniyini had made a list of twelve things. He comments:

All those things that I'd written down in my notebook while I was away, thinking that I'd be able to get them going with the Holy Spirit's help — they were already happening! On the same evening, the word spread like the flames of fire and reached the whole community in Galiwin'ku.

Next morning. . . the love of Jesus was being shared and many expressions of forgiveness were taking place in the families and in the tribes. Wherever I went, I could hear people singing and humming Christian choruses and hymns, when in the past I would have expected to hear only fighting and swearing and many other troublesome things that would hurt your feelings and make you feel sad.[5]

The changes had been building for two months and were starting to be seen by everyone.

The next week, Djiniyini got the choir together on the beach to practise for Sunday night's service. Anna Edwards, a sister at the hospital, was the only *Balanda* there. She describes what happened:

Only about fifteen people turned up and we sang a few songs and everyone made damper because we had fires going. It was a very informal occasion. Before we knew what was happening, it turned into an incredible worship time which we'd never had before in that way and it went on until well after midnight from about seven o'clock. From that night on we had them every night.[6]

The numbers at these meetings grew quickly. At the end of the first week, there were about thirty people. By the end of April, there were 150 to 200 people, meeting every night of the week for four or five hours. They would gather outside someone's house in a circle. At first, there was a single circle, but this gradually became a circle about six deep.

It was in these gatherings for fellowship and prayer that the real movement of the Holy Spirit came at Galiwin'ku. No-one stood in the centre leading the meeting. The focus was on God and his leadership through the Holy Spirit rather than Djiniyini's and Kevin's leadership. They tried to preach, teach and guide the people, but so much was happening that it was hard for them to get a word in! It was clear to them that it was God who was at work, not man.

The days of asking for favourite songs to sing had gone and there was a flow from one song to the next as the Holy Spirit led them. While the singing continued, some people would pray and worship God aloud. The singing and praying complemented each other without any competition or discord.

During February and March, Galikali had been away on leave, returning at the beginning of April 1979. Snippets from her diary entries and letters over the next few weeks give some feel of the atmosphere building up in April.

Friday 6 April: My first taste of new move of God in *Yolngu* fellowship. Find myself incredulous. . . *Hugs* from men. . . atmosphere of *love*. Can it be true?

Saturday 7 April: Took a long time to get going. . . Djilipa saying to complaining child re sore finger, 'Just praise Jesus with us — he'll heal it!'

Power 'fell'. Tears a relief. Gelung and Y [another woman] drunk with Holy Spirit. Praise you, Lord God Almighty!

Tuesday 10 April: *Yolngu* fellowship in church. . . let's get rid of the seats! And children — several lost in praise. B and Dj [two of Djiniyini's children] filled with Holy Spirit. Had a picture of the children flocking to Jesus and ministering mightily. Let it be so, Lord.

Wednesday 11 April: One of the *yawirriny*[= young men] prayed for last night was praising God in English — sounded like a quote, but whether or not it was, it must have been tongues!

The wave that's been building up for maybe a year is *breaking*. The night fellowship meetings are the most 'charismatic' I've ever been to in terms of knowing the presence of God — people in floods of tears as the power of God comes on them, others drunk with the Holy Spirit. The shouted praises from so many *Yolngu*, the passionate worship and adoration are just unreal. Reserves between black and white have melted away. . . I've never known such a flow of love.

G, Y and M [three men]. . . are so high — everyone united with their wives in a new relationship. . .[7]

The praise is incredible — just the same old songs and a few new original ones , but the Holy Spirit is the conductor. The volume rises and falls as he wills — as it rises, lots of folk break off singing to worship verbally, loudly.[8]

There's been a lot of English sung, but the Holy Spirit is giving *Yolngu* praise songs. . . Intriguing thing is they get them in Yolngumatha [their own language], then in English — the words just flow out naturally! When it's in English first and we try to force Yolngumatha words, it doesn't go the same![9]

In a letter written at the time, other community staff wrote, 'It is really good to see the *Yolngu* praising and worshipping the Lord so freely, they leave most of the staff behind, a long way.'[10]

During April, Joyce Ross, Bible translator from Yirrkala, came over to Galiwin'ku for three weeks to help Galikali translate John's Gospel for the planned mission with Dan Armstrong. A few weeks later, she commented on the fellowship meetings:

The focus was on Jesus' *victory*!. . .
'Jesus, you're alive!'
'You're not a god of stone!'
'You're not a god of wood made with hands!'
'You're the living God!'

. . .[for those affected] their whole body trembled. . . God gives them a physical manifestation of the touch of his power and, suddenly, all the spirit world that they know applies and they see Jesus as that One and the Holy Spirit as the spirit of life, joy and wholeness — much more than miraculous healings, although there are healings.[11]

As they were convicted of sin, some would start weeping and getting right with God. They would go into the middle of the circle and kneel, often with both a sense of repentance and of praise, worship and awe at God's presence and who he is. Some of the elders or other Christians would come and kneel beside them and pray with them. Sometimes, there would be some counselling and talking with them, but mostly it was just laying hands on them and praying.

Galikali wrote in her report on the revival:

Europeans who showed an interest in sharing in these meetings were warmly welcomed and frequently were asked to share in the ministry of praying with those in need — but the quickly established and acknowledged leadership was very definitely Aboriginal. There was a warmth, acceptance and openness between black and white that was quite breathtaking. . . That was also very evident between clans which had not related well in the past. Some of the first to be set on fire were the wives of quite a number of the leaders and potential leaders, who had previously been held back by this lack of support in their desire to follow God.[12]

Other community staff reported:

The excitement among the Aboriginal people was outstanding. Fellowship was more of a drawcard than the pictures, even for the children. [Open air community movies had been very popular at that time, before TV and videos arrived.] People met every night and Sunday services were incredibly well attended. I remember a visit by some church officials from Brisbane and a praise time in the church in their presence that I thought would lift off the roof![13]

Galikali described that occasion in her diary as 'spine-tingling'.[14]

As each person made their commitment to Jesus, prayer for their whole family would increase and frequently they would all respond to Christ within a few days. Sometimes, it would be a family leader who came first, but often it was a child or wife.[15] They found it all so incredible. Galikali wrote in her diary about one church leader:

Thursday 12 April: W [Christian Aboriginal leader] is very ignorant — mystified — confused about Jesus as 'Coming King'. He thought the current outpouring of the Holy Spirit must be what's meant by Jesus coming back. The incredibility of this being only a taste of heaven was too much!

Good Friday [13 April]: Midnight. . . [the] meeting [was] *high* in worship. Wow, was it high!

Monday 16 April: Meeting on beach. A real 'spirit of heaviness' and awareness that the high feelings just won't be humanly stirred up. . .[16]

Finally, the translation of John's Gospel was finished and Galikali reported in her diary:

Friday 4 May: Finished *John* last night. Thanks, Lord — actually sooner than I expected. Good time in prayer during the a.m., binding Satan and demanding the release of people's minds to use this Djambarrpuyngu Gospel. . .[17]

At one point during April, the Aboriginal church elders identified several strong spirits affecting the area and started to tell people to renounce these spirits as they prayed for them in the middle of the circle. The spirits were *Lanydjat* and *Marryulk*. In English, they are called Pride and Unbelief. Galikali wrote about it:

Tangible change in the atmosphere. This had *nothing* to do with *Balanda*. We've been on the outskirts of everything, except in prayer — not 'left out', but obviously God is doing a clean-up in his way in the *Yolngu* church so we can truly be one.[18]

The changes that resulted from dealing with these spirits can be seen in the lives of Rronang and Dangatanga.

Rronang was a fisherman, not educated in the Western world. He came from one of the more influential families in the community. When he heard about the fellowship meetings, he felt they were a waste of time. However, God was at work in his life and about the fourth or fifth night, he found himself going along to see what was happening, as he describes:

I was a Christian for sixteen years. I used to go to Sunday school, then church every Sunday. When the revival happened, I said to myself, 'I don't want to go there! I've been a Christian for sixteen years! That's enough! I'm faithful! I'm still going to the church!. . .'

But one time, God's Spirit was really talking to me — pushing me to go there. . . I was standing in the back. . . As I stood there, somebody was preaching and he said: 'I think the Lord is challenging us tonight, even if we are older Christians. We have to come and kneel down and receive God's Spirit — a new blessing, a new hope. Because maybe your life is still Christian, but you're still standing in the same place. Maybe God's Spirit is now talking to you. . .'

Rev. Dhalnganda Garawarra (Rronang) with his wife and child

And I thought, 'Hey, that man is talking to *me*! — straight to me, not to other people!'

'Maybe some of you are standing there — you don't want to come and kneel down and change your life. You may be thinking like this right now. God's Spirit is challenging you right now to come and kneel down and we will pray for you and you will receive new blessing and new life and new insight! '

'Hey, that's me!. . . Well, I can't go — I'm a Christian!. . . Maybe I will share later with the minister. Nobody can see me then. . .'

But the Spirit said: 'No! Move right now! Move! Kneel down! Don't worry about what you are thinking!'

Rronang tried to convince himself and also God that he was shy and that the inner voice of the Holy Spirit inside him was wrong:

But the Spirit was saying at the same time in my heart, 'No, *you* are wrong! I want you to come and kneel down!' And then, after that I just moved. . . put my pride and everything aside and knelt down and they were praying for me and I was really blessed! Straight after that, for four days the Lord was speaking to me: 'You've been working, fishing, for a long time. Now, I want you to be a fisher of men. Instead of catching fish, I want you to catch men.'[19]

As the pride was dealt with in his life, he felt God was calling him to train for the ministry of the church:

And I said, 'But how? I'm not trained or qualified. I didn't go to school. I'm just nothing!'
   'Don't say that you are nothing. I chose you! I appointed you!'

He struggled with that for four months, finally asking for a sign that it was right. That night, his wife had a dream about him becoming a fisher of men instead of a fisherman and going to college to learn more about God. But it was another month before he talked with the minister about it and the long procedures of the Uniting Church began. His application went through the elders' council. . . the presbytery. . . the synod committee. . . the synod.

The whole process took so long that he was ready to give up and just go back to being a fisherman and forget about it all. But God was not giving up so easily. God's fire was working on him and his pride. He was eventually accepted and trained at Nungalinya College, the combined churches' training college for Aborigines in Darwin, where he has been a lecturer in theology for a number of years, graduating with a BTh in 1996.

The next story is Dangatanga's. As his story shows, some people had dramatic changes in their lives. Dangatanga was the sort of person you really didn't want to meet in a dark street at night. He was a violent, *Balanda*-hating alcoholic who, amazingly, was to become a reconciler, with a very special way of relating to *Balanda*.[20] He tells his own story:

What made me change? — well, I don't know. That's the mystery of the Lord. Because what I was thinking for my life [was] I wanted to be doing what I want. I cut my life off from the family — I left my wife, kids.

My wife had patience all the time — she just waited for me to come back — and the kids, but I've been still struggling. . . I went drinking in Darwin — brought grog here, had arguments with family, arguments with another tribe, arguments with white people, missionaries — really bad.

My wife was praying for me. You know, we enjoyed going to Sunday school. But I didn't really see this new life clearly, personally, for me. I never experienced it like this.

One day, I went to Steven's place. I went there carrying my bottle, drinking, and I was sitting down in the car laughing. People were praising. Djiniyini and Kevin started fellowship and I was there sitting down watching and at the same time I was drinking and laughing. I was really bad. When I look back, that way it's nothing there — empty life!

Then, Djiniyini started speaking. People were singing, praising, they were slain in the Spirit: just fell down everywhere. And I was watching. What's happening?

The Lord was really speaking to Djiniyini and gave a message for me. I was sitting down on the bonnet of the car, laughing, holding the bottle, and then suddenly I felt the car shaking.

Djiniyini said: 'The Lord spoke to me. There is one man must come before tomorrow — tomorrow is too late for him. If he receives the Lord Jesus now, he'll be saved. That man is really following his own way and he doesn't want to listen. . . You know all the bad things. . . If you come forward tonight, you will have more friends and you had no friend before.'

They were really powerful words! I came forward a little bit and I was listening, but I kept on laughing. I left that bottle. I got a shock, because I knew that the Lord was there. I felt different like I never felt: I was inside a fire, with the fire all around me and I felt comfort [peace], but I was burning.

I didn't say anything, but just quietly laughed — tears, too — at the same time Djiniyini keep on speaking — keep on, keep on. Then, suddenly, I felt just like somebody punching me, lifting my foot, and I was walking. One step . . .stopped. Three steps, into the middle, close to the middle past the people, then into the inside of the circle. Then, I was knocked down — head down, legs up — sliding, like an electric shock that threw me, legs up, head down. I've never experienced this before!

I thought I was hurt, but I just felt like rubber or something. Then, I woke up and I was just like a new-born baby. Weak and crying, crying — I never cried like this. Just a new man, new man with this big pool of fire around me. The fire was still there. I can feel the heat.

I feel just like when a new baby is born. When you're inside in a mother's womb, you feel safe and sometimes you feel hard to get out — that's what I was feeling. I was inside in the seal of Satan just like big eggs and I was trying to come out. And the fire was just pushing the eggs close and, when they come too close to them, I come out. The fire just forced them and I just come out. Knocked upside down.

Next minute, they were praying for me. Elders, Kevin, Djiniyini prayed for me. Oh, I was crying. Then, I looked back at the people and I felt different. Different — just like I was just free, free just like in a new land. I walk in just like a new land, singing, praising.

Then, my life started growing, feeding. I went to see Rronang and Djiniyini one day. I still felt like I got lots of muck in me — muck of Satan's scars! I need the deliverance prayer. . . before I go for baptism in water. Then, I had this special deliverance prayer with Rronang, Djiniyini and Kevin. They prayed for me and shared a lot of things where I've been tied up in my life. . . After that, I feel fresh — like a new baby. I don't know the world — just come into it!

Then, I want the Lord to establish a new kingdom in my life, his kingdom. Then, after a couple of months, I was leading in singing and I joined with groups, joined with elders, prayed together, prayed for us to grow, grow, grow.[21]

Later, he was baptised as an indication of his changed life. Dangatanga is now one of the key church leaders in Arnhem Land and his *Balanda*-hating attitudes have changed to a desire to bring reconciliation and peace as a very special ministry to black and white today.

There was another area of the spiritual world that God placed on the bonfire for refining. One day, Djiniyini put a bookmark in his Bible and left it on a blanket in the front yard for someone who was going to read from it at a meeting. But a crow came and attacked his Bible and tore it to pieces. This was a particularly meaningful and stretching situation for him because the crow is *maḏayin* [totem] for his clan.

Galikali wrote in a letter:

After a very disturbed night following this late-afternoon episode, Djiniyini and Gelung were both troubled and *needing* ministry — and the Holy Spirit brought some people, all at the same time (about 8:30 am) — none having any idea why!

Rronang was told to drive around the Health Centre Hill, then slow down and Djiniyini hailed him. Nyiwula knew in her spirit they were in trouble and came down. Wendell and Garrawanngu turned up. Wuyatiwuy was praying for them, finding himself weeping. Djiniyini and Gelung were deeply ministered to, so the attack turned into a mighty victory. The house and grounds were thoroughly cleansed — they marched all around the house and yard, claiming it mightily for Jesus, and that's really started something.[22]

Following this incident, they continued to have visits from a crow, but also a dove. Djiniyini talked about it:

Every time when the bird came, he used to knock at the door and I said: 'Gelung, somebody is outside.' And she would see that bird fly away. Every time it came, then we can see another bird — a white one — come and chase it. They used to fight every time and we could hear them.

One day, we asked all the elders: 'I want you to come and pray, and we'll be praying that the bird will visit us.'

We locked the door and closed all the windows: 'so you can see with your own eyes and believe with your own heart'. So we were silently praying and then the beak [knocking]. And I told each one, 'I want you to go one by one to the window and just open it a little bit.'

Wendell was really good — he nearly died! Wendell just wanted to collapse! So every one of them went to the window and they saw and they believed. And then, after about ten minutes, the dove came and chased the crow away: 'Waah, wah, waah. . .'[23]

They knew that the dove represents the Holy Spirit and is a peaceful bird and wondered about the significance of it chasing away the crow, the totem of Djiniyini's clan. It caused them to search in their culture and ask God if there was something there which he wasn't happy about. What was God trying to say to them about their totem? They are now asking what deeper truth God is leading them to discover through this incident.

✦ The mission with Dan Armstrong at Elcho Island

Finally, it was time for the mission with Dan Armstrong, planned before any of these new experiences had started.

Dan and his team arrived on the Saturday evening, 1 May, 1979. They had tea with the community, then a time of worship. It was a very ordinary sort of time: there were some real tensions, as drunks came around and one woman was yelling about a song they sang which had words sounding similar to the name of her dead relative. (It was against their traditions to use any word sounding like the name of a person who has died in recent years.)

Later, a smaller group of the leaders met with the team in one of the houses and began to worship God. They felt God's presence in a powerful way. Dan spoke out these prophetic words he felt God gave him:

> My little children, over the next few days you are going to
> learn what this really means — to be my children. . . to learn
> to rely, to trust, and to depend on me. . .
>
> You will learn to be really free — to play, to laugh, to
> hope, to cry. You will see how a father loves his children
> and you will learn to love me as your Father.[24]

Next day, Sunday, during the first service of the mission,
Dan and Con Stamos, another member of the team, taught
some new songs which were well-received. Several people
came to the front for prayer at the end of the meeting,
including two *Balanda* teachers. Galikali wrote in her diary:

> Afternoon. . . R [a *Balanda* teacher] *really* getting free —
> clapping, dancing, hand-raising. . .! Lots of our 'old ladies'
> in tears! One young fellow came down from the choir stalls
> backwards with his hands in the air! Build-up of praise at
> the end was tremendous.[25]

Evangelist Rev. Dan Armstrong with Elcho Island minister, Rev. Djiniyini
Gondarra, wife Gelung and child during the 1979 mission

That evening, there were hundreds of people present, including many tribal elders. Dan preached a powerful message on the cross which brings freedom from death, sickness, demonic oppression and fears. One of the old tribal elders and his wife were the first to respond. The church leaders seemed so stunned at this that no-one went to talk and pray with them for a while.

Finally, Djiniyini's seven-year-old son, Djaybung, went over to them and placed his hands on their heads and other children joined him in praying for them. The ministry of the children had already been developing strongly as they worshipped the Lord before the mission. One of the teachers wrote:

> Dan's preaching in the meetings had solid Bible teaching, with a solid challenge to take the message of the special blessings God had given them to their people who had not yet received it. There were many messages on basic gospel truths, such as 'God loves you', 'Jesus died for your sin', 'You can be free from fear and the prisons within'.[26]

The messages were interpreted into Djambarrpuyngu and Galikali, the linguist, found most of the interpreting 'really incredible'. Aboriginal languages have a very different, cyclical structure to English, with a lot of repetition, so that it takes longer to say something than for English. Dan spoke in his very clear, simple English and the interpreting flowed so smoothly that it often overlapped — there were no gaps and waiting for one to finish. This was seen as a real work of the Holy Spirit.

By Monday night, there were so many people attending that they had to meet outside the church building in the open-air.

On Tuesday, Dan went fishing with some of the men to get to know them better. Dan is a totally dedicated fisherman: as an evangelist fishing for people's souls with the gospel, as well as catching fish with a rod. He cut his arm badly on a guy wire on the boat, requiring six stitches. That night, he asked another team member to preach. Con Stamos spoke about how God had helped him break his addiction to smoking. Galikali wrote in her diary:

> It was a very tense time, as so many of the Christians were addicted to tobacco. It was especially difficult for the interpreter and brought a negative reaction from the whole group. Dan was confident over Romans 8, verse 28: that God was working out his purposes in it all![27]

Wednesday after work, there was a meeting for the men. For a number of years, there had been no young men in the church, but there were many of them at this meeting and they experienced the Holy Spirit's touch in their lives.

For several weeks, there had been visions of tongues of fire during meetings but, during this meeting, people saw fireballs descending from the sky towards the meeting and there was a very strong sense of God's presence.

Galikali also reported there was a commissioning of young men to take the gospel to others:

> Dan had a 'word from the Lord' at the end. . . that Elcho would be increasingly the 'Island of the Holy Spirit' and that teams would go out from here all over Arnhem Land, to part-Aborigines and White Australia, throughout the continent and beyond, with lips of fire. The men — especially these scores of young men — took that seriously and nothing would stop them![28]

The church elders had decided to hold the Wednesday night meeting in 'bottom camp'. This was an area in the town near the beach, where they felt there were strong spirit-powers. They wanted to claim the area for Jesus. Galikali reports:

> Around bottom camp, there was an area recognised as having evil spirits. Some say it used to be a ceremonial ground; others that a man had deliberately given himself to

a spirit of anger and eventually killed himself there. . . During the week before Dan arrived, and in his first few days here, three young fellows from the bottom camp went 'mad'. Each has had some deliverance, but not completely clear.[29]

It had already been noticed that people classified as mentally disturbed often reacted when Jesus was being worshipped and Christians were feeling the Holy Spirit's presence strongly. They had come to believe that there were demons involved in the behaviour of these people.

It was clear during the meeting that there was a spiritual battle going on. There were many dog fights. Four of the six team members had severe stomach cramps during the meeting. One of the young Aboriginal men went beserk. Galikali wrote:

[It was] the 'highest' meeting in spontaneous flowing and claiming of victory. Three hundred to four hundred people took that area from Satan in Jesus' name and claimed mighty positive victory there and powerful ministry from the people who live there, etc. Djiniyini prayed powerfully and all spontaneously chorused 'Yuwalk!' [Yes, that's right!] at the end of each statement. There was quite a bit of deliverance that night during the altar call and more of the old men responded.[30]

Thursday was a different sort of battle. It was the last night before the team visited four other communities. They were expecting a really great night, with lots of people.

Then they heard that the Brian Young Show was flying in to Galiwin'ku for a concert that night in the large community hall. This was very close to the place where the mission meetings had been held. Aborigines in the communities had little entertainment except movie shows in those days and this style of concert would normally have an audience of hundreds. Dan Armstrong reports:

We were disappointed and I thought, 'Well, now we'll really know whether we're in a revival or not!'

So we arrived that night and there were about five hundred gathered there rejoicing in the Lord [some gave a count of seven hundred]. There were about forty people at the Country Western Show.

We saw the same thing happening wherever we went. At one place, they had to close the picture show down because no-one went: they came to these meetings. We left at 10.30 every night worn out, but they stayed until one or two o'clock in the morning, still ministering to one another.[31]

During the six weeks of the revival before the mission, about two hundred adults had committed their lives to Jesus. During the mission, another two hundred made that commitment.

Many of the *Balanda* were really touched by God. One couple who had caused many heartaches and frustrations for many of the missionaries were living together under an adopted name. The Holy Spirit drew them and they made a commitment to Jesus on Sunday night, later being officially married in the church at Galiwin'ku.

Another *Balanda*, Ross, was married to a *Yolngu* woman who had left him some months earlier for a man in Darwin. Ross caught hepatitis and a *Balanda* Christian couple were caring for his children for about six weeks. They just 'loved the socks off Ross'.

Dan went to their house on Thursday and Ross turned up. He made a very deep, tearful commitment to God, saying he wanted to make a fresh start with his wife. Dan laid hands on him and claimed her for God and the restoration of the marriage. Ross later commented that Dan has 'electric fingers'.

Two days later, his wife ('B') unexpectedly arrived for the weekend to see the children, not even intending to speak to

Ross. Galikali wrote, 'On Sunday night, Ross and B went forward hand-in-hand and B gave her life to the Lord. There was barely a dry *Yolngu* or *Balanda* eye there!'[32]

Dan Armstrong reported on their final meetings:

We came back to Elcho for a final Sunday night meeting. On the Sunday afternoon, we gathered together all the people that God was raising up to be elders and leaders in the life of the church. As we were sharing, God gave me a message that God was going to send out these people in teams to bring revival all over our land. I just *knew* this was going to happen, and I shared it with them, and a great roar went up, and they began to cheer and glorify the Lord.[33]

Dan had longed to see evidence of the Holy Spirit's work in Australia like he was seeing overseas and it was finally fulfilled during this trip to Arnhem Land. A few weeks later, he told one church in NSW that he was really impressed at what he saw:

[It was] their gentleness and their humility. They did not flood out and trample over one another. They came out gently one by one and knelt, falling upon their knees and began to weep. . . and were broken before the Lord. . . and rising into newness of life with a glorious shine on their faces.

And God was raising up ministries among them. . . evangelist. . . teacher. . . prophetic gifts. . . and it was beautiful how they flowed in this and really became the body of Christ. . . As people began to come forward, some of the people who had come to Jesus were coming out and beginning to minister with us, without ever having to be asked, without having to be shown. . . weeping with them, rejoicing with them, praying with them, on their knees with them. It was beautiful.[34]

One of the team members, Con, was a schoolteacher. He spoke to children at the Galiwin'ku school and it was arranged for one of the classes to swap letters and photos with his class in Sydney. Their letters contained statements like, 'We go to fellowship and praise God' and 'Lots and lots of people here have given their hearts to Jesus.'

After the mission with Dan Armstrong at Elcho Island, the impact of the fire of revival did not stop when the team left. One teacher wrote after the mission:

> There is a new atmosphere of happiness and friendliness around town. Some of the men who have become Christians are now actively looking for work. Families who used to do things separately are now doing things together.[35]

Another wrote, 'There is more genuine acceptance of *Balanda* by other *Balanda* on all sorts of fronts and that's tremendous. . . and a growing openness which has started very recently.'[36]

Galikali wrote in her newsletter at the end of June:

> About a further two hundred people added to the fellowship [during the mission]. So different from any previous evangelistic effort: people really on fire, lives changed radically, love flowing. Self-consciousness disappearing. And there have been many more (I'm guessing, but I'd say fifty) real conversions since the mission. Some Europeans . . .coming to Jesus mostly through what is happening in the *Yolngu* church.[37]

That made at least four hundred and fifty new Christians out of a total population of around 1200 — in only four months! But such changes don't come without struggles. On the Sunday following the mission, Djiniyini mentioned in the service that he had received a very critical letter accusing him of destroying *Yolngu* culture. He stated very strongly that he was not doing anything except what the Holy Spirit was leading him to do. The battle continued!

One day, one of the tough *Balanda* workers who lived across a back lane from the manse got to the end of everything. Djiniyini reported:

That was G's last day. He'd been drinking for a long time and had lots of troubles. He had loaded his gun and he was thinking to shoot himself. But we were praying and singing, and that song just went right into him like a melody to his insides. And he walked out of his house. He came running, crying. . . He went right inside the circle and just knelt down.[38]

Balanda church elder, Wendell Flentje, learned a lot as the *Yolngu* ministered to G:

It seemed that he was ready to commit himself to Christ and I was waiting for someone to speak to him, but all they did was pray! There seemed to be a complete trust that the Holy Spirit would do what he wanted to do — all they needed to do was pray. And, of course, the result was wonderful. The absolute turnaround in his life was probably the most miraculous event I associate with the whole revival.[39]

Years later, Rronang talked about the changes that came at that time:

We used to love only our own people and own family and own tribe more than other tribes — just a little bit for others. When God's Spirit came, he changed life. We loved each other, all tribes, more than we loved before. We loved more — we were sharing more. Our love expanded and our love and sharing life and caring life expanded from here to other places. That's more than love just for the family, for

Baptisms in the ocean at Dharrwarr, Elcho Island, 1991

one people. They tried to forgive other people.

People were working very hard — planting gardens at that time, cleaning up places, looking after children — a lot of things were happening at that time. A lot of people were coming and listening for God's word. People were praying. There are a lot of strong leaders now out of that time.

In 1970, 1971 and 1972, there was a lot of love for our own tribe, our own community, extended to other places. That's God's love, even before the revival — it was expanded love to other tribes and other people in Arnhem Land. But this is more than Arnhem Land! In the revival, this is reaching out beyond Arnhem Land.[40]

The church elders decided to hold a baptismal service on June 24. The whole community, including a number who were still non-Christians, gathered to see the baptism. They had been prepared for this through weekly teaching sessions since the mission. Galikali reported:

During the week before the service, Djiniyini and some elders interviewed would-be candidates to ensure that they understood and were genuine in taking this step. Quite a number chose or were encouraged to 'wait until next time'. There were *eighty* actually baptised, including six Europeans. . . and three couples who have been Christians for some years, but wished to take this step of obedience to Jesus' command.

What a service!

With a new understanding of the significance of the cross, the idea grew to erect a cross in the beach at low tide, so the baptisms could take place at its foot as the tide came in. Djiniyini expounded Romans 6 — being buried with Christ and raised to new life with him. He challenged everyone (not just those being baptised) to let the cross on the beach remind us whenever we see it of this passage and also of the continuous cleansing and forgiveness available at the cross. . . While groups of people were ushered to the foot of the cross, the hundreds of onlookers on the beach sang worship songs. There was a great atmosphere of praise.

The service was a wonderful witness to many non-Christians, especially Europeans (there are a lot of contractors here building a new hospital, painting the school, etc.) and much sharing has been done, questions asked, since Sunday afternoon.

Already, people who weren't thoroughly convinced that baptism was 'necessary' are saying, 'When's the next one?' Now thoroughly convinced![41]

By the end of June, every part of the whole community had been affected in a major way. There were few patients at the health centre and almost all the staff there had become Christians through seeing what God had done, especially in the health of the community. At the school, almost all of the *Yolngu* teachers and five of the *Balanda* teachers had become Christians because of the changes they could see in the children at the school.

The Christians had not even thought to pray for three of those *Balanda* teachers: they seemed to be almost beyond the reach of the Holy Spirit. Relationships between *Balanda* and *Yolngu* improved dramatically, with a new level of concern for each other.

The revival continued to refine the Galiwin'ku community and began to spread and people from all over the world came in small numbers to see what God was doing and to experience it for themselves.

5

Sustaining the hot fire

THE ARNHEM LAND REVIVAL, 1979–1981

AS GOD'S BUSHFIRE BURNED TO THE HEART OF THE THICK TREES of society, burning sticks from it were used to light more fires and sparks from it ignited dry vegetation, starting new fires. Djilipa spoke to me about the revival fire and said:

> [The word] _'gurtha'_ means 'fire', but [more than that] _'tongues_ of fire'. _'Gurtha'_ is when we go out to the bushes and light a fire in the bushes. When we look very closely, we see tongues of fire.
>
> That fire represents the power of the Holy Spirit. But tongues of fire also represents a people. In our culture, when we are singing about the land God has given us and how we have to use the land and everything in it, we are singing on that land. . . and the Yirritja moiety [group of clans] mention that name _gurtha_ in their songs. That fire is representing the Holy Spirit and representing people, because that fire goes to link people to other clans. That links clan to clan. There is a link to bring people together.
>
> It is just in the fire because, when we look at fire, there's a power. There is a link — the fire makes us into one, every clan. Yirritja have to make a special ceremony. But first of all, they have to talk with the regional clans. They talk and talk on, they have to make agreement. And second, they have to pass a message to the other clans. Then, when they come back to that clan, they have an agreement and they can start the ceremony.[1]

✦ Changes in the community

The fire began to burn very deeply, bringing changes in the whole community. People were looking for work. They took a new pride in themselves and their world. Church elder, Wendell Flentje, was the agriculturalist in charge of the community market garden and wrote later:

> From early 1979, there was a great demand for banana suckers, sweet potato runners, pawpaw seed and so on as people seemed to want to be more productive with their time and seemed to want to beautify the surroundings of their homes. The end of all gambling for about two years meant that people had more time to care for their surroundings.[2]

Galikali adds to that:

> A few places are putting non-Aboriginal homes to shame with their park-like grounds. It's not yet 'typical white suburbia' (a doubtful aim at best), but new life is helping people to come to terms with a non-nomadic lifestyle and the realities of litter and accumulated 'things'.[3]

Djilipa also talked about the change in people's lives in 1979:

> Their life is an example to their neighbours to follow. It's showing people how to look after a place so people can see it and say, 'I must do something, like this man working out there.' They might look and do the same thing. Sick people, some in a bad condition: we were going to them and we laid hands on them and then that person straightaway stood up — got up from the bed — completely better, because it was God's power. The sick people really have faith in God before they are healed, because they have heard and seen God heal other people.[4]

Petrol sniffing had been destroying people's brains and killing them, but it declined dramatically, as did consumption of alcohol and drunkenness. General vandalism in the community decreased significantly. There was also a new depth of relationship in marriages that could not be hidden. Some *Yolngu* husbands and wives felt so close to each other that traditions were broken and they held hands in public.

Galikali wrote:

One of the most significant outcomes. . . is the death blow to the custom of polygamy. So many couples have come into a beautiful unity in Jesus. . . always sitting together in the relaxed atmosphere of fellowship. . . but also in church. A couple of years ago, I would have said 'it's cultural' to the fact that mostly men sat on one side of the church and women on the other. . .[5]

However, it was not a complete death blow to polygamy. Nor did it seem to affect the prevailing lack of discipline among children. Galikali commented at that time about the total lack of discipline of children that the revival had not changed.[6]

In 1980, a missionary asked a Galiwin'ku *Yolngu* what difference the revival had made in everyday life. He thought for a moment and said, 'See that man over there? I now call him my brother.' The missionary didn't understand at the time that the *Yolngu* world view had been fairly confined to their own tribe and their land, ceremonies and law. He later came to realise the significance of the remark:

There was some relationship with adjoining tribes. . . but they had different law, different sites. But with the renewal, there was an awareness that the God who was foreshadowed in our sacred sites, who gave *us* our law and ceremony and our land, was the same God who gave *you* your land, ceremonies, truth. . . and that makes *you* my brother!

. . .It was amazing that there should have been a compelling desire to go out from the renewal at Galiwin'ku in missionary zeal. . . In the past [and still to some degree], knowledge was something to be kept secret: knowledge was power. But now it was being given away.

. . .to think that a man from the coast could bring truth

about God to people in the Centre. In the past, he would have had a spear through him! One night at the Katherine Convention, a government man said, 'If we in the government had brought this mob together even a few years ago, the spears would have been out.'[7]

In May 1979, one of the nursing sisters reported big changes in health at Galiwin'ku. 'We're getting half the number of patients at the health centre for the first time. There has been that kind of healing of people who needed tender loving care, [who had] all kinds of physical symptoms from their inner problems — they are [now] healed.'[8]

Djiniyini also talked about this change. Referring to one of the nurses, he said:

> Sister Cheryl came in two days after the revival. 'Hey! You know what? Nobody's in hospital — nobody's there, now!' She [usually] had five or six people who were drug addicts. All of them come and ask, 'Asprin! asprin!'. . . 'Tablets, tablets, tablets!' and Cheryl was arguing with them. But when that revival happened, there was no sign of those people at the health centre.[9]

There were not lots of miraculous healings. It was more a matter of people finding life and power, so they didn't get sick. They had something other than themselves and sickness to think about to give them personal attention: they were conscious of being loved by God!

Dangatanga started work at the health centre around that time. He talked to me about some of his work:

> I was praying for sick ones, praying for people with the problems. I prayed for the medicine before people take it. I used to help lots of young boys and middle-aged in hospital, telling about the drugs, because sometimes they were taking lots of drugs just for fun — you know, sometimes causing spiritual problem, sometimes physical problem. . . If doctor check you and everything's all right, might mean you got spiritual problem. You need some-

body to pray with you and deal with that problem. He can pray with you, ask God.

So I make lots of books about the drugs [for people to read]. I was making book about the headaches. Why headaches? Because there's two type of headaches. One is headaches you can get through [getting too] hot, or maybe you get angry or no food [don't eat]. That's the natural headache. But other headaches is. . . a spiritual problem.

If you see the people getting mad, they can say mad words: you know straight away that's the work of Satan. The natural headache you can have tablets, just one — it's gone. But. . . if you have [it] three or four times or six times, [it's spiritual]. You wasting lots of money taking tablets. . . You have the tablets with just no reason. Pray with them!

I explained it and we had a special service in the hospital.[10]

The fire also started to burn deeply into some of the cultural traditions, such as blaming others for causing deaths. This came to a head in September 1979, when a twenty-two-year old died as a result of sniffing petrol and drinking a mixture of acetone and methylated spirits. Galikali recounts what happened next:

Non-Christian members of his clan immediately began fear-generating talk of blame and payback. The atmosphere was tense. Older members of the clan, who are new Christians, saw for the first time that they had to oppose a traditional custom, because it ran contrary to the prayer we sing almost daily from John 17: 'Father, make us one'.

The mother of the dead man is a Christian of only a few months, but had an incredible witness as she demonstrated God's peace and even joy in the midst of sorrow, and she and Djiniyini and Kevin were powerfully used of God at a clan meeting which lasted for many long hours.

The final outcome was the conviction that death was not, after all, the result of sorcery (sudden tragic deaths have always been attributed to same). The previously angry leaders and relatives went to the leaders of the clan which was being blamed (a long-standing feud) and shook hands all around and spoke of friendship and acceptance. It's hard to describe to an outsider the significance of this event in the life of an Aboriginal community. Believe me, it's exciting![11]

Another change that many people struggled with was the relationship between ceremonies and Christianity. Earlier, we heard how George Dayngumbu was dying of emphysema and God healed him. Gradually, he came to believe that God did not want him involved in the secret ceremonies, and now he says:

All the secret ceremonies have to go, but we must keep the public ones which the women and children can see because our very life is in that.

I did the carving of the *rangga* for the 1957 Covenant with another boy. A lot of people did the painting. My father marked the lines and said, 'Do it this way.'

But now I'm giving everything to the Lord — I'm not touching anything any more. When the children say, 'Father, show us the totem. How are we going to do it when you die?' then I say, 'Well, I can't do anything any more! My hands are clean — I can't touch it any more!'[12]

This refining process has had a deep effect on George which was seen clearly during the revival meetings. Many groups would come forward to present items and lead singing. It was often like concert items or empty ritual, but George's whole group only sang worship to God and reflected a deep spirituality.

✦ Unusual events of a spiritual nature
During this period, a number of unusual events occurred that were believed to have a spiritual origin.

Shane Blackman is an Aboriginal Christian leader from Townsville who visited Elcho Island. He told a story of a group of girls at Galiwin'ku who were having fellowship under the trees, singing a song called *I Love You, Lord*, when Jesus appeared to them, standing under a tree. They all fell down, praising and worshipping God. A sick baby with them was immediately healed and a group of young men who had been hassling them immediately dropped their spears and fled.[13]

Sometimes, people saw supernatural light or fire. One time during a church meeting, people walking around outside saw a flame come down from the sky. Those inside didn't see it, but someone outside started yelling, 'Water! Water!' Somebody else went running to get water to put out the fire, but nothing was burning! When they came close, they said they saw people who had 'tongues of fire on their heads'.[14]

Djiniyini and Gelung spoke about a time when they were praying with their family:

Djiniyini: We could see this light coming in — it was about 12 o'clock in the morning. There was a light coming in and then shaped itself like a man standing.
Gelung: . . . in the light.
Dj: . . . in a gown. And everyone of us could see it.
G: We couldn't see the face.
Dj: We couldn't see the face, but the light shape.
G: Just light, shining. . . It filled the whole house.
Dj: And then we could see the hands reaching out.
G: . . .reaching out and touching those two daughters. And we could feel God's presence. He was there — oooooh! . . . God was present, was real, it was. . . in the kitchen. . . the whole house. . .[15]
It felt like being washed by the waves of God's presence and love all around us — right up over our heads!
Dj: But we didn't feel it outside in the yard.[16]

Within a few weeks of the mission meetings, there was another event that was seen as a miracle. Galpagalpa had been deformed by leprosy and had to wear shoes all the time.

His old sandshoes were worn out and rather decrepit. One day, he found a new pair of shoes, his size, at his home. No-one knows where they came from. Galpagalpa was convinced that they were sent by God. This prompted his decision for Christ.[17]

Dangatanga also told me a story about a time when he went fishing in a small dinghy by himself. He was trawling with several hooks on the line and caught two fish at the same moment, which jerked the boat and caused him to fall overboard. He swam to a nearby island. He was worried that he now had no food or water or even matches to light a signal fire. He continues:

> That fish was still on the line. . . running that way off to Milingimbi. . . Then, I started praying. . . It was really calm, water was flat. Then suddenly, wind started blowing from north. . . Then, I saw the boat — it just jumped. . . motor start twisting and it pointed this way, coming back again. . . the boat was coming very fast. . . And he come right up, right up, right where I was sitting down. . . his motor in the sand right here. Those fish were still on the line.[18]

There were many similar stories, including Djiniyini and Gelung's story of their eighteen-month-old child being saved from falling down the dozen steps in front of their home by an invisible hand that apparently placed her safely on the front lawn;[19] and a preacher who called on Jesus and was saved from being hit by a rock the size of a cricket ball that a psychiatrically disturbed *Yolngu* woman was about to throw at him.[20]

There have been many other stories that have been told, some of them drastically changed from what originally happened, but these give some feel of the unusual events associated with the revival.

✦ Changes in the life of the church
The changes in the life of the church were more significant

than these unusual phenomona and possibly even than the social changes. Galikali described some of the new life in her Christmas newsletter in 1979:

I've just returned home from fellowship. . . which has continued nightly for nine months now. Numbers fluctuate, but as usual. . . there was a good crowd — maybe two hundred. God has worked in such a way in the lives of our minister Djiniyini and his wife Gelung that the atmosphere of their home is something special. . .

Let me give you some idea of the form of this nightly meeting. Quite a band of young men are gifted with the guitar. . . The night always begins with 'jolly' choruses — you know, those action choruses which we Europeans are embarrassed to sing because it's 'Sunday school stuff'. . . After some time — when a fair number have arrived — a more worshipful song is struck up and that's the sign for those who wish to move out from where they are sitting in a wide, relaxed circle to share in a more compact circle, standing, of course, and up to half-an-hour is spent worshipping. . .

And quietly, under and over the singing, one can hear the murmur of prayer as people pour out uninhibited verbal praise. One of the leaders — usually Djiniyini if he's present — will pray out more boldly, to close this time in preparation for the preaching (on five nights a week) of the word. Sometimes, after the preaching, there is a sharing time, but often the challenge is specific enough that folk are ready to kneel and accept whatever God is saying to them. The 'standing circle' is formed again and, as the singing and praying continues, those who wish to [do so] move out and kneel in the centre of the circle and the elders pray with them.

Naturally, it's too noisy for conversation, but how exciting to hear reports of people saying, 'How did he know what was on my heart? He prayed as if he knew, but I didn't tell him.' In such ways people are learning by experience what prayer 'in the Spirit' is and [what] some of the spiritual gifts are all about.

Very often, the warmth as folk conclude by shaking

hands, embracing and greeting one another, and singing. . .
makes them reluctant to go home. But work days are work
days. . .[21]

She added more detail to that picture of their time together
later:

While everyone was singing praise and worship, people
were sometimes convicted of sins and went out shaking or
crying or talking. They would often stand up and tell a
long story in a loud voice and the volume of the singing
would increase with real excitement. It seemed that
whatever confession the person had to make had to be said
out loud, but also kept private, between them and God, so
the singing also had to be loud so that the people couldn't
hear.

A problem later developed when someone had a
prophecy. As they raised their voice, so the singing got
louder and the prophecy couldn't be heard above the singing. [Another problem was that] there were times of very
powerful public spiritual warfare with many spiritual
manifestations, but the understanding of those things by the
people was very limited and many forgot about it.
[Another characteristic was that there was also] a lot of
emotionalism — shaking for a long time before going out
for prayer, tears, etc.

The renewal made a big difference in relationships between *Yolngu* and *Balanda*, as well as within families, clans
and from one clan to another. People are much more
outgoing in establishing relationships now.

Sometimes, people would see a light above a house and
go there to find someone with a need for prayer — maybe
a very sick child or someone deeply distressed with asthma.
They came to recognise it as a Holy Spirit sign and people
would gather from all over town to pray there for whatever
need there was.[22]

Yolngu started to really want to know God more, not just
to have the good feelings of fellowship times and singing.
There was a hunger to learn God's ways and what it means

to be the body of Christ. So each week, Galikali and the Bible translation team would translate the passage that the minister wanted to use for the next stage of teaching. The following Monday afternoon, two leaders would teach from it and distributed it to the fifteen Bible study leaders. Then on Tuesday night, they would teach it to over a hundred in small groups in their own languages.

They would read the scripture passage and follow this by a set of questions checking for comprehension, relating Old Testament and New Testament and relating it to life today. This brought a depth of preparation for the outreach which followed and also meant that the translated scriptures were being used much more than in other places where Bible translators continued with their set programs.[23]

✦ The first revival thanksgiving weekend: March 1980

On 14 March 1980, the Galiwin'ku community held the first anniversary of the birth of their new life — the 'Glory to Jesus Arnhem Land Revival Thanksgiving Weekend'. Aborigines arrived from all over Arnhem Land.

A few days later, Galikali wrote:

And what a weekend! Two weeks before, we had a con-centrated twenty-four hours of prayer (and prayer for weeks before, of course) during which we especially claimed a fine weekend and smooth flying. . .

Well! It rained non-stop (cyclone Doris ensured that); Connair went on strike just when people were starting to arrive; the three speakers we believed the Lord had directed us to invite from Yirrkala, Milingimbi and Roper River were unable to come, two of them on the day the celebrations started; [and] we had preparations and accommodation organised for a conservative crowd of 150 visitors and they arrived in droves. . . 250 from Umbakumba and Angurrgu on Groote Eylandt, Yirrkala, Numbulwar, Lake Evella, Milingimbi, Ramanginning, Gunbalanya (Oenpelli), Goul-burn and Croker Islands.

But God proved his sovereignty — we had a time of blessing far surpassing our expectations. And the gift of an extension. . . the cyclone warning made it impossible for most of the visitors to leave on Monday as planned, so Monday night was a very welcome continuation of the blessing.

The hallmark of the weekend was, of course, praise. We met in a very large unfinished hall which is locally known as the 'Opera House', which (we now know) can hold comfortably crowds of eight hundred to a thousand. . . Try to imagine a crowd of that size. . . representing three completely unrelated language groups, all singing at the tops of their voices in English and [Aboriginal] languages, eyes closed, many hands raised, revelling in the presence of the Lord. I'm sure I wasn't the only one battling tears on the first night — it was unreal.

This incredible freedom in singing especially is one of the features of the revival and groups from each community had plenty of opportunity over the weekend to demonstrate the gift God has given them. . . always much appreciated by all the others. On Thursday and especially Friday as the visitors arrived, they could be heard all over town singing — partly 'practising', but mostly because they couldn't help it!

The theme of the weekend was 'One Body and One Spirit'. It was also the *experience* of the weekend.

Djiniyini and Kevin shared the preaching with Jovilisi Ragata, our Elcho community worker (Fijian), who is also a candidate for the Uniting Church ministry. Pastor Peter Morgan, a part-Aboriginal Assembly of God evangelist, was here, accompanied by his musical family. . . Their contribution was greatly appreciated. . . a further demonstration of the unity God is creating. . . In the past, Arnhem Landers would not have appreciated part-Aborigines at all, for anyone who was not part of your own culture-language group was really an enemy, or at least a total foreigner.[24]

Peter Morgan began to pray for people, placing his hand on their head and most of them fell to the ground and lay there for fifteen minutes or more. Often during that time, the Holy Spirit seemed to be dealing with resentments, bitterness, anger, hurts and such like from their past. Sometimes there were physical healings. Most of them found they were made new in all sorts of ways and their relationships with others really improved. Galikali continues her report:

It was especially encouraging to have the Western Arnhem Land communities represented, as they have been largely untouched by revival so far. Gunbalanya (Oenpelli), especially, is a sad place, but the [Church Missionary Society] Bible translator Meryl Rowe, who was over for the weekend with a couple of plane-loads of people, is just beginning to see encouraging signs, stirrings of new life. . .

Yirrkala was represented by a group of about forty, many of whom obviously received real blessing over the weekend, and we're looking forward to news of developments there. Though there are stirrings, pockets of exciting growth, the community as a whole has continued to be preoccupied

Kevin Dhurrkay conducts a choir at the Galiwin'ku Revival
Thanksgiving Weekend: March 1980

with ceremonial life, clan rivalry and the ever-present grog [alcohol] problem. We trust that sharing this weekend will be significant in God's timetable for Yirrkala. Many of the non-Aborigines (Elcho staff and about fifteen visitors) received a special touch from the Lord, too.[25]

✦ Taking the firesticks of revival beyond Elcho Island

When Joyce Ross had come from Yirrkala to Elcho to help Galikali translate the Gospel of John a year earlier, she was amazed at what she saw. To her, it had seemed absolutely impossible that this could happen at Yirrkala. But the Elcho people were praying for the whole district and what she saw gave her faith to believe God would do it there, too.

When she went back to Yirrkala with a tape of the mission, she played it to some local people They were really excited at what they saw that God could do with fellow *Yolngu*. Joyce said:

Two days later, they began doing the same thing, just meeting, singing, a little group in the camp and praying, 'God, touch our lives, too.' A young lad. . . met with one of the girls and they'd said, 'You know, God's doing such wonderful things in our lives, we're just full up of his Spirit, but there's so many people who don't know.' They asked God to bring some of those people who used to be inter- ested in Christian things to the service on Wednesday night and they couldn't believe it when they kept walking in. To him, this was a tremendous miracle from their prayer.[26]

That was a result of just listening to a tape of meetings at Elcho Island!

The revival brought a new phase at Elcho Island of looking beyond themselves and their own people. Even before the mission in May 1979, Buthimang had an experience with a rock that showed this change.

He was living out of town and came in one day to find things different: the revival had started. 'I was living at

Gulumarri outstation. I was there and then I came back to Galiwin'ku. We come by people sitting around talking, singing and praising — every night! That has never happened before.'[27]

Everything that was happening was so new and totally beyond his experience and he cried out to God about it. He said that God told him that Australia was to be set free as a country: just as *Yolngu* were experiencing freedom in worship and in their relationship with God, so every part of the whole country was to experience this and then it would be really free.

Buthimang wanted to pray about this vision. This is what happened next:

> Then, one night I had a vision of the Australian map. . . . I tried to find the people who really can get it for me — where could I get that Australian map? Maybe in the bush, maybe on a beach or somewhere. Then one man, Djaymila — he's a really clever man in the water. . . with speargun. And I asked him, 'Hey, you're the one who can swim — you will try and get some map for me, some Australian map?'[28]

He told Djaymula to look for it at Airstrip Beach, so Djaymula went there fishing and skin-diving. He was about to return to the beach when a flash of light caught his eye and he went to examine it. He picked up the rock which had reflected the sunlight shining through the salt water and was amazed at the shape of the rock. He took it to Buthimang and said, 'Here's your map of Australia.'

Buthimang really rejoiced, because he had seen this rock covered with water in his vision. It is incredibly like the shape of Australia and it helped them centre their prayers on the whole land and all its people.

Stories of the revival began to spread all around Australia very quickly, even right from its beginning. As *Yolngu* from around Arnhem Land came to visit relatives at Elcho, they joined in the fellowship meetings and experienced the presence of God. They came forward and knelt in tears of praise and repentance and their lives were changed. They returned to their communities and people could see the difference in them. They shared the story of what they had experienced and told stories of things that were happening at Galiwin'ku. Very soon, the invitations started to come from Milingimbi, from Yirrkala, from Groote Eylandt and even from Cape York in Queensland, right across the Northern Territory and Western Australia. And the Elcho Islanders responded to many of those requests.

It was not just *Yolngu* who were affected. As government officers, consultants, contractors and even passing yachtsmen came to Elcho, they saw the cross used for the baptisms set in concrete in the ocean and asked about it. Many saw the changes in people and in the community. Some experienced what God was doing. They started to say, 'We love coming here. There's something about this place. There's a peace here

Buthimang's stone map of Australia, found in the ocean near Galiwin'ku as a result of a vision

that's nowhere else. What is it?'

A young family living an alternative lifestyle on a boat arrived one day. Galikali reported:

> They had not been on land for three months. . . had an intense sense like a spiritual magnet drawing them to Elcho Island. . . a great desire to harbour here, as they sensed tremendous peace and warmth in the atmosphere as they rounded the point into the bay. They knew nothing of the 'spiritual happening' amongst the Aborigines. But the locals made them feel very welcome.[29]

So the Elcho Islanders started to travel around Australia sharing what God had done and shown them. In September 1979, a group of over thirty-five of them travelled to Alice Springs for the first Central Australian Aboriginal Christian Convention. Aborigines, Christian leaders and others from many parts of Australia were there. It was another way God used to spread the fire to other parts of the nation and the story of that convention is in the next chapter.

In November 1979, Djiniyini and Gelung led a group of fifteen Galiwin'ku *Yolngu* to a national conference and combined church crusade in Canberra. They shared their new life and soon had people from all over the nation singing 'God the Father' in Djambarrpuyngu. They were greatly encouraged and learnt much from Nigerian evangelist Benson Idahosa and his miracle ministry. It was the first time they had seen that their new spiritual life was also in other parts of the church.

It brought a greater expectancy and confidence in God's miracle-working power among the Elcho Islanders. A number of Galiwin'ku *Yolngu* who had been to Canberra committed their lives to Jesus as a result after they returned home. Galikali reported:

> One of our young men, blinded just over a year ago through drinking the lethal acetone-and-metho combination, has had his sight almost completely restored. All of the men who

went to Canberra came back freed from the bondage of smoking. Tobacco has such a universal hold amongst Aborigines that it has been a low priority amongst things that 'drop off' as the new life of Jesus takes hold. But that is changing.[30]

By the end of 1979, the Elcho Islanders had received invitations to send evangelistic teams to many parts of Australia. The trips were taking Kevin away from his work and family and a call went out for prayer for this outreach — for additional leaders to assist Kevin and for finance.

The distance from Arnhem Land to major population centres in Australia is unbelievably great and the only reasonable way to travel is by air. Galikali wrote that 'the return plane fare to Darwin is $200 for a start. . . it's not like accounts of revival in other countries, where teams could easily go by foot. . .'[31] She added that Djiniyini had also begun to find the many trips to speak in other places conflicting with the needs of the local church and his family. In her report on the 1980 thanksgiving weekend, Galikali also wrote:

I believe God is answering prayer for the outreach of the church here. God's timing was evident in the wonderful blessing at Groote two weeks before the thanksgiving weekend (significantly, the same weekend as our prayer vigil), when our visiting team of twelve witnessed 130 people come, or return, to Jesus. Many of these were part of the visiting crowd this weekend.

On Saturday 29 March, Djiniyini and a small team begin a nine-day ministry to the Urban Aboriginal Mission in Paddington, Brisbane. A plane-load led by Kevin leaves on 9 May for a week at Mowandjum and the Kimberley area in Western Australia — invited by the Kimberley Presbytery of the Uniting Church. One of the good things about these longer absences of the church leaders is that the troops back here learn to take more responsibility in leadership.

We are continually reminded from many quarters of prophecies and visions there have been for many years of

Holy Spirit fire sweeping through the north of Australia and spreading across the whole continent. Will God do the former and not the latter? Continue to pray for us, as we hold onto that vision for *you*.[32]

As the Elcho people went out to hold missions in other places, the refining process continued at home also. At the end of 1980, the government appointed a new principal of the Galiwin'ku school, Shepherdson College. She had visited the school before her appointment and the school staff and community objected strongly to her appointment. They did all they could to have the appointment changed, without success. Her belongings arrived on the barge and no-one would unload them.

Then, God spoke to them at fellowship that night. They realised that they had done all they could to change things and now they should forgive her and work with her rather than having no school for their children. Forgiveness is not a significant part of Aboriginal culture, since it highly values obedience to law, so it was a major step when *Yolngu* began to accept her and to work together with her.[33]

✦ The second revival thanksgiving weekend: March 1981

Dan Armstrong was invited back for the second Arnhem Land Revival Thanksgiving Weekend in March 1981. Afterwards, Dan reported to his church in Canberra, talking about how he had worked with urban Aborigines for years and found that many of them had become 'defeated people'. He compared that with what he saw in Arnhem Land in March 1981:

. . .the first time I went there. . . to see the difference between these people and many of the folk I've known back here. I saw within them a dignity, a strength and a courage — they weren't defeated people. . . And it is because they know his power of victory within their lives.

This time was even more wonderful, for I saw so many who were new in their faith when I was there. . . were taking leadership among their own people.[34]

Dan commented on the incredible number of items they sang. He came to realise it was their way of expressing what had been happening in their lives. Not many of them were able to learn God's way through reading the Bible, but they were teaching the words of the Bible in their own languages in songs they had written themselves. And people memorised the Bible in these songs:

There was an item from Milingimbi, an item from Groote Eylandt, an item from Goulburn Island, another item from Galiwin'ku. . . item after item. There were all these different places and they were harmonising. . .

Over the past two years, the people of Galiwin'ku have been going out. . . there were people from these other places who had been touched by the Holy Spirit, many of them through teams who had gone out from Galiwin'ku. . . And in all these different places, there is a growing number of people who are loving the Lord Jesus Christ.[35]

On the Wednesday night of Dan's visit, they had a family night and many families responded to the message God gave them that night:

We saw husbands and wives and children. And sometimes, even an uncle and an aunty would be thrown in, because uncles and aunties are very close in those family structures. They came and knelt and they committed their total family to Jesus Christ. I remember praying for one family. . . I prayed with the husband and wife and then I prayed with the three young girls. And it was so beautiful. Then, they all went back to their place and someone came up and said: 'You've just blessed a husband and four wives!'

But you know, it was precious to do that. To be able to just really cement these people into God. And I believe God is working all of that out, because many people are beginning to understand the husband and wife relationship and the depth of it. Very few couples there had ever been married before God in a marriage ceremony. I think I married about twenty couples. . . joining their hands together and in the name of the Lord Jesus Christ, bringing them to God and making their vows to him.[36]

Dan and the team left Elcho Island and went to Yirrkala where they found things were still very different. The community there has been exposed to the Western world so much more since bauxite mining began and the town of Nhulunbuy was established only twenty kilometres away. Dan used to be an alcoholic and was really upset to see so many drunk young Aboriginal men around the Nhulunbuy shopping centre at nine o'clock on Saturday morning. At lunchtime, they had a picnic on the Yirrkala beach with the families. Dan said:

There was hardly a man there. They were all in town drinking. And I just felt such a burden on my heart for those people.

That night, I spoke one of the strongest words I think I've ever spoken and challenged those men — there were many of them there, gathered out in the shadows. And I told them what the average European thought of them. That's not an easy thing to do. . . 'Drunken, stupid, dull Aborigines who were killing their lives and no-one could care less.'

And I challenged them to what they really were: precious and beautiful people of God, who can have the dignity that God wants for them — to be leaders of the nation, the first people of this land. And I believe God began to break through to some of those lives from that night on and we saw many of those men from that Saturday night really coming through to Christ.[37]

John and Trixie Rudder were part of that team with Dan Armstrong. Because they had worked at Yirrkala and Galiwin'ku for fourteen years, they knew the people — those who had been far away, those who had struggled and those 'who had been faithful through many years of hardship. . .

the people in whom we had seen the fire and flame of God in days gone by.'[38]

At Elcho, they now found people *knew* that God was victor, but Yirrkala had not found that release from their years of intense struggles. Trixie said:

> The Christians had a survival attitude — like many Christians down here. They were hanging onto the Lord for grim death to stay with it. And praise the Lord. . . we saw the people take hold of the fact that they were God's people and they were on the victory side.
>
> You know, just on twenty years ago when we went into the Aboriginal field and the Aboriginal people started talking about *mokuys* [evil spirits] and *galkas* [magic], we missionaries said blithely, 'There aren't such things and, anyway, even if there are, Jesus is stronger.' We did not realise the spiritual bondages that the people were in. And we were trained to think, 'Get rid of the culture and they'll be right.'
>
> But that's all a lie. I thank the Lord that in the Aboriginal fields now there is a real awareness of spiritual warfare and the victory is with Christ but, for some, they've not yet taken unto themselves that victory.[39]

In her report to their church in Canberra, Trixie told the stories of four people they had known for years. She talked about a struggle between ceremonial leaders and Christians over a dying man at Yirrkala:

> Aboriginal medicine men and the ceremonial leaders would gather around him and they'd pray and he would go into a coma. Then, the Christians would hear about it, so they'd gather round him and pray and he'd sit up and be as bright as a button. And this went backwards and forwards, so that even the ceremonial Aboriginals were saying, 'Well, we've got it now, we've got the best of both worlds. We've got our power, but now we've got God's magic, too.'[40]

The sick man was old and really wanted to go to be with Jesus and he managed to get the Christians to let him die.

Trixie said, 'That said to the ceremonial leaders, "The Christians have failed." On the other hand, it left the Christians with big inner, personal questions.'

Shortly after that, Laklak, a Yirrkala woman who was Aboriginal Tutor Sister at Nhulunbuy Hospital had a terrible experience:

> Her very close brother was very sick and the leaders of his family group were so entrenched in the ceremonial that they said, 'The Christians are not coming anywhere near him. We will use our medicine.' The doctor and the nurses begged to be able to give him medical attention and were refused and he died. Laklak became so depressed that she only functioned when she was at work. It was spiritual warfare.
>
> But we saw Laklak come alive. We saw her as a person emotionally, mentally, spiritually put back together again. And it was a very beautiful and a very precious thing to see. It was spiritual warfare, but God has the victory.[41]

Trixie also shared an experience from that second thanksgiving weekend that linked Yirrkala with Elcho:

> One night at Elcho, a young man by the name of Wulumbuyku came forward and knelt in the sand at the foot of the cross and gave his life to Jesus. Afterwards, together with his young wife Dopiya and their children, they came and sought John and I out and just wrapped their arms around us.
>
> The Lord took me back fifteen years before, when I had held Dopiya as a young girl of fourteen crying in my arms when Wulumbuyku, the son of a very powerful ceremonial leader from Elcho Island, had sailed across to Yirrkala in anger and in fury to claim his promised wife, who was this fourteen-year-old schoolgirl. . . the store was locked and people had taken refuge inside the store. The pay office was locked and half the European people were taking refuge inside the pay office. Wulambuyku was screaming around with his spears, demanding his woman to take her back to Elcho.

I said to Dopiya, 'Do you want to go with him?' She said, 'Yes.' And God said to me, 'Take note, there are things here that you don't understand.'

At sixteen, Dopiya did go to Elcho to become Wulumbuyku's wife. She was a Christian and she loved him and she prayed for him. But he was such an angry and dangerous young man — and such an important young man ceremonially because of his family — that when he walked up to the hospital dispensary, which he needed to do regularly, because he had very bad eyes. . . you could see the people shift back. The Aboriginal people at the dispensary would move back without a word so that he went straight in. He was treated very carefully lest anybody ruffle him.

So he walked the island like a king. All the time, this young Christian wife prayed for him. And so, fifteen years later, it was a great privilege before the Lord to see that man come and kneel at the cross and give his life to Jesus.[42]

Trixie's fourth story involved a miraculous healing:

There was another woman, Gulumbu. When we were first at Yirrkala, she was the youngest of three wives. Her husband was very important ceremonially and he regularly beat her up and he'd lock her up in the house and tell her that she wasn't to go to church — she was to go nowhere near those Christians! But we were amazed at the spiritual insight she had and what she understood of God and of Jesus. . . — in isolation, with no scriptures, with an antagonistic husband, locked at home — and God sovereignly taught her and filled her with his love.

When we went back this time, Gulumbu looked just the same. . . still that same shine of the Lord on her face. One day we were talking to her and she had a backache. You don't take much notice of backaches when you live in the tropics. . . John did not know the extent of Gulumbu's backache. She had a backache, so he laid hands on her back and he prayed for the pain and the tension — and he really didn't take any notice of the fact that he threw in the words, 'and all those bones get back into place'. She stood up straight and said, 'Oh, thank you!'. . .

Next morning, she came and she was running around saying, 'Look at me, I can touch my toes, I can dance, I can do this, I can do that.' We learnt that over the years, her husband had beaten her up so often and so viciously that she had specific bone damage in her back — and God had sovereignly healed her![43]

The team that came with Dan Armstrong in March 1981 saw wonderful miracles and ministered to many, but there was one final surprise. Dan said, 'Sunday they had an offering among the Aboriginal folk. They just wanted to share in some of our expenses. Now, they don't have much money these people — very little.' Dan was staggered when he opened the envelope: there was $1000 in it. 'The gift of generosity — and they've got it.'[44]

So the revival fire spread from Elcho Island to Yirrkala and throughout Arnhem Land. Fires started to be lit all over northern Australia and down into Central Australia as the Aborigines travelled to other communities, sharing what they experienced of God's presence.

6

Igniting the tinder-dry desert

REVIVAL SPREADS TO CENTRAL AUSTRALIA

I HAD BEEN TRANSFERRED BY THE UNITING CHURCH TO A NEW work among Aborigines in Alice Springs. My family and I moved there in January 1979, straight after my vision of revival recorded in the *Introduction*. We had an expectancy and excitement and a sense of awe about the renewal I knew God was about to bring to Central Australia.

✦ The Central Australian Aboriginal Convention: 1979

At the end of June 1979, Kinyin McKenzie came to me. He was from the Pitjantjatjara tribe which lives around the top end of South Australia. He shared with me a vision he had been trying to develop for several years: to establish a Central Australian Aboriginal Christian Convention. He wanted to hold one at the end of August and needed help.

There didn't seem time to organise it, but God made it happen. Hundreds of Aborigines came from different tribes and denominational backgrounds, travelling hundreds of kilometres. Four Aboriginal Evangelical Fellowship leaders from Sydney, Melbourne and Adelaide flew in to be the speakers.

Yolngu from Elcho Island were also invited and a group of thirty-three adults plus a number of children flew the five

John and June Blacket

hundred kilometres to Katherine, then travelled by bus the thousand kilometres to Alice Springs. They were looking for teaching and experiences that would take them further in the direction they believed God was taking them. But the Central Australians and even most of the speakers still hadn't started to move in these areas. So the *Yolngu*'s faith developed as they shared what God had taught them.

The *Yolngu* found some things rather difficult on that trip. Most of them had never travelled more than a hundred kilometres from the tropical climate of the Arnhem Land coast and had never experienced temperatures lower than 15ºC. In Alice Springs, they experienced a cold spell, with their first day only reaching a maximum of 10ºC. They also suffered a real culture shock and, as a result, no real one-to-one sharing with the Centralian Aborigines happened.

The Elcho group prayed for unity in their team — they really needed it — and Galikali wrote in her diary how some of this was achieved: 'I know that one of the special features of our group witness was that Ross, Pam and I [all Europeans] were automatically included in everything.'[1]

Pam became sick and late on Saturday night Kevin Dhurrkay asked the speakers to join them in praying for her. Ben Mason, one of the speakers, was a tribal man who had spent a lot of his life with tribal Aborigines, but the other three were having real difficulty adjusting to the tribal people. They were very Westernised urban Aborigines who spoke in fairly sophisticated English that wasn't understood very well. They found many things that were happening were very hard to take, including things like raising hands in worship.

In contrast to the urban Aboriginal speakers, the tribal people dressed very casually, many in old clothes, and they found the ancient language of the King James Version quite impossible. One speaker also had resentments towards whites from his childhood, but Kevin read James 5 and asked him to minister to Pam, handing him a bottle of oil. He anointed Pam and prayed for her. She was healed over the next day or so.

Kevin found his name on the program to speak at the Friday night meeting following the screening of the film 'Peace Child'. He gave a spontaneous message which effectively followed on from the theme of the film. A number of key men from the Pintubi town camp responded by committing themselves to Jesus that night and about sixty others over the next two nights.

The Elcho Islanders experienced another new thing: a Christian corroboree telling the Easter story, carefully prepared and presented by the Warlpiri tribe from Yuendumu. They didn't have the Bible in their own language, so they took the Good News Bible, read the story phrase by phrase in English, translated it, discussed it, then formed it into song, using traditional women's melodies. It was presented with traditional-style clothing, body paint and

Easter Pulapa

dancing, using rhythm from boomerangs rattled together. It was an exciting and unique form of Aboriginal Christianity that was starting to develop.

The work in Central Australia developed slowly, but we were hearing reports of what God was doing in north Australia which confirmed the vision I believe God had given me. I was certain God would also act in the Centre. Meanwhile, Pitjantjatjara co-worker, Wally Dunn and I carried on with our work: we fed the poor; we helped, taught, preached and encouraged; we prayed for the sick, the oppressed, the discouraged and others.

We were joined by a group who prayed expectantly for a breakthrough in Central Australia, wondering where it would happen first. I thought it would probably be at Ernabella, South Australia, with the style of work that had been done among the Pitjantjatjara tribes by the Presbyterian Church for over fifty years. But I was wrong. It was to be among their cousins, the Ngaanyatjarras, at Warburton Ranges Aboriginal community across the border in Western Australia.

✦ The situation among the Ngaanyatjarra around the Warburton Ranges

Before we hear the story of the fire of revival among the Ngaanyatjarras, we need to take a brief look at the region and some of its history.

The Warburton Ranges community (often called 'Ranges or Warburton) is in the middle of the Central Desert, about halfway between Kalgoorlie and Alice Springs. There are many barren sandhills in this desert, but east of Warburton there are also many beautiful ranges, including the famous Uluru and Katatjuta (Ayers Rock and the Olgas).

In 1933, two missionaries from the United Aborigines Mission (UAM) travelled in the blazing sun and freezing nights for ten weeks by camel, looking for a site in the desert to establish a new mission station. Will Wade (still affectionately remembered as 'Mr Wade' today) established the Warburton Mission the following year. A church, children's homes, school, trading post and various industries (such as cattle) were established over the years, run by UAM missionaries together with Aboriginal people.

Some of the Aboriginal people were receptive to the gospel and came to know the reality of God's presence. One of them, Fred Forbes, told me of a thousand kilometre trip he did a long time ago after he had taken some camels to Ernabella in South Australia:

> I came back on foot — I walked and waaaalked. . . then I lay down. . . it was really hot and I had no water. . . All the way, as I walked for days, I was praising the Lord. Finally, I thought I would praise God one last time before I died. . . Then, an angel touched me on the top of the head and I was drinking the water from the angel through the top of my head, not my mouth; my legs and arms were revived.

The angel said, 'You're not going to die.'. . . There were six, seven, eight, nine, *ten* angels lined up above each other with their feet up off the ground.

I didn't dream it — no way! He put Jesus' Spirit in me and my body came all alight. He gave that water to me and he gave his Spirit to me and it was like a flow of fire. Before that, I used to be just half a Christian.[2]

The government's policy of assimilating Aborigines into Western society affected the missions, so the 'Ranges school and church used English. Missionary Wilf Douglas saw the need for them to keep their own Ngaanyatjarra language and he developed ways to write it down, then argued to have its importance recognised by the mission council. Eventually, he was appointed as mission linguist in the 1950s and it became official mission policy to use the language.

Many teachers and also mission children's homes workers felt really threatened when they couldn't understand what the children were saying in their own language and banned its use. When the Western Australian government took over the school in 1957, they made it illegal for Aborigines to use their own language at school, using a law originally aimed at Asian immigrants. This policy continued until 1973. It did little to help assimilate Aborigines, making them feel that they were inferior to whites and English was superior to their language.

In the mid-1960s, the church was handed over to be run by Aborigines, with missionaries continuing to work in community management areas.

Within three years, small groups began going to their leaders or the missionaries to tell of their desire to get right with God. In one month, fifty people turned to Jesus in this way. The movement continued for a few years. Some people left the church after a few months, but others have continued as consistent Christians right up to the present.

As a result, five of them went off to Gnowangerup Aboriginal Bible College in the south-west of Western

Australia for one or two years' training during the period 1968 to 1975. When they returned, several of them took significant roles in the local church and translation program and one has served as a missionary to Aborigines in the north-west of Western Australia for many years.

By 1981, the people had the books of Matthew, most of Genesis, Acts, James, Ruth and some of Exodus available in their own language. However, only a handful of people could read any of it. Then the Bible translators, Dorothy Hackett and Amee Glass, moved to Alice Springs to speed up the work of translation, finally releasing the full New Testament in Ngaanyatjarra in 1991.[3]

Their move left only three UAM missionaries living in the Ngaanyatjarra area: Thelma Roberts, and Herbert and Lorraine Howell, although there were also some other Christian 'whitefellas' (the local name for whites), including the community adviser, Chris Marshall.

Ngaanyatjarra Bible translators, Aimee Glass and Dorothy Hackett

Early in 1981, Thelma returned from leave in Melbourne to find that something new was happening amongst the Ngaanyatjarras:

The people were more interested in the things of God. . . I would walk up the road and a group of older, tribal men, sitting and talking, would call me over and ask questions about Christianity. . . God was obviously doing a new thing himself without the aid of people. People had a new interest and hunger for God.[4]

The people had a sense that God was speaking to them supernaturally and a strong interest in God was developing. Maimie Butler recalls that in May that year, people were becoming Christians at Blackstone, a Ngaanyatjarra community about 125 kilometres east of Warburton:

I came back to the Lord at Pipalyatjara earlier that year and, when we went back to Blackstone, we were having meetings and there were a lot of young ladies and young men and we all got together and we sang at meetings and the old people joined in — all having fellowship, taking part in testimony. That's the time when the old [Aboriginal] man, Mr Forbes, was seeing visions and having dreams from God. God was showing him that there was going to be more people coming to the Lord and it happened![5]

The people at Warburton kept having meetings right through that year and Maimie began writing new Christian songs in her own language which she felt God gave her.

Thelma relates how she used to take Christian tapes, scriptures (mainly in Ngaanyatjarra), literature and pictures, and visit people. She had bought a copy of the Bible Panorama illustrated study and was quite surprised at the interest shown in it. After a section of a tribal ceremony ended, a steady stream of men arrived painted with red ochre and their long hair in mud curls. Many of them were not Christians at the time, but they had come to see the book and hear the story.

Jerome and Martha Ward suddenly started attending church. One night when Jerome was drunk, Yimiyarri Bates talked to him, quoting scripture and praying and gave him her Bible. Next morning, he started reading the Bible, then started trembling and dropped to his knees to give himself to God, then felt a new peace inside.[6]

Terry Robinson had been to Bible college for several years, then drifted away from God. Three days before the mission, he went to Pastor Arthur at night so he wouldn't be seen ('just like Nicodemus') and made a new commitment to Jesus. This swelled the number of active men in the church to three out of a total population of around three hundred.

Around the same time, the community staff Bible study group were growing closer to each other. Up to sixteen of the total of twenty-five whitefellas were attending regularly, including several who weren't Christians.

Despite all this, the community was developing a national reputation for being in a mess. There was a lot of fighting, drunkenness and despair. In 1980, the Federal Minister for Aboriginal Affairs described it as the most troubled Aboriginal community in Australia.[7]

In mid-1979, many things were not good in the area, when two missionaries with a concern for the Ngaanyatjarras met in Canberra. They talked about the Arnhem Land revival and the spiritual struggles that had been involved. They knew the nature of some of the spiritual powers over the Central Desert and decided to seek to evict them in Jesus' name. For the following three years, Warburton Ranges became even more chaotic than it had been. It seemed like they had removed the existing order and controls from the community before it was God's time.

The Uniting Church's Australian Inland Mission had been running the hospital at 'Ranges, but the violence — even towards the sisters — finally caused them to withdraw their staff. The government took over the million dollar hospital and locked the gate through the two-and-a-half metre high barbed wire fence around it. There was a buzzer to ring when help was needed, but children played with the buzzer until the staff turned it off and, at times, the only way to get their attention was to throw rocks on the hospital's iron roof — but the children did that for fun, too.

Ron Williams, *Nyoongar*[8] missionary who has worked with the Ngaanyatjarras for years, said in his book:

Many young people were sniffing petrol, people were getting drunk and fighting, and death had become very common. During this time, the Lord gave me a vision of either possible revolution and destruction, or revival if my *Wangkayi*[9] friends repented.[10]

Wilf Douglas, the missionary who started the Bible translation program at 'Ranges, was asked about the situation by the editor of *Australian Evangelical* magazine. His reply described how things had been at 'Ranges in the late 1970s and into 1980:

The local community was probably at its lowest ebb socially, economically and morally. Flagons of wine were being brought in by what we called 'the grog runners'. . . The government, instead of encouraging self-help projects, had yielded to the practice of simply handing out social service benefits to the people. So few were working and everybody had money — a bad situation.

When the wine was brought out (allegedly sold for up to $70 per flagon), the most horrifying kinds of fights ensued — people being hit over the head with crowbars and flagons (and boomerangs). . . Children from nine years of age were petrol sniffing and so damaging their brains that they were doing crazy things. (Older children were actually forcing younger ones to sniff.) It seemed that years of work at Warburton mission had gone down the drain.[11]

However, by 1981 things were improving. Unemployment benefits had been replaced by the Community

Development Employment Program where people had to do some community work for their pay. Chris Marshall had been appointed as community adviser during 1980 to sort out the mess and this was having its effects, although Warburton was still a troubled place. A spiritual breakthrough was needed.

✦ The coming of the *Yolngu* team to Central Australia: 1981

Warburton Ranges missionaries, Herbert and Lorraine Howell, were hearing stories of what they thought was extreme behaviour amongst Elcho Island Christians and at other places. They were very happy that Elcho Island was so far away from them at 'Ranges. They felt this movement would 'probably take a year to reach Darwin, then another year to reach Katherine and then it would probably never reach the Centre because it was so far to Alice Springs, so we were quite safe because we were a thousand kilometres from Alice.'[12]

Then one day, Herbert said to Arthur Robertson, the Aboriginal church pastor, 'It's getting close to August and we still don't know who is going to speak at the Bible school.'[13] The Bible school had been held for four days every August since 1972 and they always had one or two visiting speakers.

Arthur had heard stories from two local men who had visited Elcho Island a few months earlier and had been told some of the *Yolngu* were coming to Alice Springs. He wanted Herbert to write to invite them. Although Herbert was really worried about doing this, 'we [nevertheless] felt that something needed to happen in our lives'.[14] So he sent the invitation with some trepidation; meetings with Pitjantjatjaras and Ngaanyatjarras in South Australia and Western Australia were added to the *Yolngu*'s trip for the 1981 Central Australian Aboriginal Christian Convention in Alice Springs.

The convention in Alice Springs was held in August 1981. Speakers were Dan Armstrong with a team from Canberra, and Kevin with a team from Elcho Island. God's preparation included some visions seen by locals involved, some real encouragement and also some struggles.

After one time of prayer before the convention, an Aboriginal man said the meetings should be held at a park near Heavytree Gap. Alice Springs is bounded on the south side by the MacDonald Ranges, a straight line of very steep, high hills with very few gaps where travellers can pass through. He said this was a significant place in the old days and Aboriginal men had refused to allow women or whitefellas to pass through this gap, forcing them to climb over the range or divert over twenty kilometres to the nearest gap.

The Assembly of God pastor in Alice Springs didn't know about this discussion, but shared a vision he had experienced of Christ standing towering above these ranges outside Heavytree Gap, asking for permission to enter the town. These revelations became focuses of prayer in the preparation for the convention.

So it was decided to hold the meetings there at the park just on the town side of Heavytree Gap.

Many people came from all over Central Australia and a large group came from Elcho Island. Many made commitments to God or were touched in some way. One of them was Albert Lennon.

Albert is a big man, both physically and tribally. His wife had remained a faithful Christian over many years, but he had lost interest. She wanted to go to the convention, but they lived at Fregon, 500 kilometres away, and Albert had too much work to do. Finally, Albert decided he would drive her to the meetings, but he stayed in his vehicle in the carpark.

When the appeal was made at the end of the meeting, he was the first to respond and came forward, weeping. He told how God had washed him inside and out from the top of his head right down and all the rubbish in his life was washed down into his boots. So he took them off and threw them away in the river!

After the convention, a team of five *Yolngu* flew to some of the Pitjantjatjara communities in South Australia. The team was led by Kevin Dhurrkay. My Pitjantjatjara co-worker, Wally Dunn joined them, and David Sidey and I went as pilots of the two small planes and as prayer support.

It was Kevin's first visit to the area and he used Wally as his interpreter. Kevin later spoke to me about the trip, about the first meeting at Fregon and about Wally's help:

> He was like a right hand man to me, interpreting — and we preached. . . I didn't know how the people would respond to the gospel. . . most of these people hadn't been worshipping God in the way that we expressed it. . . I thought I wasn't going to make it, but I knew the Holy Spirit was there and I think there was just about 100 people [out of a total community of 250 plus visitors] came to the Lord Jesus that night.
>
> One of the things that almost frightened me which I discovered (that no-one ever told me until you told me later at Ernabella): there was a lot of fear around. This needs to be broken in the community. Not only that, but a lot of other things like witchcraft and secrecy. If they break down the fears, I'm sure the Holy Spirit will work.[15]

There was a slow response at the meeting at Ernabella the next night and it seemed to many God was breaking some spiritual bondages. The next morning, Friday 28 August, 1981, we set off for Warburton Ranges.

Both of us whitefellas in the team were afflicted with laryngitis. David didn't even get halfway to Warburton before Air Traffic Control asked him if he had someone on board who could do his radio work for him because they couldn't hear him!

I was a much less experienced pilot and had found the weather conditions very difficult on the previous two days flying from Alice Springs to Amata and Ernabella. My voice lasted until we landed at Warburton and I was able to speak enough for the few tasks which God had for me through the weekend. Our voices returned just before we left for home. I believe God used this to silence us so that we couldn't get in the way of the Aborigines' ministry.

On our way to 'Ranges, we had to fly over some of the most ceremonially significant country in Australia. When we landed, we found there was an air of expectancy. A day or two earlier, nearly 300 men had converged on Warburton. They had been at tribal ceremonies further east and the men were now travelling through to Mt Margaret in the ceremony.

Herbert Howell reported: 'The Christian leaders were expected to accompany them. . . As it happened, word came through that the Elcho Island team was on the plane from Alice Springs to Warburton.'[16]

Stanley West, who was not an active Christian at that time, was the driver of one of the trucks carrying these men. He decided that he wanted to stay in Warburton to hear what 'these strange men have to say'. Others agreed with him, so they all stayed and listened.

✦ The *Yolngu* team's mission to Warburton Ranges

The meetings were held in an old corrugated iron store which had just been handed over to the church, since they no longer had a building. A new shop had been built and the old one was cleaned up only a few hours before the team arrived for the meetings. The first meeting was held that night and the building was packed out, with most of the people sitting on blankets on the concrete floor and many standing outside.

Herbert wrote in his diary:

Much opposition with stone throwing on the roof and general noisiness in the building, but people impressed with the visitors' authority and praying. . . Most were ceremonially attired. Despite much overt physical opposition, the meetings became progressively more and more quiet so, at the last, people would barely move or be upset when a disturbance did occur.[17]

Herbert commented that in all the years of holding meetings he had never once encountered the kind of opposition that occurred at these meetings:

[In the past] people might walk past being angry, but they never tried to disrupt the meeting. Throwing rocks on the roof was normal, but not during a service. You could sit in the mission house having breakfast and have rocks on the roof all the time. But this time the opposition was intense. Sometimes down the back, we couldn't hear the speaker — there was just too much noise on the roof and kids running round rattling a piece of wood on the corrugated iron walls.[18]

The rocks were so big that they really startled everyone and after each one the fear increased.

There were also the usual number of dogs with the people inside the building and the noise of their fights echoed around the unlined tin walls and roof. Each disturbance seemed to bring a wave of unrest and uneasiness on the people, but the *Yolngu* continued to lead the praise and worship, raising their hands to God, in whom they put their trust, despite every attack. Kevin reported later:

When I looked at that, I was sure that the devil was really there and he said, 'I'm not going to let them go.' I think the devil was really frightened because he knew it was the time the people were waiting for. He was really disturbed the first night.[19]

Djawangdjawang preached the first night. His English was far too sophisticated for the desert people and it wasn't translated, yet somehow God spoke. Some of the staff commented that it was not a really strong message or a powerful meeting, yet a lot of people responded.

Some who responded were community leaders with their

hair in ceremonial mud curls, maybe covered by a beanie or hat. The *Yolngu* came and prayed with them, laid their hands on their heads and loved them.

Philip West was one of them. He had turned away from God a long time before and his son had been drinking and petrol sniffing. They both responded that night. Quite a group of them came forward, many of whom had been outside listening, but not wanting to get too close. Some of them were quite drunk or high on petrol during the meeting, yet they responded.

Many of the whitefellas present were quite puzzled and concerned about what was happening. So David and I met with some fifteen to twenty of them on Saturday afternoon, while the Aborigines met together separately. Most of them had never experienced anything like it before and some had heard a bit about weird things that some Christians were doing that 'you have to be really careful about'.

I said that what was happening was humanly impossible and irrational, but pointed out that Westerners try to communicate rationally to Aborigines' minds, whereas Aborigines communicate more by spirit.

Even though the people couldn't understand all the words that had been spoken to them at that first meeting, they could discern the 'spirit' of what was being said. Their response was the result of a communication of spirit to spirit through the Holy Spirit working in people who were so open to him. We talked about the need for the power of the Spirit of God in our lives and the different ministry gifts he brings. I also shared how some people single out tongues and make a big blockage out of it when it's just *one* of the gifts. There were many questions and we tried to answer them gently and patiently.

I knew some of them really wanted more of God's guidance, love and power in their lives and I wanted to pray for greater evidence of the Holy Spirit in their lives, but I was running out of time and voice, so I just said:

> I know that some of you have real needs. You've got tremendous responsibility because of what God is doing in this place. You really need the power of God. I think maybe as whitefellas we need to swallow our pride and be able to go forward and receive ministry from Aboriginal people — because all the time we've had the attitude, 'We're the missionaries.'
>
> That pride is the number one enemy of God. But you have to ask the Aboriginal people to pray for you. In the past, it has been the other way around, so it's hard for missionaries and staff to do this — we're not used to having to ask them to do things for us, but this is God's way. He wants to bless you. Please don't let pride get in the way.

Some of them did go forward humbly at meetings or privately to ask Aborigines to pray for them and they were greatly blessed.

There was a real barrier between the *Yolngu* team and the Ngaanyatjarra people. Herbert had wanted them to stay with Aborigines rather than the missionaries. *They* had invited them into their territory. Arthur replied: 'Oh no, they're strangers. If strange Aboriginal people come into this country, we should spear them. But we can't spear these people because they are bringing God's word to us. But *you* have to look after them.'

And so they stayed in the literacy building behind the mission house and that proved to be a real encouragement to their hosts, Herbert and Lorraine. When they finished their meals, they would sit around and pray together.

Herbert reported:

> They'd say, 'Now we're going to stand up, all hold hands and we are all going to pray.' And this was so new to us. We stood there and we'd pray and feel really embarrassed, hoping that nobody would come to the the door and see us through the window.[20]

On Saturday, before the morning meeting, the people started to drop their shyness with the *Yolngu*. Kevin had said to them, 'Feel free, forget about the shame, the shyness or "you way up there and we here". Just make yourself free, just come and meet us — come in, everyone.'[21]

So the locals gathered to talk with them between the meetings. But there was also a language barrier that had to be overcome, so Wally Dunn became a very important part of the team. Wally's English was better than many of the Ngaanyatjarra people's and they could understand his Pitjantjatjara better than Kevin's English. (The Pitjantjatjara language is about as similar to Ngaanyatjarra as Dutch is to German.)

Kevin later commented about Wally: 'I wouldn't have left *him* behind!' Bible translator, Amee Glass, pointed out that Ngaanyatjarras would only understand spiritual things in Wally's language if they had had a *lot* of contact with Pitjantjatjaras — especially the children. Kevin replied: 'I noticed that but, when Wally was speaking to the children, they were quiet and listened and looked straight at him as if they knew the language.' Amee responded, 'It *must* have been God!'[22]

On Saturday night, there was alcohol in the community (which was illegal) and the police also arrived. (They only visit occasionally from Laverton, about eight hours' drive away.) Cars driving past the church had no mufflers and made a terrible din.

There were many children sitting on the floor right up to the stage at the front of the building. Fairly early in the meeting during the singing, one young boy, in playing around, had kicked another in the mouth, causing screams and blood when his tooth went through his lip. Through it all, the *Yolngu* kept worshipping God and preaching, without paying any attention to the distractions.

During the message, a big local man entered the building

carrying a spear in one hand and holding his young son's hand firmly in the other. He called out loudly as he picked his way among the people seated on the floor, till he came right to the front of the building where most of the children were seated. Kevin kept preaching and ignored him.

The man looked for the boy who had kicked his son in the mouth, but God seemed to blind his eyes from seeing the boy who was still sitting there shaking with fear. Eventually the man left, but returned again and again, calling out loudly each time and coming right to the front of the meeting.

Then suddenly, the whole team felt we were being challenged by the Holy Spirit: 'Why are you letting Satan destroy what I am trying to do here tonight?' The question shot through our minds and startled us out of curiosity and fear into prayer! Kevin started praying while he kept on preaching.

The children had already been squashed over to one side and people had begun to stream forward to kneel at the front when the man returned once more. The man walked right to the front again, then turned to the children and threw a handful of sand in their faces.

Without thinking, I stood up and walked over to him as he began to leave. I had never spoken a word of their language or studied it. *'Mamu, wiyarringu!'* [= 'Spirit/devil, you're finished/dead — go!] I commanded with a confident use of Ngaanyatjarra language that had to be God-given.

The big man turned and glared at me and I repeated the command, again with an authority that was not my own. The man paused, then turned and left. After the meeting, he came to see the team and apologised, saying he was upset because of his boy and was doing what their law demands: 'Blood requires blood'. We put our arms around him and told him we loved him and accepted him, and I apologised for having to speak in that way to the spirit that was with him. The following night, he gave his life to God.

Herbert wrote in his diary:

The meetings became progressively more and more quiet so, at the last, people would barely move or be upset when a disturbance did occur. We witnessed great numbers of people going to the front, kneel and be prayed for. It was overwhelming to see the way God was moving people and convicting them and bringing them to himself. The authority and gentleness of the visiting speakers and the way they gave themselves in ministering to people here was astounding and people were aware of the great power they had. Praise the Lord![23]

The people had never seen this sort of power to deal with these common outbursts and disturbances and were incredibly impressed. And they really needed that power.

In my prayer time the next morning, I read I John 4, verse 18: 'There is no fear in love. Perfect love drives out fear.' I suddenly realised that fear controlled the area, that Jesus had confronted it and won a significant victory in the region that weekend. I became really excited and went to the morning service expecting this verse declared to everyone in their own language.

When Arthur asked me to lead Communion that morning, I realised that this sacrament actually proclaimed God's perfect love. It is a message that speaks in a language that everyone can understand — it doesn't need words. Suddenly, that sacrament took on a new depth of meaning for me.

After the Sunday morning meeting, there was a lot of talk at the mission house. There hadn't been a baptism at Warburton for twenty years and they had been wanting to have one for weeks. Arthur wanted the team to baptise some of the Christians who had been faithful believers for many years before they left. But there was no water that could be used except a slimy water hole some distance out of town.

A small group gathered that afternoon at the church. Many of the others were asleep, but Arthur and the locals were very keen on action. They asked me to talk about the meaning of baptism. The next thing I knew, Arthur produced a bucket of water and Wally and I were baptising about twenty-two women and an old man. We did it together, as one person: not each of us individually. Both of us took a mug of water, baptising them, using our own language at the same time. It was really beautiful — I've never experienced anything like it before!

Sunday night was the last meeting and the people were waiting for the team. When Kevin finished preaching, he sat down and the team looked at each other wondering what to do next. There was no appeal for commitment, but suddenly, lots of people came forward and the team were totally overwhelmed: there were men who hadn't yet made a commitment, many who had been outside the church; there were lots of children and some of the whitefellas. We ended up with everyone standing in a huge circle, lifting our hands up to the Lord as we sang.

Alwyn Bates tells of his experience that night:

> I was living at 'Ranges when the Elcho mob came. I'd been living on the booze [alcohol] and all that and, at the meetings, I'd been sitting right at the back there or outside. At the last meeting, one of the blokes gave an invitation and the Lord really spoke to me there. Then, I went forward. I started to walk around — I couldn't sit down — walking backwards and forwards. I tried to go back home and I'd keep going back. So I started going right through then — right through to the front.
>
> I couldn't explain that, but all of a sudden everything inside felt changed and I felt happy inside — the next day, I was still the same.[24]

Maimie Butler was another who went forward for prayer that night:

> When I saw them [the Elcho Islanders], I was happy and excited. They were a bit different to us. We used to sing shy-way, but they had something in them: something strong and there was no shame in them, praising the Lord, praying for people.

. . . when they start talking in tongues, some of our people started asking, 'Hey, what they saying? Is that their language?' Mmmm, somehow, I sort of knew it wasn't their own language — it was something different, you know? I just say to them, 'It's not their language, it's Holy Spirit.' Talking to them, I just *knew* that!. . . You felt the Holy Spirit was there.

I went forward so they could pray for us, they prayed and I felt it was something that came in me gently — this quiet feeling and it's still the same — I feel the same. . . Yea, everybody came for prayer that night. I reckon it was the same feeling for everyone, 'cos after that everything was changed — drinking, fighting, swearing. They never use swear words in the camp.[25]

After the meeting, the team and some of the local leaders met at the mission house for supper. Pastor Arthur and Herbert and Chris — in fact all the local leaders — were asking, 'What do we do now?'

We could only give one answer: 'Ask God! Look to the Holy Spirit for every answer! But *don't* try to organise things yourself without him, at all!'

The team flew out of Warburton at 6.00 am on Monday, less than three days after arriving. Kevin had told the people both planes would circle the community twice while we prayed for the people of Warburton Ranges. As we circled, the people knelt at their homes and *wiltjas* (bush shelters) and prayed for the team.

Talking excitedly with Lorraine and Thelma later, Herbert said, 'It was like blessings were sprinkling down from the planes as they left. We were sad to see them go, but something greater had been left behind.'[26]

'There was a vast sense of something huge having been accomplished and that a new era had started,' Herbert wrote in his diary.[27] Ten years later he commented, 'And that's true, you know, and the new era hasn't gone away — it's still here.'[28]

7

Lighting many new fires

THE RAPID SPREAD OF RENEWAL IN CENTRAL AUSTRALIA

IT BECAME APPARENT TO MANY that God's timetable was for faster action in the Central Desert than it had been at Elcho Island. They had a total transformation in one weekend rather than weeks of build-up before a ten-day mission. It seemed that God quickly took firesticks from the fire to light new fires.

✦ Amazing events soon after the mission

There were amazing changes in the people of the area after the mission. Mamie Butler, whose story we heard in the last chapter, told me:

> After the Holy Spirit came into all the people they was really changed — we were no longer shy or frightened if somebody was running with a spear to spear someone. They didn't take any notice of people swearing at them. Those people who had bad tempers — if someone swears at them they used to get wild and start a big fight, but they are really changed.[1]

Thelma Roberts reported:

> Warburton Ranges was beginning to change to be a happy place, with music and singing much of the day and night.

It seemed people were given a new freedom or release as they lifted hands in worship and praise to God, praying with those who had responded.[2]

Immediately after the mission meetings, all the men left 'Ranges for their tribal ceremonies at Mt Margaret. They would normally have stopped to buy alcohol on their way home. Wilf Douglas met them on the road and found they had refused to go to Laverton for alcohol, because they wanted to get back to 'Ranges for more of the blessing. He and fellow UAM missionary, Ian Lindsay, arrived at 'Ranges to find amazing changes. Ian wrote:

We were at once aware that something had happened — everywhere gospel music was playing!

. . .it had caught everyone by surprise. How like our wonderful Lord!. . . We had been praying for revival, almost giving up hope that God could do anything with a people who had turned their backs so completely on him when suddenly, in a way most unexpected and unplanned by us, he reached out and gathered to himself hundreds of precious souls.[3]

There was an enthusiasm and life the missionaries had never seen before. Thelma had some Christian books arrive in the post. Terry Robinson saw them and wanted them. That was the beginning of thousands of dollars worth of literature, Bibles and tapes being sold.

They found that shyness had gone and the people had so much to tell the missionaries. When there was sickness, leaders were asked to pray as a group and there was healing. The hospital staff noticed the difference in the number and type of needs of patients.

One man collapsed and was taken to the hospital very ill. A Royal Flying Doctor Service (RFDS) plane was on its way to transport a sick baby to Kalgoorlie and the sisters thought he would probably go out on it, too. A group was asked to go to the hospital to pray for him. They laid hands on him. He felt something else touching his head apart from their hands and, a few minutes later, got up and went home healed.

In February, there was a crisis at the hospital. It had rained all day and the creeks were flooded. A baby was brought in very ill needing fluids, medication and the help of doctors. No-one realised that the only person at 'Ranges who knew what to do was Jeanette Balfe, a Christian nurse who had worked in remote areas of Africa. But she was in bed at the nurses' quarters with pneumonia.

Jeanette heard the emergency bell from the hospital ring in the nurses' quarters, but thought it was a mistake. Then, it rang a second time and she decided that they must need her, so she got out of bed and paddled over to the hospital through the storm.

The procedure that the nurses were trying to do for the baby was impossible in her condition. Jeanette suggested another way which no-one else knew about or could do. Despite the weather, they managed to make radio contact with the doctor in Kalgoorlie for instructions from paediatricians in Perth about the fluid and drugs that the baby needed. Jeanette managed to get the infusion going, then lay down alongside the baby and they both went to sleep while the other nurses went back to their other patients.

The following morning, the sun was out, but the 'Ranges airstrip was still unserviceable. The patients were driven to an old airstrip about thirty kilometres away. By the time the RFDS doctor had examined each patient and they were all settled in the plane, the incubator for the premature baby had flattened the plane's battery!

They jump-started the plane from the vehicle. It was quite an experience for all involved, with praise for the nurses. But one thing was totally amazing: no-one had rung that emergency bell! Jeanette and others saw this as a miracle, as part of the revival amongst the people, and felt that the praise belonged to God.[4]

During this period of dramatic change, the missionaries found the pace exhausting, but God gave them extra strength. Herbert had always found it difficult to teach and help before, and Kevin had prayed for God's Spirit to help him. Herbert found that the prayer was answered immediately:

> When Terry or others came, I would find all this stuff pouring out of me — the very next day, just pouring out of me! And I'd sit there and almost listen to my own voice.[5]

They came to realise that the Holy Spirit's supernatural power did not end when the twelve apostles died. They had always thought it unfair that they had to struggle when the apostles had the Holy Spirit's power — but now they knew that was all wrong! Herbert also told me of the changes in his own relationship with God:

> I used to address God as Lord God Almighty, quaking in my boots lest he might zap sinful me, but after the revival I found myself addressing him as *Father*![6]

It was clear to all who lived in 'Ranges or knew the community well that something totally beyond human understanding had happened that weekend. Amee Glass reported:

> The group at Warburton continued to meet almost every night to praise the Lord and share the word and more were continually added to the group. They also visited Jameson and Warakurna, where almost everyone turned to the Lord. Pastors were appointed from among those groups who continued to lead services on Sundays and most week-night evenings.[7]
>
> New leadership emerged from among these newer Christians. They tended to be mainly younger, bilingual men who were not able to read in Ngaanyatjarra. So the preaching was mainly based on the English Bible even when the passage was available in Ngaanyatjarra.[8]

✦ Renewal comes to Warakurna

A month after the *Yolngu*'s visit, Aborigines went from 'Ranges to Warakurna, a community near the Northern

Territory border. They felt God was leading them to go and share what they had experienced, and went in an old bus the Christians had bought earlier that year. They wanted to share what God had taught them through the Elcho Islanders — they sang the songs they had learned and told what God had done. Terry Robinson, who led the group, tells what happened:

> Only a few people came for the meeting. We were disappointed and discouraged. I was thinking, 'What's the use of coming here? We may be a fool to come here! Nobody is taking notice.'
>
> So I turned to the Bible and in front of me was a passage about Jesus talking to his disciples, telling them to throw the net a bit further away, and the disciples caught a lot more fish.[9]

They felt the Lord was encouraging them to throw out their nets and try again. Their meeting that night was very different.

Many people came to their open air meeting, but it was disrupted by a community leader who was angry at the meeting being held. He drove wildly round and round the group in his car expecting everyone to run away, but they stayed sitting there. This is a common way of expressing feelings of anger — and it always scatters people fast!

He staked a tyre, but continued to drive madly around them. Then a second tyre went flat. A car with two flat tyres is undrivable, so he went to his house and got his spears and woomera (spear thrower). As he ran towards them, he tripped and fell, breaking most of his spears. As he got up, he began to put a spear into his woomera to throw it into the middle of the meeting. Instead of running away, 'they all just got together and stood and raised their hands and praised the Lord and sang. That staggered the people at Warakuna just as it staggered the people at Warburton.'[10]

One of them even said, 'You can do anything you like — we

are not frightened, because Jesus is here with us.' Another said, 'We're standing in the name of the Lord.' Locals joined in the rejoicing and made commitments to Jesus, staying around for many hours talking about Jesus and their new life in him.

The battle over the spirit of fear during the *Yolngu*'s visit has been effective and lasting in the region.

Robin Smythe was one of those who came forward that night. He had been present during the meetings at 'Ranges also:

When the Elcho Island mob came I was there, but I was outside — I just stood back and watched. . .

[Then at Warakurna] God spoke to me when I was watching TV [actually, a video — this was before TV was available in the area]. I knew the team was there and I tried to duck away again like I did in Warburton Ranges. This time God spoke to me and I feel something leading me that way. . .

I was coming back from watching TV and I had to go past the meeting — they were in the way so I had to walk through the meeting and the invitation was given just then. Even though I never heard all the message, I went out to the front there and knelt down, crying because I came back to the Lord. I was thinking about all the bad things I was doing and I was happy to come back — crying with the joy and to forget about the past — and God's family.

I never felt anything inside me like that before. I gave my heart to the Lord when I was going to school at Leonora, so I knew about *Mama* God ['*Mama*' is the Ngaanyatjarra word for 'Father']. I used to sing song — wake up every morning singing, 'Walking with Jesus, by his side I'll stay'.

So I've been listening to God right through when I've been growing up and when I got older I came back to the Lord and I think, 'Oh that's good; I've been brought up in Christian way,' but never really made that real repentance. Now, I'm glad. . . I've felt the power. . . [11]

✦ The ongoing renewal at Warburton and Warakurna

The Holy Spirit's presence continued to be felt in the area. On Monday 17 November 1981, I received a phone call from Chris Marshall with the news that there was a real revival at Warburton. Another fifty to sixty people were baptised on Sunday and an old man told of a vision that was 'like the Revelation of John all over again!'[12]

There was no water around, but the Christians had prayed for rain so that they could baptise some of the new converts. It rained, so they were able to go to a creek about twelve kilometres from 'Ranges to hold the service. The following weekend, the 'Ranges group again visited Warakurna and held a baptismal service for the new Christians there.

Some of the opposition continued, especially those throwing the rocks. Thelma wrote:

> Sometimes a drunk would try to disrupt. One night, the choir was singing and a large stone was hurled and hit the wall and shattered above their heads. Sometimes the meetings were broken up, but some stayed and prayed against the fierce opposition. In my case, this intense praying would turn into praise even while the stones and shouting were still in force. It became a warfare.
>
> Sometimes, when an appeal was given later in the meeting, one of these troublemakers was the first to respond. One young mother testified one night and spoke of the change in her life. She simply said, 'Jesus took the rocks out of my hands!'[13]

✦ The Elcho Island team returns to Warburton

Before the Elcho Island team had left Warburton in September, Kevin told the leaders that if they needed them and asked for them, they would return.

On Thursday, 10 December 1981, Chris Marshall rang me saying that the people were gathering for meetings and they wanted Djiniyini and the Elcho team to visit the next Tuesday for three or four days of teaching meetings. Would I please contact them and arrange the visit?

That would need an incredible number of miracles! There were many major difficulties: Djiniyini's program was always very busy, the only phone at Elcho Island was unavailable, planes were often booked out — and we only had a weekend and three other days to get them there, at least two days of which would be travelling.

Then, there was the matter of finance. Offerings from the last mission were excellent — $720. But the cost of hiring the planes alone was over $1200. We had been absolutely amazed at the way God had provided this and also Kevin's airfares from Elcho Island.

How could we organise all this in such a short time? This organisational nightmare was actually all sorted out within twenty-four hours! Plane bookings were confirmed and a light aircraft booked. The team was Djiniyini, his wife Gelung and Rronang. I went again as pilot/prayer support.

The Ngaanyatjarra people had already taken up a collection of about $1500 to go towards the Elcho Islanders' expenses and further offerings were added to it during the trip.

The Howells were away on leave and could not therefore provide accommodation, but the Ngaanyatjarra Christians no longer regarded the *Yolngu* as strangers. They saw them as brothers and sisters in Christ and wanted to look after them themselves.

Hundreds of people had travelled for hours to be there. Albert Lennon, the Pitjantjatjara leader whose life-rubbish was thrown into the river in his boots, had been personally transformed since he came back to God in August. When God spoke to him about going to 'Ranges for the meetings, he gladly drove for over twelve hours to get there from Fregon with a group of his people.

There were far too many people to fit in the church, so the meetings were held outside it, where a platform had been made from an old truck tray — something that became standard procedure throughout Central Australia.

The singing and testimonies went on and on — there was so much that God had done that they wanted to praise him for and tell others about! Warburton Ranges is in a part of Australia that goes on 'daylight wasting time' — the official time zones don't cater for them and people were normally in bed by 7.00 or 8.00 pm — especially in those days before TV.

Djiniyini taught on the nature of God and the church. By the second night, he was teaching about the Holy Spirit

Djiniyini Gondarra speaking to Aboriginal pastors at an outstation, 1993

and asked me to share some of my testimony on the difference the Holy Spirit had made in my ministry. He then asked all the church leaders to come out to the front, so the team could pray for a new outpouring of the Holy Spirit on them for their ministry.

Gelung and Rronang began to minister in song as about a dozen leaders came and stood before the platform. The Holy Spirit ministered to them by removing bondages and hurts and anointing them with his encouragement and the fruit of his presence — love, joy, peace, patience, kindness, goodness, faithfulness, gentleness and self-control.[14]

Djiniyini spoke to the crowd: 'Now, the rest of you people who want to receive the power of Holy Spirit for your life and ministry, you come forward.' No-one moved. Djiniyini repeated his invitation and, for the next two hours, people streamed out to stand before the platform while the four of us in the team prayed for each one and the Holy Spirit touched them.

Gelung told with real excitement how she felt the Holy Spirit's power:

> We started praying for healing and also for the baptism of the Holy Spirit and, as I stood there, I heard Rronang started speaking in tongues, but then all of a sudden I could hear God's voice — feel God's presence was there.
>
> One old lady — she came forward. She knelt down and started to pray, then Djiniyini came forward and I started praying with her then. Suddenly, we could feel God's presence was there and she was baptised by the Holy Spirit for the first time.
>
> She stood up and started shouting, 'Come, come, come; God's still present. . .' It was like a fire burning in her life and she could feel the presence. . . she could feel it there. I heard her say, 'Come, come, come; as soon as you come here in this circle here, you'll be healed completely.' . . .[She was] jumping and jumping and praising God . . . Then, we saw all this crowd of people.[15]

I have no idea how many people we prayed for in this way that night — there must have been three to four hundred people at the meeting and it seemed like every one of them came forward for prayer, with the same results. Around midnight, some of the children started to come forward for prayer also and we started to pray for them, but I started to feel concerned and suggested to Djiniyini that the local leaders and parents should be praying for their children. The meeting closed soon after that.

Djiniyini, Gelung and Rronang were busy for a long time after that meeting. 'That night we couldn't sleep — people were so excited. . . After the service was finished, people came and we were ministering late in the night. . . until 3 o'clock in the morning!'[16]

Chris Marshall had gone home very early with a splitting sinus headache and he heard the news when I arrived home from the meeting. Suddenly, he was wide awake with the headache temporarily forgotten and said: 'And I missed out!' He made sure he didn't miss out totally: he had been wanting this for himself for a long time! The next day he found Djiniyini and asked him to pray for him. He fell down under the power of the Holy Spirit. Later he said, 'It was wonderful! I was filled with the glory of the Lord and I couldn't move if I wanted to. I just lay there praising the Lord and then gradually I was able to get up.'[17] That release made a real change for Chris as well as for many of the people — there was a new power to do the things God wanted.

The following evening was the final meeting. Everyone who was vaguely interested but had missed out the previous night was there that night. It was a very unpleasant, windy night with lots of dust, so the meeting was crammed into the church. Djiniyini had pressured me into giving the teaching on the church, then he went on to talk about the churches in Revelation chapters 1 to 3 and how God knows each group and meets their needs so they can be truly his people.

At the end of the meeting, those who had missed out the previous meeting came forward to the front of the building for their touch and some fell down on the floor. But God was doing something different and we were struggling to know exactly what it was. We felt we had to invite the leaders forward and Djiniyini began to speak about God's desire to use Aboriginal people in ministry beyond their own town and tribe, even to other races.

Everyone came forward and stood in a big circle, three or four deep, and the team prayed for God to make them truly the church. As the meeting closed, the people began to sing, filing around to shake hands with each of the team members.

As they came to each of us, we sensed an anointing flowing into each person. I remember one very old lady with no teeth, rather crippled up, coming to me — and I sensed God saying: 'I will use her in taking the gospel to people far away from here.' I felt absolutely amazed by that thought, but I saw it happening in Geraldton seven months later — over 1500 kilometres away!

During the meeting that night, some people were driving around in a car, yelling out. Djiniyini went out and talked with them, warning them, 'You can curse Jesus. . . but you cannot curse Holy Spirit, because Holy Spirit cannot forgive you. Because you are dealing with something, something. . . *fire* burning.'[18] He talked about God's love and the foolishness and the stubbornness of people: 'We have a precious life that belongs to him. He can take that if he wants to, if we aren't careful.'

There was an awesome prophetic note in his words. The next morning, we flew home.

✦ Tragedy sends the gospel out
As we landed in Alice Springs, the Ngaanyatjarra church was being really put to the test. Father Christmas had arrived at 'Ranges and it promised to be a beautiful day. Everyone was very happy, when suddenly the air was cut by wailing and yelling.

Seven young men were in a car having fun spinning around on the oval. Because of a hole in the fuel tank, they had a drum of petrol inside the car with a hose feeding the engine. The car rolled over, petrol sprayed all over the boys and the car exploded into flames. Two of them died on the way to hospital in the plane. Three others were flown to Perth for treatment, where another one died three months later. One escaped unhurt and another had minor injuries.

Thelma Roberts was there, later writing that they all knew God was present in very special ways. One young man was given special strength to get the last victim out of the flames on his second attempt. A doctor had landed to refuel his plane just before the accident. An RFDS plane was nearby and another came out later. There were relief nurses still there after others had returned from holidays and each young man had a nurse to care for him.

Normally, people would had bashed their heads with rocks until they bled as a sign of mourning, but a calmness came over the place and there were only some small commotions. Pastor Arthur was a close relative of some involved, so tribal taboos prevented direct action. He went to the church and cried out to God. Thelma prayed and talked with him, reading Psalm 23 with him. Verse 3 particularly helped him: 'He gives me new strength.'

The Aboriginal Christians gathered around the beds of the boys and prayed for them. They went around the camp to relatives, supporting and praying for them. Thelma also went around visiting various groups of people:

Some were just sitting or standing around in shock, some were praying. . . I knew I would also have to visit the parents of the boy who was the driver [he would be blamed for the accident and his family punished]. I felt completely drained physically and spiritually — not knowing what to expect or would they even want to see me? As I walked, I prayed, 'Lord, I've nothing left to give. Fill me with your Spirit to go to this family.'

It was late afternoon. They beckoned to me to enter their camp. I was filled with the love and compassion of Jesus. They told me they had been hit with rocks and sticks 'just like Stephen in the New Testament' — and they just sat there and took it. Usually, they would have retaliated strongly.

I knew their son had become a Christian not long before — as was his cousin. Both were badly burnt. As I left, a younger sister called me saying her father had seen a 'cross' over his son's bed at the hospital — it was a help to him, I'm sure, to prepare them that his son might die.

One boy saw another person in the burning car with them [like in Daniel's day] — he had white shiny clothes.

Several of them had seen the Lord in the car. Another tough teenager said, 'If it wasn't for Jesus, we'd all be finished by now.'[19]

When news of the deaths came on the hospital radio next morning, large groups gathered around the families. Thelma's report continues:

We sat with them and cried, sharing deeply their hurt and sorrow, praying with them. As I held the mother and prayed through the tears, after a while I couldn't believe what I was hearing. . .'I can see his face [her son]; he is happy! Yes, Lord, you are Lord, even here — thank you, Father.' There was joy in her sorrow, in the depth of experiences shared. This couple had lost four children before and she had been beside herself in grief. This time there was composure — God was helping and strengthening them in a new way.[20]

Thelma later said, 'I don't understand it but, when the accident occurred, it was those people who had fallen down [under Holy Spirit's power in the meetings] who had the strength and the courage to go to the car and pull the boys out of the burning car. The others couldn't go near it.'[21] And it was these ones who went and ministered to others, whose faith remained strong for years.

After the accident, Thelma had been asked what was her summary of all that was happening at Warburton Ranges — all the incredible things. It wasn't until after the funerals that God showed her the answer to give them: 'Beauty for ashes, the oil of joy for mourning, the garment of praise for a spirit of heaviness, that they might be called trees of righteousness, the planting of the Lord, that he might be glorified.'[22]

Many people went bush or to other communities to mourn and 'Ranges became a sad, quiet, almost deserted place. But a deep bond of love had come through the joy and then the tears.

A few weeks later, there was a shooting accident where a

young boy died at an outstation in the area. Thelma was approached by three church leaders, Arthur, Terry and Alwyn, asking her to drive them out to all the sad, grieving people to comfort them with the word of God.

Thelma wrote:

> It was the beginning of a number of conventions held in the outstations over a very hot summer! They would head off in their old, beat up cars and somehow arrive there and back again. Even that was a miracle. It was so hot that the petrol was evaporating, even in the mission vehicle.
>
> This was where the revival began to spread: reaching out where the need was, with the word of God under the leading of the Holy Spirit. . . Good did come out of tragedy![23]

✦ The Ngaanyatjarra visit to Elcho Island

Then the invitations began to come in from other places that had heard of what God was doing.

The *Yolngu* had invited the people from the Ngaanyatjarra church to join them at Galiwin'ku for their third annual Revival Thanksgiving Weekend in March 1982. Twelve adults and two children, led by their pastor, Arthur Robertson and his wife, Phyllis, flew up from Alice Springs for a time of learning, experiencing the presence of God through his people. Robin Smythe was one of them:

Pastor Arthur Robertson at Warburton Ranges

> After I came back to the Lord, I start to get involved in the church — doing

church work, taking up the offering. . . God gave me strength to do little bit bigger things, so I went to Elcho — went there because God has plans for me. . .

The leaders prayed for me at Elcho Island for that gift and I was anointed for that gift of healing. . . I came back and I prayed for sick people — started at Alice Springs and they were healed and all around the Goldfields. . . I prayed for one old man, a young girl at Sid Ross hostel. I prayed for a lot of sick people and, even when drunken people come out at meeting to give their hearts, [I would] pray for them and they feel different: they were sober; all the argument and that was finished — changed! God's power is real — even people who fall away now, they know and they cry for God's power.[24]

✦ Changes in a Ngaanyatjarra leader

Another man whose life was changed was Bernard Newbery, a very gifted Ngaanyatjarra man from Warakurna, a man whom God touched when he was young. He described his experiences this way:

Looking back over a few years when we became Christians, back in those days it was different. You can become a Christian, but you really can't feel that you've changed. After I became a Christian, I decided to go to the Bible Institute. Just going through the really hard work. . . It was just beyond my knowledge. I just couldn't understand — just couldn't get the meaning of 'everything become new'.[25] I couldn't place myself in 'everything made new'. All I knew was that I was a Christian.

I came out after a few years of training at the Bible Institute at Gnowangerup. . . and I tried to memorise what I'd learnt at the college. I stored those precious memories of the time I spent at the college — the lectures and the people I spoke to, the people who taught me and helped me — and tried to make it clear so I could understand.

Anyway, I came away with very little knowledge of the meaning of the scriptures. I kept reminding myself that I was a Christian and I couldn't do this and that. Later on,

I went back to Warakurna and went back to living my own ways, which I never used to do. All the time I used to feel that I was living in the wrong place. Drinking and gambling wasn't my kind of activity.

Then one day along came that mob from Elcho Island and I saw there was a lot of people made a stand for the Lord and they all wanted to be preachers and all wanted to do this and that. I never saw anything like that in all of my lifetime.

They were all talking at one time. I had just never seen it happen in any other convention in the Great Southern [south-west corner of Western Australia], in Perth and all around that area. And I've never seen people flock in like a moth being drawn to the light, and children and old people all coming. They were all high in spirit and they all wanted to say something and know the Lord.

I sort of stayed back in the background and I talked to people and asked what it's like. The people I talked to — they were talking in a different sort of way from normal speaking; suddenly, I realised that there must be something behind all this. I should switch over and feel it myself and I will know it rather than just getting it from those people that I talked with.

I sat there for a while after the Elcho Island people had gone and I made a comeback — and suddenly, just like that, it was so different! The atmosphere changed — a new being — changed! The people you talked with were changed and I felt the coming of the Holy Spirit. I was baptised into the Spirit and everything turned out like everything was new. I felt it: that everything was new.

My mind couldn't understand and grasp what was being lectured at college. All became real — came out and became reality, and you could feel and touch. You can feel the power behind the words in the scripture; the meaning from the scripture became alive instead of just being words.

You know they talk a lot about Holy Spirit — that you can never be baptised into the Spirit, or some people say it can't be another Pentecost. But for us people, it was the first time for us and it was something different, a change in the people's approach, a change in the communication. People never used to talk to each other too much — but now everybody wanted to share this wonderful feeling that they felt when the Holy Spirit came upon them. The very ground that you stood on — it came just like walking on heaven. The feelings that really our mind or your tongue can never tell. It's beyond. . . beyond. . . beyond!

Everything is changed and it felt so good. With that feeling, we went out, not because someone told us to go, but it was that same Spirit that compelled us to go and share that feeling — the heavenly feeling.

So we grouped ourselves — some went west, some went south. And, from what I was hearing from other groups, signs and wonders followed them wherever they went. And the people — hard people — came to experience the first touch of being baptised into the Holy Spirit.[26]

✦ The Ngaanyatjarra spread the gospel far and wide

Jesus commissioned his disciples in Acts 1: 8, saying, 'But the Holy Spirit will come upon you and give you power. Then, you will tell everyone about me in Jerusalem, in all Judea, in Samaria and everywhere in the world.'

God, through Djiniyini, commissioned the Ngaanyatjarra people as firesticks to take the whole gospel to the world. For them, 'Jerusalem' meant their own families and people. 'Judea' was their more distant cousins and family. 'Samaria' was the distant relatives they didn't want to have anything to do with, but still in the Central Desert. 'Everywhere in the world' was the foreigners and strangers in other parts of Australia and other countries.

Two teams went out to be witnesses to Jesus. One went to the goldfields (their 'Samaria'), led by Terry Robinson, and eventually covered most of Western Australia. The other team went north, led by Bernard Newbery. But first they had some more of 'Judea' to be covered.

Early in 1982, Ian Lindsay again visited the 'Ranges and

asked Terry Robinson and the church if they would go to Mt
Margaret for Easter. Terry said, 'We told him we were only
thinking about it — we never gave him a decision. We told
him if the Lord lead us down there, we'll go.'[27]

While they were waiting to hear from God about it,
someone had a dream that they should go to Mantamaru
(Jameson) for meetings and they all agreed. Terry reported:

> We were all of one accord — everybody had this sort of
> feeling that they had in their heart — they all wanted to go
> to Jameson. So we went away. Then, we had a big meeting
> there and a lot of people from South Australia and some
> from Northern Territory were there. We had a lot of people
> who experienced the power of the Holy Spirit. People that
> were sick and had pains and were crippled — they were
> healed; they found that power of the devil was no longer
> in them and they were delivered.[28]

Bonnie Yates tells the story of one of those healings:

Terry Robinson with his family

Les Cameron was sick and today he's walking around himself. He used to get funny in the head — he'd go off and wander away and people would have to go and find him and then lock him up so he wouldn't keep wandering away. He couldn't talk at all. He was a good man as a young man, but something happened to him. He got mad and cranky; he'd chase right around — chase all the kids, men. His father would lock him in the house. They prayed for him and now he doesn't do that any more. Today, he's walking around fine — no sickness at all. He can sit down and laugh! He's listening to the Lord.[29]

Realising the need for teaching, Bernard Newbery took a team around the Ngaanyatjarra communities in May that year leading Bible studies, spending a few days at each place. Then, they went right out in the desert to Kintore on the Northern Territory–Western Australian border — 'Samaria', for them.

On the second day of their meetings, they were gathered at around sunset with these really 'uncivilised' and 'wild' Pintubi people. Bernard said:

We shared the fresh touch of the Holy Spirit. A lot of people accepted the Lord and there was joy in the community. People who were really hard or can't believe in God — they felt the touch of the Holy Spirit.

I always keep saying you need to be baptised into Holy Spirit and, when we first got there, I gave the word and many people — even before the invitation — were making a stand for the Lord.

Then there was something like a big willy-willy [a whirlwind] — you can't see it, but you could hear it. If you had heard it, you would expect to see leaves moving, but there was hardly any movement of the leaf — it was just a gentle southerly wind. And people started flocking — of their own accord people started coming when that noise was on. We didn't even get halfway through the message and didn't make any appeal at all — people just came![30]

It was just getting dark, when suddenly they saw a bright light in the sky and there was a man with a book standing in the light! The whole group were sitting totally amazed and wondering what it was, when they heard this wind coming through the trees.

In that country, you can hear the wind coming for miles through the mulga trees — and they could hear it coming closer and closer, until suddenly it was right there. They were looking at the trees and the sound of the wind was right there, but the trees weren't moving! The leaves were quite still! Suddenly, the whole group were aware of God's presence and fell to their knees, pleading with the Lord for forgiveness, cleansing and a new life!

That's the sort of thing you read about in the book of Acts, but most Christians never expect to experience! Acts 2, verse 2 talks about 'the sound of a mighty wind' — and that is exactly what they experienced at Kintore as the Holy Spirit came powerfully to do his job of bringing them to repentance!

A few days later, a young man was telling Herbert Howell about what had happened at Kintore. This young man had been a real criminal — always in trouble and people dreaded what he would do next. But here he was telling this incredible story to Herbert. Then, he said to Herbert, 'Let's pray.'

> I don't know where he learnt to pray. . . he hadn't been involved in church in any way as far as I knew. He just prayed in an amazing way — it was incredible! He just sat there praying for a quarter of an hour: praising the Lord, thanking him and telling the Lord how wonderful he was. . .[31]

Herbert was still wondering about this, when Bernard Newbery met him and told him exactly the same story. Bernard is a careful, thinking man, not easily carried away with excitement, but Bernard was totally impressed at the reality of what had happened!

'There's still a strong group of Christians up there at Kintore. . . We started to feel after a while that we were living in the book of Acts,' Herbert said.[32]

But God's bushfire was only just starting!

8

Fuelling a raging bushfire

THE CRUSADES ACROSS WESTERN AUSTRALIA

BUSHFIRES OFTEN SPREAD THROUGH SPARKS AND WIND, but this one didn't spread accidentally. God took firesticks from the desert fires of the Warburton Ranges area to light bushfires all over the land and God's bushfire cracked open seedpods to bring renewal.

The story of the firesticks was told in a song that was written by an Aboriginal couple, Len and Stella Wicker, from Mt Margaret Mission in the goldfields of Western Australia. Len and Stella have sung it in many places across Australia, really touching a chord in many people's hearts — because so many Australians really wanted to see Aborigines rise up to be the people God made them to be, rather than just drunken down and outs filled with shame:

Chorus: There's a fire burning from the desert,
There's a fire burning thick and bright,
And it's starting to reach further out
As God's Spirit moves across the land.

Verse 1:   Now I wonder if you've ever noticed,
The people the Lord used that day;
They came from the north, Central Desert,
With the message from God up above.

Verse 2:   They came right down through the Goldfields,

> Down south and further along the way;
> God's Spirit is moving the people,
> With the message from God up above.

Verse 3: Now, I wonder if you've ever noticed
> God's calling and what it means to you:
> Of Jesus — he's coming back again —
> Are you ready to meet him in the end?

Verse 4: Yes, there's a fire burning from the desert,
> There's a fire burning thick and bright,
> And it's starting to reach further out
> As God's Spirit moves across this land.

The Goldfields was a natural direction for the Ngaanyat-jarra people to go to share their new life. Their mission settlement at Warburton Ranges was started from that area and they are related to Goldfields Aborigines. The Goldfields around Kalgoorlie is tough country. The gold rush began in 1893 and gold mining has been the major industry ever since. But it brought all the heartbreak, sickness, death and problems of gold fever into a very hot, dry, remote part of the land. For Aborigines, the struggles weren't just the greed, rape, prostitution, violence, murder, drunkenness, curfews in town and racial prejudice of the invaders. They also had their own tribal fights.

Aboriginal pastor, Ron Williams, tells of his great grandmother's tribe visiting Skull Creek in Laverton during World War I. Her tribe speared the local Aborigines while they were asleep. The police simply dumped the bodies down a deserted mineshaft and filled it in.[1] Life was tough!

✦ Preparation for renewal

God had been preparing the way for his bushfire in Western Australia for many years, with little fruit from the hard work of many missionaries. In 1921, Rudolphe (Rod) Schenk, a missionary with the United Aborigines Mission, arrived at Laverton in the Goldfields. He had ridden his motorbike from the eastern states — 4 000 kilometres of dirt tracks!

Aboriginal pastor, Ron Williams, records that Rod 'was told by the Western Australian government that the Goldfields Aborigines have no hope. They are the lowest Aborigines in the state of Western Australia and nothing can be done for them.'[2] But Rod felt a calling from God burning in his heart that he had to take the love of Jesus to these people, bringing them courage and hope.

Ron Williams frequently expresses his feelings of gratitude to the many missionaries who brought the gospel to his people. He tells of Rod Schenk's work that took ten years of struggles before he was able to welcome his first convert, with both black and white trying to get rid of him.[3]

Ron wrote a number of songs about Rod's work. One of them tells about an Aborigine who accepted Rod's good news — Mulga Joe, or Mulgatjanu, father of Aboriginal evangelist, Pastor Ben Mason. Mulga Joe lived kingdom of God values. At one time, he wanted to show Ron a reef of gold and a reef of copper which he had discovered, but Ron was more interested in people than that sort of treasure. Mulga Joe said, 'Well, we'll leave them. Can't take all that gold and copper to heaven when we die.'[4] Mulga Joe was once told to stop talking about Jesus and he replied, 'I don't want to be like a windmill tied up. I want to be pumping water for the thirsty sheep.'[5] So, Ron wrote a song about that, too.

Another of God's Aboriginal servants in Western Australia was Bob Williams, a tribal leader from Carnarvon, who became a Christian at sixty and spent his last fifteen years travelling around the state taking the gospel to his people in an Aboriginal way. He tried to help his people to realise that Jesus was not just for the whitefellas. Some people were calling him the 'king of the Aborigines';[6] the tribal law men didn't understand or like what he was doing and threatened to spear him.

In October 1965, a law meeting was held at Meekatharra to sort out the matter. Bob told them that Jesus is not against Aboriginal ways, for he 'came, not to destroy the law, but to fulfil it'.[7] They came to believe that these words of Jesus apply to Aboriginal law as well as Hebrew law, and he described Jesus as 'the in-between one' — the One who stands between the races. Bob was granted freedom to travel anywhere in the the Murchison, Goldfields and Central Desert with the gospel. He once described himself as 'the one who made the cut line' — the pioneer who blazed the first trail so that others would later follow.

Rod Schenk had established a mission settlement at Mt Margaret, which became a centre of Christianity for Aborigines in the region. Bobby Scott, Aboriginal pastor at Mt Margaret, told me:

> The people that came in from the desert were living out on the outskirts of the towns. . . The mission has been having trouble ever since Mr Schenk established Mt Margaret in 1921. When he got this ground he prayed: 'Lord, bless this place, Mt Margaret, so that from here people might go out.'
>
> This is where I was bought up here in Mt Margaret Mission. And the missionaries trained us so that one day we might become missionaries ourselves, that we would go out and tell the people about the love of the Lord Jesus Christ.[8]

As a result of government policy, Mt Margaret was handed over to Aboriginal leadership by the United Aborigines Mission (UAM) in 1976. Bobby said:

> The missionaries all went away because the government put pressure on them to leave Mt Margaret. We said: 'Well, we're not going to let Mt Margaret just fall away into the government's hands!' So we formed a Christian committee. We called it the AMOS Committee — Aboriginal Movement for Outback Survival. We started this off without the support of any government, but then we got funds from the government and we bought this place. . . it was Christians like Pastor Ben Mason, Tom Murray, Les Tucker, Cyril Barnes, Arthur Stokes — we was on the committee.
>
> All the time during Mr Schenk's time there was a lot of pressure and when we took over the pressure seemed to

Bobby Scott, who was pastor at the Mount Margaret community
at the time of the crusades

come on us: the devil wanted to take over, destroy this
place and we just about gave up hope. We knew that this
was God's anointed place and we wanted to carry this on
as a mission — a Christian centre, a place where people can
come and find the Lord Jesus Christ.[9]

By the early 1980s, there was real hopelessness, drunkenness, social disintegration and lawlessness amongst
Aboriginal people in the Goldfields. Retired UAM missionary,
Claude Coterill, saw this as part of God's preparation for
revival. Claude has worked with Aborigines in the area for
many years and still lives at Leonora, helping the people:

Just before the revival came here, you can feel people
coming to the Lord — *Wangkayi* people [Aborigines from the
Goldfields and Central Desert]. Lindsay — the biggest drunk
going, a whitefella — wanted to know more about the Lord
and become a Christian. The Holy Spirit coming on people
— you could feel it in the air, people becoming friendly. . .
putting things right. . . you could feel it in the town.[10]

The year 1981 had been a time of special preparation for the bushfire of revival in the Goldfields as well as in the desert. In August, around the same time as the first *Yolngu* visit to Warburton Ranges, Mt Margaret held its annual convention. This convention attracted people from around the Goldfields and other areas. Ron Williams, who has worked in this area for many years, was one of the speakers. He did a painting and shared a vision that he had in July 1979. Ron had seen the mess that his people were in and felt God speaking to him about the situation:

> The Lord gave me a vision of either possible revolution and destruction, or revival if my *Wangkayi* friends repented. I had this vision of muddy, swirling waters rising up and a picture of a lifeboat, which was the gospel of Christ. Then, another picture came into my heart like a river coming down from the Northern Territory. This river would join the eastern Goldfields and go right through to Kalgoorlie and on to Esperance. Another river would join up from the Kimberlies through the Pilbara region.
>
> The verses the Lord gave me in July 1979 were in Isaiah 43, verses 19 to 21: 'Behold, I will do a new thing, now it shall spring forth; shall ye not know it? I will make a way in the wilderness and rivers in the desert. . . I give waters in the wilderness and rivers in the desert, to give drink to my people, my chosen. This people have I formed for myself, they shall show forth my praise.'[11]

Bobby Scott tells of some of the outworking of Ron's vision at the Mt Margaret convention:

> We were holding a convention service here. . . and the Lord gave brother Ron Williams this wonderful vision. . . He saw a stream come right down to Warburton and coming straight through here. He was sharing that vision and, before the convention was finished, we had a big rain here and it looked to me like the revival started at that time.
>
> It was a vision and a sign to show us that one day we're going to expect a big revival to come through — and that's

what happened! When the convention was over, he dug a big hole on the side of the creek and he baptised about six young people. . . and it was real cold, too![12]

Early the following year, the people from Mt Margaret began to develop a real expectancy that God was about to do something. Bobby told me:

We heard this revival is coming through from Elcho Island and they were saying a big revival is happening in Warburton Ranges and they going to come this way soon — any time now — going to come through to Mt Margaret and come to Leonora.

The Lord was giving us verses from the Bible, and one of the verses was 'Pull down your tents and stretch the ropes out so that you can make more room — enlarge the place of your tent'[13] and that's what we had to do. That verse came when the revival started to leave Warburton because that's what's going to happen here at Mt Margaret. . .

They were 'singing' in Warburton to us — people were saying there's a big revival happening at Mt Margaret — it was like an echo that we could hear those people singing. . . And the air: there had been a heaviness in the air. When there is trouble, there is a heaviness in the sky. . . The Aborigines say that, when you get heavy, that is the devil up there. . . the prince of the air. When the revival came, the burden seem to have lifted. . .[14]

By 1982, almost all of the AMOS committee had moved away from Mt Margaret and were living elsewhere. There was some stirring and questionable tactics by well-meaning whites in an attempt to hand control to a local group, removing the Christian influence from Mt Margaret management. Bobby said:

The government formed another group — they called it the Wiltjanet Group. They wanted the old law to be here in Mt Margaret — initiation law. This was a central place and they wanted to establish it as a centre for tribal law business for Coonnana, Cundelee, Warburton Ranges and Wiluna. . . But we fought hard against that. We prayed and asked the Lord to keep us strong and give us wisdom and knowledge to hold this place.[15]

All the formalities were to be completed at an official handover to the Wiltjanet Group in March 1982, with government officials present. But God intervened. Ian Lindsay, UAM missionary at Leonora, tells of two of his regular visits to Mt Margaret:

A fortnight before this changeover was to take place, I took a group of young people there one evening to show a film and hold a gospel meeting. When we arrived, there was fighting going on all over the place: cars were being smashed into each other; bottles, bars and rocks were flying. The white community manager had his arm broken. We did have a meeting, but only because the people came to the church for refuge when the police arrived.

One week later, four men arrived from Warburton; the Lord poured out his Holy Spirit and on my next visit practically all were following Christ. All week the meetings had continued all day; people were just bubbling over with the joy and love of the Lord. This was to be the day of the changeover of control. Imagine the surprise of the government officials (and their embarrassment) as the people said, 'Oh no, we want to keep the old AMOS Committee; we are all Christians now.'[16]

✦ The first crusade trip

The Ngaanyatjarra team arrived from Warburton Ranges to share what they had received from God through the *Yolngu*. Terry Robinson was the leader of what became known as the 'crusade team'. He tells of their arrival at Mt Margaret:

. . . the first living thing that we saw was two nanny goats in the church, so we drove the goats out of the church. . . and swept it out and cleaned all the windows and then we had a meeting there. The locals came along. They wanted to see what was happening — what kind of Christians we are, what kind of ministry we had.

We were telling them we were filled by the Holy Spirit, the power of God is taking us, living in us. . . and a lot of people came to know the Lord. There were a lot of drunks and we were able to defeat the evil spirit of drink and we claimed the people for the Lord. They were all amazed! They said, 'These ordinary people come up from the desert. . . they don't have fear!'[17]

Bobby spoke of the response:

People were starting to ring from Kalgoorlie and that's 300 kilometres away. People started to rush in from Leonora. We were just camping out and came into Mt Margaret and we saw all these desert people. When we saw them, we asked, 'What's going on? What's this? We're not going to be taught this way!' People were raising their hands and you could see the smile on their faces.

This church was packed. . . When a creek is running and it rains — way down at another place you can hear the creek coming, you can hear the water coming. The revival sounded like the water was coming, roaring along. People would ring up and say, 'What's going on at Mt Margaret?' We said, 'There's a revival here. You've been praying for revival — well we've got revival here! The prophecy has been fulfilled now. The vision that brother Ron got from the Lord — it's here now, the river is starting to flow here!'[18]

One of those converted was Alwyn Bates:

I was in Mt Margaret drunk. The crusade team was having a meeting, playing guitars and praising the Lord. I got this old fella with me and he was wanting to go to town. I jumped in [the car], put the key, tried to start him, and the key just disappeared in my hand!. . . Mucking round trying to find the key — na, nothing. I went to the church — oh, I accept the Lord, then. We were singing there, praising the Lord and I went home. I was still thinking about the key. I went to sleep. Next day, I went to have a look for the key — just on the floor there: the key is there! I looked everywhere! But now the key's just laying there![19]

After the Mt Margaret convention, the team stayed around for a while, living off the land — kangaroos and emus. Terry Robinson said:

> We used to rake around to scrape our pockets to buy a bag of flour and we shared it around. What the Lord was doing was separating the Christian people to go home and the ones who were to go further on. One morning when we were at a meeting, we looked and there was a thick, dark cloud pointing towards Kalgoorlie. In the midst of the cloud was a mark, a white mark — just like a cross. The Lord was telling us to go to Kalgoorlie. . . So the Holy Spirit led us, just like when God was leading his people by the cloud, and the Lord went with us.[20]

❏ *The team goes to Leonora and Kalgoorlie*
On the way to Kalgoorlie, the team stopped at Leonora for meetings. Shortly before he had moved to Leonora, Ian Lindsay stood on the corner opposite the Leonora UAM hall at daybreak and said later he had 'felt moved by God to claim the town in [God's] name'. Just twelve months later, 'suddenly these people arrived and stated that they had come to tell the people of Leonora what God was doing'.[21] There were too many people to fit in the church building, so they met outside, right where Ian had stood and prayed a year earlier. He wrote in his book:

> The first night was rather quiet; people just stood and looked. But the second night, there was much opposition. Shouting, fighting, rocks flying and police carting away drunks. Then, the Holy Spirit took over. There had been singing, a simple testimony and message from God's word. Then, as the group stood there softly singing, an appeal was given — not an emotionally-charged oration, but a simple appeal to turn and trust the Saviour. A hush descended on the town — a quietness you could almost touch, the peace of the Spirit of Peace. Many, who minutes before had been causing trouble, now came forward in tears to kneel at the front and confess their sin and need of the Saviour.

This continued throughout the week. First, the camp people came, then the townspeople; the gaols became empty, crime ceased and the pubs reported a twenty per cent drop in sales. (The white fellows drank the rest.)[22]

Local Aboriginal leader, Les Tucker, told me:

They had some real good powerful singers. Marlene, a blind girl, had a beautiful voice. Unknown to us, her voice went all over the community and into the homes. People would say, 'Who's that beautiful singer that you had down there — her voice was really lovely!'[23]

Even the police couldn't believe the changes in people, and publicans became frightened because they were losing their customers. There was a new spirit in the air in the whole region, even over one hundred kilometres away in Laverton. Ron Williams tells of meeting a young woman from Europe in Laverton and asking how she became a Christian. She replied, 'The atmosphere around Laverton was electrified and I just couldn't help but turn to the Lord.'[24]

Wilf Douglas told me that the team came to the Little Sisters of the Poor, a Catholic Order who work with Aborigines in Kalgoorlie. They gladly gave them the use of their property, the Roundhouse. Wilf said the team looked quite bedraggled at the meetings, 'but when they opened their mouths to sing, it was like heaven and the Holy Spirit really ministered through them'.[25]

One of the Irish Sisters said to Wilf, 'Pastor Douglas, you've done a marvellous job with those people out there!' He protested that it was God who had done it and she said, 'We gave the people the sacraments, but you gave them God's word in their own language!'

They held meetings in several other venues in Kalgoorlie, including Boulder Town Hall. The Kalgoorlie mayor was so impressed that he said he would arrange a venue any time they wanted to hold a meeting.

The team had travelled 600 kilometres over very rough

dirt roads to reach the Goldfields and found their people were lost and in a mess — and ready for their message. Excerpts from newspaper stories give some of the impact of their crusades in the Goldfields.

The West Australian of 10 April 1982 reported:

Since last December, more than 1000 Aborigines from the Goldfields to the border have committed their lives to Jesus Christ. The impact on law and order has been astonishing. At remote stations and settlements, in towns like Laverton, Leonora, Menzies and Kalgoorlie, violence has subsided and hardened drinkers have thrown away the bottle. At Warburton, where the Western Australian revivals started last August, purpose and calm have replaced violence and terror.

The most amazing thing about the revival is that it has happened entirely in the absence of white influence. The recent Kalgoorlie Fair, notorious for Aboriginal revelry, was peaceful as crowds of visiting Aborigines instead attended daily Christian revival meetings at Victoria Park.[26]

Perth's *Daily News* of 26 March 1982 reported that:

Leonora missionary, Mr Ian Lindsay said: 'Nobody's making them give up drink. They're just losing the desire to drink once they accept Christ.' On Wednesday, the constable in charge at the Leonora police station said: 'There's nobody in the lockup. But the number of arrests on Pension Day will tell the story.'. . .

The Kalgoorlie-based area officer of the Department of Aboriginal Affairs, Mr Cedric Wyatt, said the effects of the movement had been dramatic.[27]

After Kalgoorlie, the team returned to Leonora and conducted meetings over the Easter weekend. A few of the people wanted to be baptised. Les Tucker told me:

There had been some rain and all the gravel pits were all full of water. The Lord sent the rain, allowing these baptisms to take place and, when they started baptising a few, they just kept coming to get baptised. They finished up with four or five people baptising all the people.[28]

The Crusade team in Perth in 1982: photo courtesy of *The West Australian*

On the last night there, some of the team were keen to return to Warburton and they needed guidance once more. Cyril Barnes told me, 'Some of them were saying, "We've got to get back to Warburton to look after things there." Others said, "No, no! Got to do what the Lord says." But they didn't know where to go.'[29]

After the meeting that night, Bobby Scott told me: '. . .we prayed and asked the Lord where we going to go next. Then, we were singing and singing and someone looked up in the sky and said, "Ey, look there's a big arrow pointing up that way."[30] Ian Lindsay described it as:

. . .a large arrow made up of cloud — it pointed to the north, to Wiluna. I had heard the people talk of signs in the sky, but quite frankly I was sceptical, putting it down to imagination, but there was no doubt as to this — I saw it as did many others present.[31]

Bobby commented:

A lot of white people couldn't believe it. Some missionaries in Perth were saying: 'Oh, it must have been an aeroplane.' If an aeroplane was flying around, we could have heard it or seen it. It was very low — no other clouds, nothing, only that big arrow there — and we knew that the Lord wanted us to go to Wiluna.[32]

☐ *The team goes to Wiluna*
The crusade team was very large by the time they arrived in Wiluna. Many people from the Goldfields had joined them to travel with them and be part of the excitement. Ian Lindsay and his wife were in Wiluna for their monthly visit when the team arrived. He was confronted by an Aboriginal man from Strelley Station who told him, '. . . he had been sent to stop the "Mission mob" from preaching at Wiluna. I told him he could not stop God.'[33] Phil Bodeker, journalist with *The West Australian* newspaper, recorded some of the impact of the team's arrival in Wiluna in his 'Good News Column':

The team arrived at Wiluna on the Tuesday after Easter and stayed there until the following Sunday night. They conducted two meetings a day on weekdays and three on the Sunday. Up to 350 people, almost all Aborigines, attended. Up to fifty a night responded to a call to the front and gave their lives to the Lord. Many of the team and some new Christians from Wiluna gave testimonies [that] through Jesus they had beaten the drink and would never drink again. On the Sunday afternoon, more than 200 Aborigines were baptised in the school swimming pool.

The local Justice of the Peace told Ron Abbott that Aboriginal offences dropped to nothing during the week. On the Easter Saturday, there were forty-six people in the court, but on the following Saturday there was only one. The nursing post sister reported that casualties from drunken brawls had virtually ceased. On pension night, when the town was usually littered with drink cans, bottles and bodies, the town was clean, quiet and peaceful.[34]

On their first night, they met in the park and the locals came; many of them responded to Christ. The next day, the police sergeant came to the newly arrived Uniting Church community worker, Ron Abbott, and said that the prisoners in the lock-up could hear the guitars and singing and wanted to come to the meeting. He suggested having the rest of the meetings on the lawn outside the police station.

That night, all the prisoners lined up, looking through the wire fence at the meeting, and about twenty of them made a commitment to Christ. Counsellors went in to them in the lock-up.

Sometimes, the meeting would only just begin and someone would come forward — long before any appeal was made. And the Holy Spirit not only drew them, but changed them. At the end of the baptisms, one of the leaders said, 'Look, we're different now. Please don't leave any rubbish here!'[35] And you wouldn't have known anyone had been there, except for one thing: the colour of the water in the pool. The water had turned to red mud!

The new life really showed in many other ways as well. It was a radical transformation of the whole community rather than something that affected individuals. Some of the people were out of town and had missed out on the meetings. Afterwards, they saw Del Abbott, Ron's wife, walking down the street and chased her, calling out, 'We were out of town. We missed out and we want to be part of it!' 'Where do we get the blessing?' 'We want the blessing!'[36]

Aborigines were going to the hospital to convert the staff, saying, 'We've found Jesus Christ.' The flying doctor who had been visiting the town for years couldn't believe that it had changed the people so much in their appearance, cleanliness and attitudes. He sent for Ron Abbott, saying: 'We want to know what's happening, because I've been coming here all this time, trying to advocate cleanliness, and it just happened overnight. They're a different people!'[37] The shire clerk reported in the newspapers that the litter in the streets was down by sixty per cent.

One man really stood out in it all. Ron and Del Abbott told me about Willy. 'He was very significantly involved in the law — the keeper of the site. But a very gentle sort of a bloke. . . He was touched in a most remarkable way. He never ever drank again.'[38] When Ron asked the police sergeant what Willy had been like before his conversion, he stated that Willy had never spent a fortnight without going to gaol, mainly for drunkenness. He wasn't a very robust man — rather quiet and shy. But after the change, he stood up for his beliefs. Even when the lawmen wanted to take him off to a law meeting, he made them wait until he came back from church!

He maintained a very significant witness in every aspect of his life. Ron often said: 'Willy doesn't have to preach, because his life is telling the story.' One night, Willy got up and told the church: 'A lot of you people think I'm rubbish. I'm not rubbish any more; I've got Jesus Christ inside of me. . .'[39]

One day, Ron introduced Willy to a whitefellow, who said, 'I can see Christ in his face' — the joy was just bubbling up!

It's not surprising that the publicans were rather alarmed at their sudden drop in revenue or that a number of stories did the rounds about how the publicans reacted. It is hard to substantiate the truth of these stories, some of which have been hotly denied, especially on programs like *60 Minutes*. Much of the legend centres around Wiluna, where Aboriginal drinking was the major proportion of the hotel custom. Some of the stories claimed that the publicans were offering free meals or free beer, and many people believe the stories are true.

Terry Robinson reported: 'When we went to Meekatharra, we heard that the publican was going round with cartons of beer to all the Aboriginal drinkers in Wiluna and they were saying, "No drink, no drink." He wondered why they was all saying "no".'[40]

Ron Abbott told me that one publican went to the police demanding that something be done about his loss of trade, saying that he might as well go back north. The loss of revenue was such that he was really considering selling the hotel. The police were unsympathetic, replying that it was the best thing that ever happened to the town and they were thinking of closing the police station because of lack of work!

❐ *The team goes to the south-west*
From Wiluna, the team went west to Meekatharra. After the last meeting there, they again prayed about what they should do, then went to bed, leaving it to God. Dark clouds came over the sky and it was clear that heavy rain was coming. They were travelling light and had no tents. Bobby says:

> The old people that couldn't read or write all got together and asked God to stop the rain. That cloud came right up to them, and they seen a hand come and push the cloud — [it] went around the camp that side. . . and this side and the camp was dry that night![41]

A young Aboriginal man in Adelaide had heard of what God was doing and travelled over to join the group. God answered their prayer for direction through him that night. He had a vision where God rolled out a big scroll with a map of Western Australia and pointed to various places showing where they were to go, stopping seven days in each place.

So the team travelled around the south-west of Western Australia: Cundeelee, Esperance, Perth, Geraldton and finally arrived back at Mt Margaret in August. During this trip, the team developed and learnt a great deal. A real strength developed as Bobby Scott joined Terry Robinson and a few others in the leadership.

As the team travelled around, many people recognised some of the Warburton guys from prisons around the state. They had a reputation as wild, fearless warriors. The *Nyoongar* Aborigines in the south-west are frightened of the *Wangkayi* of the goldfields and Central Desert and thought they were coming to attack them in some way. The team said, 'No, we're Christians and we wanna share with you what the Lord is doing and the power of the Lord.'[42] They quickly saw and experienced for themselves the dramatic changes God had brought.

But there were problems. Many of the churches in the south-west of the state were cautious of them and their doctrine; the very large number of people travelling with the crusade team became a real hindrance; and there were also tensions in the team at times.

When they arrived in one town, one of the white churches was going through an explosion. Bobby said:

[They were having] a big argument — they. . . [were] arguing among themselves. The Lord sent just two or three people from the crusade team there and they preached. Pastors and elders just broke and cried, forgiving one another, and that church is still going.[43]

The team spent three weeks in Perth sharing a concert called the 'Big G: grace, growth, grit, gumption and glory'.

Ron Williams tells how they were surprised when a police car pulled up one day and a police officer came over and warmly shook hands with them, saying, 'Praise the Lord! I've heard so much about you and what God is doing throughout the state.'

Seven policemen from the Police Christian Fellowship shared with them in one of the concerts. The hatred of Aborigines and police, black and white melted as 1400 people listened to the Warburton choir sing, 'We are gathering together unto him'.[44]

☐ *The team returns to the Goldfields*
Some of the team had been on the road for over six months when they returned to Leonora in August, a week before the annual Mt Margaret Convention. Huge crowds arrived — normally, they would have expected about 200 people, but they came from everywhere in their thousands, including a national current affairs TV crew. Convention organisers, Les and Kathy Tucker, said that people were camped all over Mt Margaret area and all around in the bush:

> If we'd rung up *60 Minutes* to get them to come, they wouldn't come! But they were ringing us!
>
> We had to have meetings outside because the place couldn't hold everyone. The people put blankets down and sat down all over the creek area. People could stand up there and lined their vehicles around the whole meeting, standing on their cars on the back of it, the top of it — wherever! We usually had the convention over the weekend, but this went on for the whole week![45]

Terry said it was like the Jewish leaders in the first century when they chased the Lord Jesus round: 'He was healing a lot of people. They wanted to see the working of the Holy

Spirit — miracles. They want to see people getting healed in front of everybody.'[46]

There were many problems facing the organisers with such huge crowds. Bobby mentions just one: 'They said, "You can't have a convention at Mt Margaret: there's no water there; the water there is no good!" But the Lord gave me a verse clearly, "I will heal your waters".'[47] Bobby was confident that God would undo the excessive chlorination of the community water tank — and he did! Ian Lindsay recorded that there were up to 3 000 people present, writing of a baptism service:

> . . .at Cement Creek which had been filled by rain just prior to the meetings. As we stood and watched hundreds entering the water to be baptised by the leaders whom God had raised up from among them, is it strange that even hardened TV crew members were awed and even shed a tear?[48] Jana Wendt, compere of *60 Minutes* TV program, interviewed the crusade leaders, asking Terry Robinson if he was a black prophet:

> I should have really said 'Yes', but I didn't know nothing about that, so I just said, 'I don't know. If the people call me as one, well I can be one. Nobody call me an address like that.' [Later] I was looking at the epistles — and that's one of the gifts in the Holy Spirit, the gift of the prophet. And I said to myself, 'Well, if God called me to be the prophet, I will be one.'[49]

The team arrived back at Warburton shortly before their annual Bible school in August, the first anniversary of their revival. When they got there, they found another current affairs TV crew had already arrived and these meetings were also featured on national TV.

✦ Further crusade trips
The Warburton church had already received an invitation for a team to visit the Kimberleys, so Bernard Newbery's group

was commissioned to go north, leaving a few weeks before the Bible School that was now called a convention. They passed through Alice Springs on 7 and 8 August and travelled via the Tanami Desert to Hall's Creek for about a month's ministry. Alwyn Bates reported:

> My brother wrote a letter from the Kimberleys and it was to the leaders to take the crusade up to the Kimberleys, because he heard what was happening. We all gathered in the church and we prayed and it was the Lord's will that we had to go to the Kimberleys — not [of] our own free will. So we got all our vehicles ready, loaded up and we were gone.
>
> We went to Warakurna — we had a meeting there and we had to pick up a couple of Christian people there and we kept on going then. We had a meeting in Alice Springs, at the riverside, and the people there heard about us coming so people had passed a message around so they all came in that night. We had a big meeting there and kept going to Yuendumu.
>
> Every place we went to we had a meeting and the Lord was really with us. From there we were going to Halls Creek. We camped at Rabbit Flat and gathered together and prayed there for guidance to show us the way and from there we kept on going. . .[50]

The team travelled through to Halls Creek, Fitzroy Crossing, Noonkenbah, Kununurra, Wyndham and other parts of the Kimberley area with similar results to the earlier crusade. Bernard Newbery reported:

> Wherever we went, we had enough — not too much, not too little, but enough. We left with enough money to get as far as Halls Creek, but we were invited to go to the west Kimberleys and the north Kimberleys and we got as far as Timber Creek. We shared the same feeling, the same ministry with the people there and, since then, there's been a lot of changes. They keep coming back and telling us the fire's still burning in the Kimberleys and there are still a lot of changes taking place in the hearts and lives of people.[51]

There were a number of other trips, including the Pit-jantjatjara area in the north west of South Australia. In 1983, Terry Robinson and a team went through Wiluna to Jigalong, Strelley and Port Hedland, communities which are very strong in traditional law. Terry reported:

> There was trouble at Strelley — they were going to lock us up, but we said we came as Christians, we came in the name of the Lord, you can't lock us up! We thank God, because the Lord undertook at those meetings — all those elders from Strelley usually come and belt their people, break their legs and take them home. They were very strong old men.[52]

Like the apostle Paul, they were able to say to these tribal lawmen: 'Look, I've been circumcised, I'm an Aboriginal citizen.'[53] And the people, including a lot of the old men, followed the team to Port Hedland to join in the meeting.

Around this time an old Aboriginal man called Snowy Barnes found a rich gold deposit in a rabbit warren near Leonora. He heard that the local crusade team had collected some money to buy a bus, but found they didn't have enough to get a reasonable one. Snowy paid $13 000 for a good bus, and loaned it to the crusade team. They made an agreement that ten per cent of the crusade income would be spent in maintaining the bus. It was used for several years to take the gospel to other places.

One of these trips was to South Australia, Victoria and New South Wales. The Aboriginal Evangelical Fellowship asked Bobby Scott to bring a team across to the east from the Goldfields. Bobby asked Wiluna missionary, Ron Abbott, to go with them — especially to help with organisation, but also to help with preaching and ministry. They drew up a set of conditions: those who went had to be recommended by the church. Smokers couldn't go, because they didn't want anyone who might be a bad witness. The trip lasted eight weeks. Bobby said:

> They took us to all the old missions that were closed and where people were just drunk, and they were battling with them for a long time. We visited all the churches — Roman Catholic, Church of England, Pentecostal, Seventh Day Adventist — we didn't care what denomination.[54]

Ron Abbott said they went mainly to Aboriginal people, 'but we did get into quite a few white churches. Their intention was to minister wherever there were people who would receive us.'[55] The team were given about $1 000 before they left Leonora. They made some music tapes which they sold. Offerings were taken up for them, so that the Lord supplied all they needed.

Their ministry turned people round and brought deliverance. There were some miracles and healings — even church ministers were saved! Bobby said they were praising the Lord in Bairnsdale [Victoria]:

> . . .this old bloke's sitting out smoking and laughing at us — mocking. He was sitting outside and talking to this fellow in our team and he's telling him about the Lord. Next minute, he went over, finished. He dropped dead — had a heart attack! He had a weak heart and been a sick man all the time. We sang the last song, went out there and prayed over him, lay our hands over him and he started coughing again and got up!
>
> We tell him: 'Look, the Lord saved you! You was dead — no pulse, all finished! Next time, you might die when we not here and you know you can go to hell! You can't go your own way now that the Lord raised you up: you must give your life to the Lord!' There's a revival out there now![56]

They ministered at an Anglican cathedral and everybody came forward at their appeal, leaving the minister wondering about God's ways! Ron talks of some of the impact:

. . .it really hit church leaders as well — people that suddenly realised they'd met something beyond their experience. 'There's something that these people have that I can't explain, that the church needs.' We were in a big church near Berri and Lenny and Stella sang. I guarantee there wasn't one dry eye there! It just disarms the people. They're used to hearing about people that are drunk in the gutter and, suddenly, they're confronted by somebody that's got more of God in them than they'd ever dreamed of.

Afterwards, Ben Mason commented to me that the people we were affecting didn't go backwards. It was a more lasting experience. Bobby made the comment when we came back that they'd been many times before and he'd never ever been where they'd had that kind of success spiritually and physically. . .[57]

Most places they went asked them to come back and they intended returning to help people take further steps in the Lord. But somehow, it never happened. Ron said that before this, teams had always run out of money and had to send a message home pleading for help. His dream was 'that God would raise up and equip a crusade team that would become independent in resources. I really did believe for a long time that we might have been able to help them to achieve that. This is what holds them back.'[58]

✦ The learning that took place with the crusades

The crusade teams found there were issues which were raised that they didn't have any clues about. Terry Robinson talked about these:

The Lord was using these obstacles — these divisions within the crusade [team] — bringing us closer together in unity. And we started to learn about the Charismatics and Pentecostals. We started to hear about the revival church. And they was asking me, 'What kind of church did you come from?' And we didn't know anything about that. But we always looked in the Bible.

We discovered there were gifts in the church and tongues and prophecy. And we started looking about the baptism of the Holy Spirit. And we found also, if you want to heal the people, if you want to command the devil to leave people who are being possessed by the devil, if you are filled by the Holy Spirit, if you have that power of the Holy Spirit in you, you are able to do all that. And the question I want to ask you today, is your church having the experience like this?

. . .[at] Pinjarra [WA], that's the first time we had the experience of deliverance, when I met this woman who was demon-possessed. We went to the house and she was telling people not to let me in the house. I was telling myself, 'She mustn't like me,' and the devil was blinding me. I could easily cast the devil out in the name of the Lord, but at that time I didn't know about all that. . .

These are the deep things of God and we were discovering new territory. We were taken to where we could decide which spirits were true, just like when the Lord was healing that man that was demon-possessed and the demon-possessed man said, 'Can I follow you?' And Jesus told him, 'You go back and tell the people what great things the Lord has done for you.'[59]

Bobby Scott told of one occasion:

We prayed all through the week for this woman — every night after the meeting, because she was demon-possessed. About fifty different demons. One said: 'I'm Bobby Darren' — the singer. She'd sit down and listen to Bobby Darren music. She'd been in love with one *Wangkayi* man long time before when they're young. [But at the meeting] he was tired and lay down. We were praying and next minute a demon grabbed hold of him and lifted him up and chucked him on the ground — two feet high off the ground![60]

The group had other challenges, as Terry Robinson describes:

We moved to Gnowangerup, and that time we had no food.

There was nothing in anybody's car. It was just finished. We had no money at all. At the time, we had about eight cars travelling. We had just one slice [of bread] each, but we cut it in half and we were praying to the Lord to make us full through that.[61]

Donny Robinson said his brother Terry had one dollar:

The Lord spoke to Terry, 'Go and buy cool drink!' Then, the Lord spoke to that shopkeeper to give us seven bread and lot of stores, and the Lord supplied us, because some of the people on the crusade was grumbling that Terry brought the people out with no food. The Lord spoke to the baker to give us seven loaves of bread a day. . .[62]

Terry Robinson continues:

The farmers were touched and they brought some sheep for us, and they said, 'As long as you stop here, we'll keep on giving you.' And we had a wonderful experience of the Lord at that time. The Lord was providing food, like the Lord was providing food for them in the wilderness when Moses was leading them to the promised land.[63]

Elaine Munroe described another occasion when they had no food and prayed and God met their needs.

I said to my cousin Alwyn, 'Hey, we're still without food. We've got nothing.' But my cousin said, 'No, we have some food. The Lord will soon give it to us.' And I went and saw a big bag of sugar — one hundred weight, a box of tea, tins of food, bread and flour. The white man said, 'Come and get it, because this food is for you.' And we took the food and said, 'Thank you,' to the Lord. . .

A white man brought a trailer load of emus and kangaroos! You see, the Lord told him, 'Go out there and shoot some meat for them. They're part way there, on the road.' He kept bringing things and doing everything for us. That food and meat lasted a long time. The Lord was really doing wonderful things at that time, because he was travelling with us. . . and even when cars were broken down, he was helping us and showing [us what to do].[64]

While the whole revival move of God was so clearly seen as his work, there was a lot of prayer undergirding all that happened. Goldfields Aboriginal leader, Les Tucker, commented:

It was the prayer life that was the heart of everything that was done. It was prayer before the meeting — it was prayer after the meeting. The team also had their early morning prayer times. There was a general discussion of what we had to pray for and then everyone would start, simultaneously. You were not waiting for one to pray and you finish, then the next one. There was a great volume of people praying. . . and everyone was doing the same thing at the same time in their own language. . . I believe that was the key to the whole ministry. We were battling to get into one room in the back there.[65]

One night, there had been a misunderstanding between several of the leaders before the meeting. They called everyone together and confessed it, putting things right publicly before they went on with the meeting.

They also had to struggle with things that God did which didn't make sense at first. One of these was the experience of falling over under the power of the Holy Spirit. It had happened at Warburton, but had not happened in the Goldfields or during the crusades.

Ron Abbott tells about one occasion when it happened in Victoria: 'It spooked the Aboriginal team. They'd never been in that experience before and it really spooked them. They were saying: "Maybe it was time to go home". . . [Others said] "if a person falls forward, it's of the devil, but if he falls back it's of God." A local Christian helped them by saying, "You should never say that anyone is 'slain' in the spirit because, if you're slain, you don't get up. They're 'resting' in Jesus and God is doing something in their lives."'[66]

I have been told stories of a number of miraculous healings and fascinating supernatural events, some of which are included in this book, but it was surprisingly difficult to get concrete details of some of them. It wasn't those things that people remembered easily. It was *people things* that they remembered, especially changed lives and new relationships: people becoming what God made them to be, freed from all the misery of sin and broken relationships. They were the biggest miracles of all! And all those 'supernatural' physical events seemed unimportant compared to lives made new!

As Bobby Scott put it:

Oh, we seen a lot of miracle happening. I don't know what's stopping us from going out, even going out right now and telling the people, because the Lord has told us 'to go out into all nations to baptise'.[67] He's talking about nations, not only Australia.

This is my vision, to go out and tell nations of the power of God. We believe it's going to start again. But you see, we believe we've been making a mistake because, you see, we've been saying we want to keep that old one going [the 1982–1984 revival]. We want to see the new one — the Lord's got another different one going to start again.[68]

9

Stirring the smouldering embers

THE FIRST YEARS AFTER THE ABORIGINAL REVIVAL

WHAT HAS HAPPENED SINCE THE REVIVAL FIRE BEGAN? Has the fire really burnt out, leaving only smouldering embers?

In 1986, Djiniyini Gondarra wrote about the revival experience and the vision of renewal in Australia, saying:

> I would describe these experiences like a wild bushfire, burning from one side of Australia to the other side of our great land. This experience of revival in Arnhem Land is still active in many of our Aboriginal parishes and churches. We would like to share these experiences in many white churches, where doors are closed to the power of the Holy Spirit. It has always been my humble prayer that the whole of Australian Christians, both black and white, will one day be touched by this great and mighty power of the living God.[1]

The revival movement has been a wild bushfire burning in many parts of the nation, touching the north, south, east, west and centre, but affecting some parts much more intensely than others.

In these last chapters, we will look at what has happened since the mid-1980s and give a brief idea of some recent happenings at Elcho Island and in the Central Desert, some conflicts that the revival movement has stirred, some encouraging indicators of continuing revival and some signs of new life.

It is important to be aware that beliefs and attitudes are dynamic: they are changing. What is described here may no longer be the same by the time you read this. And it is fairly easy to look back in hindsight and see the mistakes of ourselves and others.

What follows in this section is not an attempt to be critical and denigrating, but rather to analyse so we may learn from history. I have a very high regard for the missionaries who worked in both the Central Desert and in Arnhem Land — some of them for many years under incredibly difficult circumstances.

The secret of a good bonfire or barbecue is to get the right temperature. A roaring blaze attracts people and moths and burns food and people. But when the fire dies down to red hot coals, it cooks well and warms people. This balance is needed in the spiritual fire. Some have talked about the 'froth and bubble' of the early days of the revival that died down, leaving real maturity. In 1991, Amee Glass wrote about the Ngaanyatjarra region in this way:

> Gradually over the years that followed the revival, the fires have died down. Some of those whom the Lord raised up as leaders at that time have fallen into sin and drifted away from the Lord. Others have continued to quietly look to the Lord even if no regular fellowship meetings are held in their home community. However, despite the downturn, there are still more committed Christians in the area than there were prior to the revival.[2]

This was, I believe, God's bushfire, not a controlled barbecue or bonfire, and it had to be allowed to burn when, where and how he chose.

We began this story with Wirriyi's vision of the consuming bushfire and the new life which grew immediately after it.

He explained how God spoke to him saying that he and all *Yolngu* needed to be consumed in the fire so that new life could grow:

> That fire is my word! Anybody who believes my word will do that.

They needed to *hear* and understand and to *believe* and obey this word from God. The challenge, Wirriyi felt, was whether he would allow himself to go through God's refining fire and trust God for the new life. This was the decision Aborigines and others faced in the revival — and they found there were things they wanted to protect from the fire.

Thousands of people heard and many believed; but many ran from the flames; many rushed to grab firehoses, wet blankets and buckets of sand to smother the flames; some tried to beat out the flames with branches from green bushes; and others spread out the fire to reduce its intensity. As they reacted to the heat, most of them didn't even realise they were really quenching the Spirit of God.

But still the fire burned.

✦ The value of the Bible in each person's own language
The extent to which the fruit of the revival can be seen today is strongly related to the availability and use of the Bible in language that Aborigines can understand.

At the time of the revival, some Aborigines had printed portions of the Bible available in their own languages, but mostly they had to rely on English. Some now have Bible tapes available with songs and sections of the Bible being read in their own language, but these are fairly recent. Many of them also have to rely on others reading the Bible to them because they can't read fluently in any language.

English is a foreign language for them, not their own heart-language, so very few of them have a reasonable understanding of it. Misunderstandings often arise. This is made worse by two facts: white Australians are generally very reluctant to learn and use other languages, and many Aborigines have come to regard their own languages as inferior to English. Government policies have seldom encouraged any other attitude.

It is also amazing how many people working with tribal Aborigines use versions of the Bible that are not everyday language. Many preachers and teachers still prefer to use the 400-year-old language of the King James Version which is so foreign to Aboriginal English.

On one occasion around 1989 at Elcho Island, Galikali experienced some of the joy and wonder of people discovering God's message in their own language. She had been taken to an outstation for an overnight stay. After damper and tea, George Dayngumbu asked her to lead a Bible study, but the only scriptures she had with her were in English. Rrakminy, one of the translation team ladies, then produced a copy of the book of Romans which they had finished revising that morning. Galikali reported:

> . . .some of those ladies were new Christians and you don't give Romans to new Christians! I went through chapters 6, 7 and 8 with them, and we stopped and discussed things. In chapter 7, 'the good that I would I could not do', they were just rolling around in the sand laughing, prodding each other!
>
> I didn't mean this to be funny! But I've found lots of things in the translation come through and they identify with it so strongly that it hits their funny bones.
>
> It happens time after time when they're looking at something and you know it's the first time any people in the group have seen this — I mean really seen it because it's in their own language. . . How can they grow without this stuff?[3]

Several Gumatj Aborigines from Arnhem Land said to a Bible Society worker in North Australia:

When you read the word of God in our own language, it

The Bible translation team bringing the Djambarrpuyngu mini-Bible for dedication:
Elcho Island, August 1992

speaks to our hearts. You know, if we want to escape what
God wants us to do, we read the Bible in English. But if
we really want to know what he wants us to do, we read
it in Gumatj.[4]

Translating the Bible into Australian Aboriginal languages
is a very difficult job: there is no direct way of expressing
many of the Bible's concepts in their languages and care is
needed over the hidden meanings of many terms. But thanks
to the work of a small, very dedicated group of people, the
number of translated books of the Bible is growing steadily.

Galikali had only been a Bible translator for two years
when the revival began and they had finished translating
John's Gospel a few days before the mission in 1979. She was
then able to translate the passages that Djiniyini felt were
needed each week.

At Warburton Ranges, much more of the Bible was available in the Ngaanyatjarra language at the time of the revival,

Members of the Djambarrpuyngu Bible translation team:
Galikali, Nancy, Milindirri, Rräkminy

but the Aboriginal leadership in the church was not as literate
or as well-trained and their crusades took the leaders away
from home for much longer periods, so the teaching wasn't
as effective.

Reading the Bible is a more reliable way for Christians to
hear God speaking than teaching, preaching, visions or sharing experiences. That may be why Satan has been attacking
translation teams so severely. There have been many deaths
and resignations through illness, both among the missionaries
and the Aborigines involved. Galikali died in March 1993
and, within six months, two other Bible translators working
with Australian Aborigines also died of cancer. At the same
time, another four or five Bible translators in Australia were
facing death or withdrawal from the programs because of
health — out of a total workforce of only twenty or thirty in
the whole nation!

Nevertheless, it seems that God is turning this situation

around and is using it for the people's good. Aboriginal translators and assistants are rising up with a new maturity, but these Aboriginal workers seem to be more developed in north Australia than in the west and centre.

Galiwin'ku church elder, Maratja Dhamarrandji ('Alan') has completed some of the Summer Institute in Linguistics (SIL) course in translation in Victoria and is a key person in the translation team at Elcho. SIL commenced an Aboriginal translators' course in Darwin in 1995, which is government accredited. The use of computers has increased the accuracy of translation work and reduced the time needed for the task by many years. Videos and tapes are being produced to help Aborigines learn to read in their own languages and Aboriginal education workers employed in Aboriginal schools are being trained in teaching literacy. And it is mainly people in Bible translation teams who are making this possible.

Since so few Aborigines can read for themselves, the Bible's message also comes through other people: reading,

Member of the translation team, Alan Maratja Dhamarrandji ('Alan'), and his wife, Gapany

preaching, teaching, prophecy or various other types of spoken word. In recent years, few Western staff stay long enough to learn an Aboriginal language very well, so they can't communicate deeper concepts. This has increased the use of English in Aboriginal meetings. In 1979 during the revival, Galikali and a *Yolngu* friend became very concerned: even some of the *Yolngu* were reading the Bible and preaching mainly in English!

After one meeting where this happened, they prayed together about this. The next morning, there were extra *Balanda* visitors present. They were very surprised to find the *Yolngu* leading the service. They spoke completely in Yolngumatha [= Aboriginal language] and read the Gupapuyngu Beatitudes — probably the first time he had read Yolngumatha scripture from the pulpit.[5]

Straight after this, Galikali felt challenged about her own shyness in using Yolngumatha publicly and she preached her first sermon in Djambarrpuyngu the following Sunday.

Far too often, Aborigines have not heard God's word accurately. This is partly because of the language barrier. One of the results has been the development of an Aboriginal folk religion with some incredible misunderstandings of the message of the Bible. Bob Capp recently quoted some he has heard among the Pitjantjatjaras in Central Australia:

> Christian drivers should not speed, because Jesus condemned the Pharisees for 'fasting'.
>
> Jesus will soon return, so we don't need to work any more.
>
> One frequently comes across Aboriginal people who have come to the front at an altar call, who will tell their counsellor that they have stopped being a Christian and now want to become one again.[6]

Some Aborigines believe *Balanda* are so powerful that they don't suffer. When Dan Armstrong cut his arm badly while fishing at Elcho Island in 1979, he was asked to preach in a long-sleeved shirt so people wouldn't see the injury, because of their belief that 'ministers don't bleed or get injured — they are too powerful'![7]

Recently, Aborigines described one *Balanda* missionary as being 'so powerful: he just prays and bread appears in his kitchen!'[8] There was no awareness that God answered by the missionary picking up surplus bread from the bakery free of charge.

In this folk Christianity, some Aborigines believe that if you just go to church God will bless you physically: your hunting trips will be successful and money or food will be given to you without any effort on your part. (This attitude can also be seen in the Western church!) One Arnhem Lander even said to a missionary: 'We pray to you for healing. Many times, I've prayed to you and been healed!'[9]

Some Ngaanyatjarra Aborigines also have an attitude that Christians should carry a Bible even if they can't read it, because it has a magic power. When they are praying for someone, the Bible should be placed over their head to release God's power. Recently, one commented that a situation needed so much power that they had three Bibles on the head![10]

In 1981, I could see these dangers and longed to be part of the solution, but the Uniting Church didn't have the finance to continue all its work in Central Australia and we felt God was leading us out of the scene for a season into parish work in Western Australia.

There have been very few Bible teachers with training and language to overcome these beliefs and guide the movement. Linguists in Central Australia have often commented on the misinterpretations they have heard when Aboriginal interpreters are used and very often no attempt is made to translate at all when a message is given in English.

However, there is an increasing number of people committed to helping with Bible teaching by interactive methods. Twice each year, Ngaanyatjarra Christians gather in a quiet bush setting with a small group of linguists and other missionaries for a bush Bible school, learning God's message in Ngaanyatjarra. In their communities, a few of them meet each day to learn to read and to understand the Bible in their language.

There are still Westerners making a commitment to train and serve Aborigines. One senior business executive who came with us on a recent safari to an Aboriginal Christian convention has resigned his job to go to Bible college so he can serve the Aboriginal people. Others have made similar commitments. Many more people are needed to make long-term commitments to building relationships, developing their communication strategies and techniques and standing alongside the people rather than dominating them.

Since there are so many language difficulties with the written and spoken word, many people receive messages from God through visions, dreams and experiences. This can be influenced by their own feelings and cultural understandings, as well as being influenced by many different spirits. So visions and experiences need to be checked against the Bible.

Herbert Howell teaching at a bush Bible school near Warburton Ranges

However, these experiences have always been a major way in which God speaks to Aborigines. Sue Armstrong recently wrote:

> Visitations, dreams and visions are still occurring. Often, after the death of a loved one, someone will have a dream about seeing them in heaven.
>
> One lady had a dream that she died. At the time, she was not walking closely with the Lord. She dreamed that she arrived at the gates of heaven to be told that her name was not written in the Book of Life, and she was to return and make sure her people knew that they needed their name in the Book. She wrote a beautiful song about this dream, which is often a tool in bringing people to Jesus when it is sung.
>
> Many times their dreams relate to pending danger. One lady dreamed that men were throwing spears at her and she was led into a safe place. This dream related to a 'pay-back' situation and gave her wisdom in dealing with it.
>
> Another man who was sent home from hospital to die was walking down a road. Jesus came and walked beside him and told him that he would be fully restored, but he was to spend the rest of his life bringing his people to Jesus. He was healed and went to Nungalinya College to be trained for the ministry.[11]

In various ways, God continues to speak to Aborigines today.

✦ The importance of believing the Bible's message

We have heard something of what is happening in Aborigines hearing God's message, so let's look at the believing part of it. Believing implies that it is also accepted and it affects our actions. There have been some struggles in this area, particularly through the firefighting actions of outsiders.

In 1981–1982, when reports of the revival at Warburton Ranges arrived at the United Aborigines Mission (UAM) office in Melbourne, their council was very concerned. They had had some difficulties in other places with Pentecostalism. So they wrote an extra section for their Statement of Faith on the Holy Spirit and asked their missionaries to sign it. Some found it unacceptable.

By mid-1983, the UAM had no staff left in the Ngaanyatjarra area and several supportive Christian staff had also transferred out of the area. The mission has not been able to replace any of their staff since then. Most of the ex-UAM missionaries formed a Ngaanyatjarra Bible Translation Project, working from Alice Springs and Kalgoorlie. Herbert and Lorraine Howell eventually moved back to Warburton in 1991 to support the church, still working with the translation project.

The UAM Council has since taken a hard look at what happened and they have learnt from the experience something that Gamaliel said to Jewish leaders: 'I advise you to stay away from these men. Leave them alone. If what they are planning is something of their own doing, it will fail. But if God is behind it, you cannot stop it anyway, unless you want to fight against God.'[12]

Dorothy Hackett, Amee Glass and Wilf Douglas help new readers of the Ngaanyatjarra Bible develop fluency and understanding

But what sort of effect did all this have on the Ngaanyat-jarra Christians?

They became very confused. They couldn't understand what it was all about — and they had received so much from God through the revival. They had always trusted and respected the missionaries and the mission, and they owed so much to them. Now, their much-loved missionaries were leaving when they didn't want to go. They had believed God's messages to them and seen great things. They knew they needed to learn more, but the people who could help them all left. At the same time they were being criticised and told they were wrong in some of their beliefs.

✦ The importance of encouragement

Many Christians — even missionaries and ministers — were real wet blankets to the revival. They were there, but didn't really join in or encourage the people. One missionary went to a crusade meeting, standing right back in the shadows of the trees to watch without getting involved or be seen (something Aborigines often do). He said later: 'I couldn't see exactly what was happening, because there was a tree in the way.'[13] One said: 'It's happening all around me and yet I feel like I'm sitting on the edge and it's all going past me; nothing's touching me.'[14]

Ron Abbott told me a minister said to him:

'I'd give my right arm to be part of that!' He'd stand right back and Trevor went to him and said, 'You look like a policeman standing there. . . Come in and be part of it!'. . . But he also said to Ron one day, 'Can't you stop them? Can't you stop them saying "Praise the Lord" and raising their hands?'[15]

At the very time when the Ngaanyatjarra Christians needed support and solid biblical teaching, they were criticised by ex-missionaries and Aboriginal Christians from the Goldfields and Perth whom they respected.

There was criticism over issues like Christian involvement in traditional ceremonies and not being married in a church by 'whitefella' law. One Ngaanyatjarra leader, who was totally committed to his wife, struggled with the criticism. Then, he read a verse which I believe the Holy Spirit really used to encourage him, telling him, 'Don't try to change what you were when God chose you.' He felt God was saying not to listen to those who wanted him to do things their way.[16]

There were many who wanted to label what was happening as 'pentecostal' or 'charismatic'. That immediately put God and Aboriginal Christians into a box, dumping a whole load of expectations and feelings (both positive and negative) onto them. I believe these labels have been very misleading, unhelpful and even destructive of what God was doing in this revival. It has been a privilege to see Aborigines discovering God with a childlike trust, without the church's doctrinal hang-ups.

Ngaanyatjarra Christians became very upset that the missionaries had not taught them about the Holy Spirit and the things they were experiencing, so they had not been prepared for God's work. Herbert Howell told me they did teach about the Holy Spirit, but until the revival they had never experienced the Holy Spirit, so didn't know him and were scared off by the reports from other places. Herbert (and other missionaries) also told me that they had been taught in Bible college that when the Bible spoke about the baptism and experiences of the Holy Spirit:

> . . .it didn't really mean what it said. That's what we were taught at Bible college: that the apostles did experience it and, when they died, it died with them. We weren't to expect it. It was always there in the Bible, but we couldn't see it. . . although sometimes I used to wonder what those verses meant.[17]

Christians tried to tell Aborigines that baptism in the Holy Spirit only happened at conversion. Bernard Newbery said:

You know, they talk a lot about Holy Spirit, that you can never be baptised into the Spirit, or some people say it can't be another Pentecost. But for us people, it was the first time for us. . . Some people disagree with me on the baptising into the Holy Spirit. I felt it! I was baptised into the Spirit! And everything turned out like everything was new![18]

Many of them knew that what they had experienced was real, even if they couldn't understand all the details or answer their critics. Bernard continues:

So, my experience of being baptised into the Holy Spirit, I can only tell a little bit: it's beyond what the tongue can ever tell — it's beyond, beyond, beyond. . . I strongly say that people need to be born into the Holy Spirit, baptised into the Holy Spirit to get that first touch.[19]

Herbert Howell added:

. . . suddenly, we realised God is far greater than I knew him to be, therefore I can be freer than I have ever been before. . . suddenly, it freed us to be receptive to what he was doing. . . and we were able to worship him. I suppose up till that time I had no idea what worship really was — I assumed it was singing the 'hymn sandwiches' with Bible readings that we had in a normal church service.

Suddenly, to actually address the Lord. . .! The Pitjantjatjara hymns we sang spoke directly to God and that opened me to worship. One day, we didn't know what it was and the next we did and we found ourselves thrown into worshipping![20]

In the Goldfields, some of the leaders grew stronger through all the criticism. Ron Williams went through its fire, but was purified in his ministry. He is a powerful influence in the whole region and the nation. Bobby Scott has also served God faithfully despite opposition, until his health began to restrict him severely during the last five years.

At Wiluna, Ron and Del Abbott tried to encourage the people in their ministry as they all learned about the Holy Spirit together. Ron usually went with them to help in their crusades, but admits: '. . .every time they mentioned going somewhere, I would mention that the real job was to establish a church *there* [at home in Wiluna]. So I slowed them down to some degree.'[21]

What God was doing was really unique and new — totally beyond the experience of all involved. But there were things that were not what God wanted. Unfortunately, some people became so concerned about what was wrong that they failed to encourage and help the people to grow beyond personal sin and doctrinal error. The Bible should have been used to encourage and fan the coals into flames rather than for firefighting doctrines.

✦ Starving the fire
The revival fire ran out of fuel through lack of support and encouragement.

The church either took too long to respond or didn't see the movement to be important — the place where God was at work. Few were prepared to rewrite their budgets and agendas, sell off some property, make appeals or do whatever was necessary to really support it financially, to give them encouragement and teaching and to support them in prayer.

Support came mainly as a result of personal letters and reports from Westerners to their friends. Aboriginal Christians began to feel that the church and missions had plenty of money and support for their own programs, but none for what Aborigines felt God was doing among them. They felt it was the greatest thing that had ever happened among them, but maybe they were wrong?

Within three years, the fire in Central Australia was out, leaving just a few smouldering embers. The confusion, criticism and discouragement had caused their leaders to back right off and many people left the church. It was too hard for them. But in north Australia, the roaring flames had quietened to a healthy fire.

10

Fighting and lighting fires

THE LATE EIGHTIES AND EARLY NINETIES IN THE
ABORIGINAL CHURCH

THERE HAS BEEN A LOT OF DISCUSSION and even fights over
how Aboriginal (or Western) culture fit together with Christianity. Ron Williams recently said to me:

> The Lord through his Spirit exorcises the demonic in the
> culture and makes them free. There needs to be exorcism
> of the culture, purifying: a fire burning so the gold will
> come out.[1]

But are the traditions and ways of Aboriginal and Western
culture being held back from the refining fire? Are people
building up the fires or putting them out?

✦ The church and the fire of revival
The situation at Galiwin'ku was quite different from Warburton Ranges. Many of the missionaries and *Balanda* Christians
had already been baptised in the Holy Spirit in the months or
years leading up to the revival. They encouraged and did all
they could to support a work they believed came from God,
though making many mistakes.

As a result of the revival, the Uniting Church (UCA) sent
a number of new Aboriginal students to Nungalinya College
to train as ministers. There, they were encouraged to explore

their own culture and find parallels between their ceremonies and biblical stories.

❑ The wider church weakened the local church

The UCA also appointed Aboriginal leaders to positions where they could make their contribution to the wider church. But this took them away from leadership in the revival, especially in the local church.

Djiniyini Gondarra was appointed as a lecturer at Nungalinya College. He was to move to Darwin less than a year after the revival began, but this was delayed for a year to give the Galiwin'ku parish more help in the revival. Ten years later, he told me it was a mistake to accept this position:

> [I was]. . .responding to the church and not listening to the Lord in what he was asking me to do. If I had remained at Galiwin'ku, there would have been more fruit, more depth. After I left, people had no direction and now, when I come back, people come to me a lot, looking for direction.[2]

This appointment was the beginning of a large number of national and international jobs for him, which included membership of the central executive of the World Council of Churches in Geneva. He has been constantly pressured to lead missions and speak at meetings in Aboriginal communities and in the wider church throughout Australia. In 1989, the pressure of all this caused him to take twelve months' leave to find himself again: his health — and his relationship with God and his people.

Christian Aboriginal leaders were also in demand for top jobs in government and the community because of their ability and stability, with the attendant high salaries, high status and big responsibilities. Ian Lindsay wrote about such from Central Australia: 'They were the natural ones for jobs of trust as they no longer drank or stole.'[3] This diverted a number of them from church leadership.

One of the most tragic diversions was Kevin Dhurrkay, evangelist of the Galiwin'ku church. He was appointed to a senior administrative job in Darwin in the Aboriginal arm of the UCA. Late in 1990, he could only spare a few minutes to talk to me, but he took the time to pour out his heart to me over how discouraging his present work was and how he just wanted to be an evangelist. He promised to give me a whole day to tell me his stories of the revival next time I was in Darwin. But he was never able to. Kevin died of a heart attack in December 1991, only forty-seven years old. It could literally be said that he died of a 'broken heart'.

❒ *The wider church engaged in paternalism and control*
Another form of fire control has been paternalism: treating Aborigines as children for too long. The role of missionaries has changed and Aborigines are fighting to get away from mission control and paternalism. In a recent message-tape to me on the current state of the Aboriginal church in the nation, Ron Williams talked about this:

> . . .a lot of our people are frightened of what the whitefellas say. One time, when AEF [Aboriginal Evangelical Fellowship] was in full swing and we had a number of our fellas from the tribal land who had been involved with the Spirit moving, we had three to four thousand people at our convention. Charismatic and conservative were all together.
>
> We said, 'Why don't we get Yonggi Cho?' The mission we were associated with at that time, where we held our convention, said, 'If you get Yonggi Cho, you won't be allowed to have your convention here. We don't want a charismatic influence.' That was when the AEF split up. The charismatics and the conservatives split up. We need to let the Holy Spirit guide us.
>
> At Alice Springs [Convention], we have conservative and charismatic together, and mission control is still very strong. In 1995 when we had our convention there, I spoke to some of the Aboriginal leaders about an important meeting with

missionaries and Bible translators: 'Even though we're different we can share, have a network of sharing, because our people are inter-marrying, they are getting together for tribal law groups, they're together in ATSIC [an Aboriginal government organisation] and tribal culture is becoming a uniting factor. Now what about we as Christians share together. We may be Baptist, Lutheran, Uniting Church or other little interdenominational groups, but it's as we share together that we're one in Christ.'

At that time, there was a flood in Alice Springs and all the little creeks were running into the main Todd River. One of the tribal fellas said, 'Well, too many rivers no good. We want one river flowing like Todd River and we don't want to be divided; we want to be together as Christians.'

So we presented our case to a lot of white mission workers and one said, 'How can Aborigines teach white fellas anything? Most of them are drunkards and no-hopers and they haven't got that responsibility or initiative.'

As an Aboriginal pastor evangelist, I sense very much that patriarchal influence is still there. We thank the Lord for our missionaries: I know their labour of love — I've been a missionary twenty-five years. But there is still that sense of controlling the Aboriginal people [that says], 'They're our children; we can't let them go.' But children need to grow up and we need to have a big vision.[4]

Aboriginal Christians *were* being led by God's Holy Spirit, but too many Westerners still looked at them as children and failed to recognise and encourage his leading among them.

❏ *The Aboriginal church needs new structures*
The church has had to adjust to rapid change, with Aboriginal leadership rising up and pushing aside old structures and traditions. But in many parts of Australia today, the Aboriginal church structure seems to be in total chaos. Church services are held only occasionally and pastoral care only happens sometimes.

Aboriginal pastors are not being supported financially by

their people or the church. Aboriginal Christians have tried to use the Western structures and styles they have experienced and learned from the missionaries for their own services and worship. They have found they don't work. They are irrelevant, but they don't understand why and have struggled with finding how to use their own structures and styles.

Aboriginal ministers who have been trained as a result of the revival have also found they have been squeezed by the wider church or their own people into the expectations of models of ministry used by Western missionaries. The model where a minister rules and also does everything in the church does not suit Aboriginal society, which has elders rather than kings and servants.

I mentioned new structures such as the Uniting Aboriginal & Islander Christian Congress (UAICC) earlier. The Pitjantjatjara Church (Uniting) and Arrente Church (Lutheran) in Central Australia are developing new models based on 'community ministers': local Christians who are recognised to give leadership. Training is by short courses rather than years of training away from their people. They are not paid a salary to set them apart as the one who does everything in the church. But there is something even deeper than any church structure and models. Sue Armstrong recently wrote:

> Another exciting development arising from the growing confidence in using the gifts of the Holy Spirit and listening to God is the slow emerging of a truly Aboriginal Church — one that will not need a whitefella title or ethos, but reflect Aboriginal Christianity born out of what God has been revealing to them over the years. It is in embryo at present, but will emerge to touch Aboriginal Australia and to challenge white Australia.[5]

❏ *The Aboriginal church needs new knowledge and skills*
Some quenching of the fire also came through lack of knowledge of how to live and operate as Christians, particularly in Central Australia.

Aboriginal Christians learnt as they went, mainly through trial and error. Meetings had lots of items and testimonies, with every group patiently being given an opportunity to contribute, regardless of the spiritual or musical quality. So the meetings were very long and very late. Often the speaker wouldn't reach the platform before 10.00 or even 11.00 pm.

With so many new Christians, there was often a lack of knowledge of how to help them to develop, especially where sin needed to be confronted by the leaders. Confrontation is always a difficult thing for Aborigines if there is not to be a fight, so sin was often ignored. As Ron Williams put it, 'Babies' messes weren't cleaned up.'

However, I know of several cases of adultery by Aboriginal pastors where Aboriginal leaders suspended them for a year. Western pastors in similar situations in the same denomination only had 'pastoral discussions' with their leadership. There is a maturity developing in the Aboriginal church.

✦ Aboriginal social change and the fire of revival

Some of the the firefighting and firelighting struggle has been in the area of 'culture'. There have been seminars on 'gospel and culture' held by the United Aboriginal and Islander Christian Congress (UAICC), with some very stormy meetings. But it is a much wider issue than the church or religion.

Just as the Western world has gone through massive changes in the last twenty or thirty years with technological and scientific developments bringing pressure on traditional values, morals and ethics, so also alcohol, motor vehicles, satellite television, videos and other aspects of materialism have had a drastic impact on Aboriginal society.

Social changes have affected all of life, bringing poor nutrition, disease and deaths. Church and community business is often dominated by constant demands from the outside world or local family matters, especially deaths. It is hard for Aborigines to work through important issues resulting from the changes because of these demands.

One of these demands has been a constant pressure to allow mining in Aboriginal areas. Sometimes, there has been a positive relationship between Aboriginal groups and a mining company, but often there has been little attempt to work together. This particularly applies to many Westerners who are arrogant and narrow-minded in their commitment to their own agendas.

Recently, the Ngaanyatjarra Shire Council was totally crippled for nine months by a company wanting to explore and mine for gold in their area. The company put around one million dollars into complex legal attempts to overthrow the council, discredit and sack its employees, and manipulate through 'gifts' to Aborigines who had very little idea of what it was all about.

❏ *The land and Aborigines*

Another controversial area of Aboriginal identity involves their relationship with the land. Aborigines are similar to the Jews in this relationship: it is a spiritual, as well as economic and legal relationship. Aborigines believe they are part of the land, rather than owning or caretaking it. Some of them talk of the land as their 'mother', feeling that it has produced them; their identity is always tied up in the land.

In 1980, Djiniyini Gondarra wrote:

> The land is my mother. Like a human mother, the land gives protection, enjoyment and provides for our needs — economic, social and religious. We have a human relationship with the land: mother-daughter/son. When the land is taken from us or destroyed, we feel hurt because we belong to the land and we are part of it.
>
> When we become Christians, we see more clearly our relationship with the land and with God. It was God who entrusted the land to our ancestors. We were living in a land of plenty, like first creation people. We had our own technology, our own social laws, our own patterns to follow.

Life was so beautiful before.

I'm sorry to say it, but I picture oppressors, both *Yolngu* and *Balanda*, coming into our garden of Eden like a snake. Satan used the snake as his instrument to tempt God's people and to try to destroy God's plan for his people. The bad influence came in breaking our relationship with God, with man and with land.

. . .Satan is working through their greed and selfishness, driving us out and making us blind. They are breaking what the Bible says by stealing and destroying the land. I think it's time for our black theology to interpret the scriptures in our way — and that is not something about the past only, but a struggle for today and tomorrow. It was the same God in the struggle with the children of Israel who was with the Aboriginal people all along. It might be a bit hard for politicians and government people who only act on what the law says and not on what is true justice for people.[6]

When the creation story in Genesis was translated and used in Bible studies at Galiwin'ku in 1980, one man said, 'We can see now that we are not the owners of the land — but we are the caretakers and we must protect the land.'[7]

Since the 1967 Australian referendum granted citizenship to Aborigines, much has been done to grant land title to them. The 1992 High Court 'Mabo decision' recognising traditional title in the Murray Islands in Queensland has produced much reaction: fear and division has come from the lies, distortions, misunderstandings and lack of clear answers of how it affects many people.

The year before the revival, Arnhem Land Aborigines were granted title to their land. Almost immediately, the government forced them into agreements over uranium mining on some of this land. Kevin Dhurrkay preached at Galiwin'ku in 1978 and said: 'Until we Aborigines start to remember that the land does not belong to us, we are not going to get anywhere. The land belongs to God and he gave it to us in trust. But the white man must realise this, too.'

This issue has distracted and confused many Christians and is a continuing struggle. In their struggle for identity based on the land, not all of them look to the God who entrusted the land to them. It is similar to the Zionists who are fiercely fighting for their political and physical identity based on the land of Israel without regard to the spiritual issues.

☐ *The Western economy and Aborigines*
There are often misunderstandings over finances and the Western economy. Most Aborigines have not been able to grasp a real understanding of this, although some real progress has been made in this area in the last few years by some of the Uniting Church's UAICC staff in north Australia.

Often Aborigines have borrowed money to get to Christian meetings or to get home again. Loans are not really part of Aboriginal traditional world view, so they seldom really grasp the need to repay the loan.

Most Aborigines believe that Westerners will not tell their secrets of where they get money from. They say things like, 'All you whitefellas have so much and we have so little.' In 1992, many well-educated Aborigines in responsible jobs in the church and government still believed that every Westerner had their own magic printing press to produce money!

Local Aboriginal churches are often subsidised by the wider denomination, generally with definite expectations over the purposes for which this finance is to be used. Aborigines don't always have the same concept. At Galiwin'ku, this has caused tensions because Galiwin'ku *Yolngu* have spent up to $200 000 a year of their own funds on attending conventions and other outreach meetings. Few Western churches of less than 200 people would spend anywhere near this amount on outreach and growth.

But often, the Aboriginal minister was not paid because

the local parish was broke. One UAICC staff member said to me: '. . .the pressure put on them to go to meetings, to take their [traditional] dances to conventions for whitefellas is incredible! And we're honing in on two or three guys, and it's draining their families and health.'[8]

☐ *Breakdown in Aboriginal family authority*
Social change has also brought breakdown in family authority. There is widespread petrol-sniffing, vandalism, alcoholism and truancy from Western and traditional schooling. Many hundreds of children have died from preventable illnesses and substance abuse. Traditional mentoring is no longer happening, where an older Aborigine trains and encourages a young person like an apprentice in all areas of life.

One major issue in disciplining children has been the struggle over initiation. Some Christians found they lost their desire for things of God when they attended traditional ceremonies and determined not to have anything more to do with any of them. Others asked, 'How can we bring up our children without discipline? Our discipline is totally based in our law and ceremonies!'

Many Aboriginal Christian leaders have not known what to do about it all, especially in their own families. They have felt shamed by the disregard for authority and lack of discipline, and the resulting deaths have discouraged them so they have not taken leadership in their family, church or community. These pressures have driven some of them to alcohol.

Some have given in to the temptations of adultery or pressures to take a second or third wife, resulting in feelings of shame in the church.

The incidence of sexually transmitted diseases is extremely high in many Aboriginal communities. Arnhem Land has been called 'the syphillis capital of the world' by health workers — it even occurs in young children, transmitted sexually as well as from mother to baby before birth. Short of God's miraculous intervention, AIDS is set to bring almost total genocide to Aborigines.

But God is refining them and some have been grieving and interceding over this. On one occasion in 1990, when I was at Galiwin'ku, Djiniyini preached on 1 Samuel 4. God had been speaking to him personally about his family and about things which he had to deal with so that God was honoured in each one's life. The message was also for the church: '*Ichabod* — God's glory departed'[9] because of family life that is not in order and honouring God. It was a powerful message that spoke to many people.

That night, the children were out in force: many mobs of ten to twenty each, aged from around six to twenty, roaming the streets, bored and looking for something to do. Some were sniffing petrol stolen from cars. Some were playing music loudly on their 'ghetto blasters'. Some of the boys found a quiet place with a girl. Some of them were still raging at 5.00 am. I believe the enemy was hard at work to

Children and young people praising God at Dharrwar outstation: 1994

negate what God was doing in the church that night.

Almost two years later on a Sunday night, Djiniyini and Mawunydjil stood on the lawn between the community office and the church at Galiwin'ku conducting communion together in an open air service. Mawunydjil felt God speaking and telling them to pour out some of the communion wine on the ground as a sign that Jesus' blood cleanses both the land and its people.

Djiniyini sensed the Holy Spirit's direction at this point, and the whole church called on God to break the power of Satan and promiscuity over their young people who so often used that very place for sex at night. Today, there are real signs of God's life among some of the children at Elcho Island, as we will see in the next chapter.

However, there has been little sign of hope among the children in the Central Desert. At Warburton Ranges on the night in December 1981 when Djiniyini and the team were praying for the people, hundreds of adults were touched powerfully by the Holy Spirit. But it was not only the adults that were affected. Children started to come forward for prayer at the end of the meeting. I felt that the parents and families should take authority by praying for their own children, rather than the team doing it for them. But, somehow, the children missed out and we can now see that their spiritual needs have been neglected. I feel some responsibility for this and am now praying for a new release of God's Spirit amongst them.

✦ Various spirits and powers and the fire of revival

Through the revival, many people have chosen to go God's way, so other spirits in the land have lost power. There are still those who follow those evil promptings — and even those who have given themselves so much to anger, violence or other spirits that they are out of control, needing deliverance through the power of Jesus.

But there were also those who opposed the revival, using traditional spiritual powers. Terry Robinson talked about a curse placed on his brother:

> We went to Geraldton and my brother Donny — somebody put a curse on him from Kalgoorlie. . . The devil was trying to make me weak because this was happening to my oldest brother. The devil was attacking his mind and his body, but we continued because we knew my brother was in the hands of God. In the history of Aboriginal people, no man can live when this curse was put on him. But Donny, he's living today to praise the Lord who delivered him from the power of the curse.[10]

UAM missionary, Ian Lindsay, tells of a man who went to Bible college, but later became a tribal killer. He came back to God during a crusade meeting. One day, he was helping prepare for a convention, when he became aware of an evil presence. They found out that the ceremonial leaders 'were trying to sing him back to perform a killing'.[11] The pressure was too much and he got drunk. Ian 'confronted the old men and told them to leave him alone; they just laughed'.

Ian also describes a confrontation at a convention at Wingellina, where Ben Mason felt there was a 'prince of evil' present. The Ngaanyatjarra Christians were puzzled over this concept and Ian led them through a study of Daniel 10, Ephesians 4 and Romans 8. They then rebuked the spirit in Jesus' name, experiencing an immediate and powerful release of the Holy Spirit through victory in the meetings.

On another occasion, a spirit showed itself in a house where someone had died. As they studied the Bible, they came to see that it was not the spirit of the dead person, but an evil spirit. They rebuked it in Jesus' name and again found victory.[12]

There is a constant spiritual battle. On one occasion, Ian Lindsay was preaching at a Warburton convention. Something stirred some anger in one man, who threatened him with a rock, then tried to disrupt the preaching by throwing a spear. The spear was heading straight for Ian, but Christians were praying and it miraculously broke into three pieces in mid-air and fell to the ground![13]

The revival brought a change to the spiritual climate of the land that affected everyone in it. Government officers at one revival meeting in north Australia told a missionary that the government could never have gathered such a large, diverse group of Aborigines together in the past because they would fight each other.[14]

During the last few years traditional ceremonies, especially initiations of boys, have involved groups of several thousand men travelling together. The men have come from the Pilbara (around Strelley) down into South Australia (around Fregon) and up into the Northern Territory (around Papunya). One Christian commented that the spirit of peace which Jesus Christ has brought to this land has made this possible: nothing else could have brought such violent groups together.

But there are still many other areas needing the victory of Jesus Christ. Shame is one. Aboriginal pastor, Peter Compton, recently described shame as a form of pride. Others include jealousy, backbiting and gossip — often, in fact, absolute lies.

Breaking the power of fear was a major release in the revival at Warburton Ranges. In 1992, a young man became violent and had everyone in one Ngaanyatjarra community gripped by fear. Herbert Howell managed to get some Christians to overcome their feelings and pray and the situation changed very quickly. Herbert later commented about the change that came at Warburton Ranges with the first revival meetings in 1981:

> . . .nobody got up and ran outside [any more] when any of those fear-producing things happened. People today go and watch the fights again, but they don't go and stir it up

any more. At the time of the revival, they wouldn't even watch: they would sit down and pray where they were, or get together with other Christians and pray for the two people fighting. They've lost that now and they go and watch, and then people really put on a show.[15]

The more disruption they cause and the more people come and watch, the more it gives power to those people and spirits causing trouble.

There is a strong spirit of death. In June 1985, Amee Glass and Dorothy Hackett wrote about the high number of deaths in the Ngaanyatjarra area:

This has been a hard time for Christians, some of whom have been related to more than one of these people. They have suffered attacks from Satan while they were grieving for these relatives. . . Other Christians are suffering from guilt after being persuaded against their consciences to take part in tribal ceremonies. Some have seemed to turn away from Christ, because of these pressures. . .[16]

Six months later, there was a tragic car accident. This is what Amee and Dorothy wrote:

Eleven people were killed. Seven were from the Warburton area. From a population of just over 900, the latest accident brought the death-toll to thirty-three in twelve months. . . One woman, in the space of a year, has lost two sons, her husband, sister and niece. . .

It was wonderful to see how the keen Christians had gathered around the grieving relatives — praying with them and reading the scriptures, as well as providing for their physical needs. . . Several of the bereaved parents spoke of their experience of the Lord's peace.[17]

Death is never far away from Aborigines, whether for themselves or a close relative. Infant mortality has often been described as 'third world'. An undertaker in Alice Springs said to me around 1981 that he calculated the average life expectancy of Aborigines in Central Australia to be thirty-three years, not counting deaths of children under five years old. In 1995, the adult death rate in north-east Arnhem Land was actually around seven times higher than the national average according to one *Balanda* working in this field. Most of this was alcohol related in some way or through preventable illness.

It seems there is a spirit of death over the land and Aborigines. At times, it seems like death is all they celebrate. Funerals have always been really big events for Aborigines. In some communities, it is often weeks before a person is buried — and then there are 'reburial' ceremonies later, although they have reduced the length of mourning ceremonies for most people. At the end of 1979 Galikali wrote:

> Where the deceased has been a Christian, the joyful assurance of their whereabouts has come through on a way far, far different from ever before. Because of the Aborigines' sensitivity to the spiritual world, it almost seems as if the separation of death is much less traumatic than it often is even for Christian Europeans.
>
> There is a decided difference at the funerals of Christians. . . there's a gentleness, a marked difference. . . a sense of victory that really does undergird the mourning. . . a much lighter atmosphere.[18]

There has certainly been a heaviness in funerals at Galiwin'ku and most other Aboriginal communities. Grief has to be seen to be expressed. So, during the ceremonial songs and dances associated with the person and their totems, women gash themselves with knives or sharp objects, hit themselves over the head with rocks and throw themselves on the ground.

In 1988, there was a 'big cutting' at Galiwin'ku. The next day, Gulumbul called Galikali over and sat her down next to her on the mattress on the ground, and ' . . .took this little scrap of paper out of her handbag ceremoniously and put it into my hands and said, "You've got to turn that into Djambarrpuyngu for the Christians in this church.'"[19]

It was Deuteronomy 14, verses 1 and 2: 'You are the people of the Lord your God, so when you mourn for the dead, don't gash yourselves or shave the front of your head as other people do. You belong to the Lord your God. He has chosen you to be his own people from among all the peoples who live on earth.'

Galikali's translation assistant, Rräkminy, insisted it be translated immediately and Dangatanga used it for four nights in a row at Bible study. He spoke to his people very strongly, saying:

> There's some spirit forcing them to chop themselves with a knife. . . God showed me that some people were thinking that they wanted to die straightaway. That's Satan's words! That's a short cut for them to put you in a coffin straight-away. That's wasting the blood that's produced for God, that God wants. Those people don't think, but just follow that songleader.
>
> We want to cast that spirit out! Some people are saying strongly, 'That's our system! That's our culture!' That's not your culture — it's devil culture! [20]

✦ Traditional ceremonies and culture and the fire of revival

Some Westerners believe all Aboriginal culture is evil; others that it is all good. If Aborigines were to abandon their culture, what would they do: become Westerners? That is impossible, just as Westerners can never become Aborigines. There is something in our heart and world view that comes from many generations. Almost every Aboriginal baby adopted by Westerners at birth finds that conflict as a teenager or young adult.

Is George Dayngumbu right? 'All the secret ceremonies have to go, but all those that the women and children are allowed to join in must be kept.' Many Aboriginal Christians don't agree. What is God's way? Are pride, fear, secrecy and lies the prime spirits that must be dealt with in each of our lives and the land? They seem to be the spirits at work in humanity's first sin in Genesis 3. These are difficult issues that Aborigines are working through with the Holy Spirit's guidance.

One Central Desert Christian who has taken a strong stand against traditional ceremonies has been beaten up because of it. He said to me, 'It's getting harder.' I have been told of *maparn* (spiritual 'magic') being used in the Centre against Christians and people who have died or 'disappeared' because of it, but I have no evidence that it really happened.

In 1984, Sylvia Richards wrote this to Amee Glass and Dorothy Hackett:

> At the moment, all we Christians at Blackstone are feeling sad, because the old men from here and Wingellina have growled at us. You see, at the moment a few — just the older men — are participating in tribal ceremonies here. And they are telling all us Christians from this place to go to another place [because we're not participating].
>
> And so we got ready to leave. But then they stopped us. You see, it is all God's children who are working at the shop, the clinic, the petrol bowser and the school. We don't know if we will stay or perhaps we will go somewhere. The Father [God] is the only one who knows and we are asking him.[21]

❐ *Name taboos after death*

Another struggle with culture comes after a death. The name of a dead person or any word sounding like it becomes taboo. This may go on for over twenty years. One missionary commented that 'it seems to be an effort on the part of bereaved relatives to control others' lives for a long time.' Houses are vacated, objects belonging to a dead person are destroyed — sometimes including all photos of the person, their motor vehicle and house.

If relatives of the dead person are present, someone reading the Bible aloud must change the words. The book of 'John' may have to be the 'Gospel of No Name'. At one time at Warburton Ranges, the name of Jesus became taboo. In 1991, Ron Williams went on a prayer safari with a group from his church through the Ngaanyatjarra area, holding meetings and talking with people in the camps, showing photos and slides from the 'old days'. He did it to help people appreciate their past and their ancestors who have died, even using their names quite deliberately, saying, 'That's okay — we need to remember them.' Some of these people had died fairly recently.

In many places, this would bring out anger and spears, but God had prepared the way. People cried, lovingly held photos of their relatives and gave Ron money to get them copies of photos.

❏ *The Elcho covenant*
One of the most significant events in the gospel/culture contact happened at Galiwin'ku. In 1989, Djiniyini's health and work pressures were so great that he took a year off in the bush — fishing, hunting, reading the Bible and listening for God to speak to him. Towards the end of it, he had some unusual experiences, felt God speaking strongly to him and spoke in parables to his people.

He felt God was speaking about some of the secret things in his culture and about the 1957 'Covenant with God' that his father and Batangga had led the people to make. That was when they brought their totems into the open next to the church as a sign of submission of all of life to God (chapter 2). Djiniyini felt God was speaking about some powerful totems, especially one that seemed to be the evil spirit of Queen Jezebel in the Bible.[22] He also felt God was speaking about the use of blood in a ceremony; about the taboo phrase 'tongues of fire', that is really God's term for the Holy Spirit; and that one of the ceremonies had 'stolen' their covenant with God. Djiniyini Gondarra felt God say to him:

You lay down every totem and ceremony. In each of them, there is good and bad. All of them must come under my lordship — be washed by the blood of Jesus Christ — and then you will see a new Aboriginal culture. I don't want to destroy and leave you empty. I will restore and renew what is good.

You are the man to get the covenant back that was stolen but, before you get it back, I'm going to cleanse you first. . . I am asking you to wash, so you can bring it back. . . There are good things in your culture, precious things there which belong to me. They have been stolen and they have been hidden: things that belong to me. I want them put back![23]

In talking about some of the ceremonies, George Dayngumbu said to me:

When I dance in a ceremony, who am I singing about? God or somebody else? I challenge lots of young boys: 'You've been baptised, changed your life, and you went to that ceremony, but you've still got that mark of Jesus. You went to that ceremony and you were washed with that blood, but that blood belongs to Jesus!' They know what's going on, but they're scared to say: [they're] full of fear.[24]

Djiniyini commented:

God is revealing himself in different forms to particular clans — in terms that are important and meaningful to each one. To one group, he says: 'I am the *Warungul* power!' *Warungul* is a very sharp spear used for spearing people, but Jesus is saying: 'I am that, now! It is no longer for spearing a man — that is a two edged sword for me' [i.e. God's word]. To another, he has been revealing himself as a tongue of fire! That is very, very sacred! You cannot speak about that in public, but we have been using that during the revival. . . we're talking in the faith of Jesus and saying that 'tongues of fire' is the Holy Spirit — stolen in the ceremony![25]

He and Gelung told me it was not the ceremony itself which stole the covenant. It was the greed and other evil in people's lives in that ceremony which caused them to lose what God was saying to them through the ceremony.[26]

The annual Revival Thanksgiving Weekend in 1990 was held a few weeks after Djiniyini's new revelations. The church had special times of prayer for months before it, including a thirty-hour period of prayer and fasting leading up to it. There were some signs, wonders and other special revelations of the Holy Spirit before it. Record crowds attended, with an incredible sense of expectancy.

The weekend began with Djiniyini leading a victory march. They stated that it was to 'Lift up Father God the Creator', affirming Christ's victory over Satan. It was part of reclaiming their covenant with God.

A large flag-waving crowd marched from the house where Djiniyini received his revelation down to the old totem poles of the covenant. Christians carrying a gold banner with the words of the covenant led the march. Eight of the tribal elders made speeches before the crowd moved up the hill to the community hall for the meetings. There, each clan knelt at the foot of the cross to affirm their commitment to God and his covenant with them.[27]

✦ The continuing experience of refining by fire
Just a few months earlier, Galikali had written this about the struggles:

> . . .there are many hurting and strained relationships in the church because of gossip and trouble-making. One feels at times so oppressed by the lashings of the enemy that it's unclear how to pray. The community is in the doldrums with awful financial problems (bankruptcy), rampant vandalism and shameless sexual freedom amongst even the youngest teenagers. There is widespread apathy so, when community meetings are called, they're poorly attended; no-one seems to have the emotional stamina even to think any more. And all this with very little help from the grog!
> . . .Some months ago, Mawunydjil began to speak out

The Covenant banner in front of the old church,
with the 1957 rangga poles on the right

about culture conflict in a new way, using the translated
scriptures and boldly proclaiming God's holiness and his
call for his people to be undivided in their loyalty to him.
A very few men were standing with him, but he's getting a
confused reaction and subtle opposition from many others,
as his message is different from some of the things that have
been said here in the past about these matters. He is being
accused of denying his culture/Aboriginal identity, which
of course he is not doing. . .[28]

It seemed that God was taking them through his refining
fire and in August 1992 Galikali said:

The big jump in maturity in the church has been in the last
five years, not in the first five years of the renewal, even
though some of the leaders have dropped away with second
wives and other things. There are new leaders, like Maratja
who came to the Lord in 1984. The new thing we have been
expecting and praying for during the last five years is
already here, but it's slower and deeper.[29]

One of the significant points of encouragement and growth for the people has been gathering together with Aboriginal Christians from other places in conventions. It is like a Christian form of their traditional gathering in a corroboree, with dancing, singing and sharing together. It is a spiritual celebration which fits their culture and is much more Hebrew and Old Testament than a weekly church service with the Western rational style of 'hymn sandwich and sermon' that started to develop, with Hellenistic influences, in the New Testament.

For urban and some Pitjantjatjara Aborigines, the AEF's convention in Port Augusta has been a major annual corroboree. For the Top End of the Northern Territory, it has been the Katherine convention — and there have been other regional gatherings.

But probably the most significant gathering for tribal people and many others has been the Central Australian

Dramatic song telling the story of the sacrifice of Abraham's son
and God's Son, Galiwin'ku: 1993

Christian Convention. I mentioned the first two of these in chapter 6. After I left Central Australia, they stopped until the late 1980s, when Ben Mason was appointed to Alice Springs by the UAICC. They became an annual event held there each January. They have been an important link between Elcho Islanders, Centralian Aborigines and other Christians from across Australia, as well as the South Pacific, Asia and beyond.

It is a significant spiritual meeting, with major battles being fought 'in the heavenlies'. The following report on the 1991 convention gives a little of the story:

Aborigines from about twenty tribes — as well as Irish, English and people from many other nations — attended the convention, some large groups travelling thousands of kilometres to be there. There were evangelicals and charis-

Ben Mason, Bobby Scott, Ron Williams and Herbie Laughton play a hymn on gumleaves at the Central Australian Christian Convention in Alice Springs: 1993

matics and Christians with all sorts of other labels (or no labels), all joining together without hang-ups. 'It is the most inspiring Aboriginal meeting in Australia today,' reports Ron Williams, Aboriginal pastor from Kalgoorlie.

The daily sunrise prayer meetings on Anzac Hill were attended by thirty to sixty people of all races (about half Aborigines), where God led the battle in strength with his incredible wisdom. This included prayer for Australia and the Gulf War situation, and there were real spiritual breakthroughs.

There were stories of incredible difficulty to get there. Ron Williams led a group of about thirty from the Great Southern/Goldfields area of Western Australia through the desert. They had repeated trouble with tyres and shock absorbers — and with their trailer, which had many of its welds crack under the strain of roads which, after prolonged drought, were the worst for years.

At one point, the trailer broke free from the bus and came to rest upside down, twisted and mangled in a sandhill. They called on the angels from heaven to help them and saw thick metal straightened, as non-human forces pushed the heavy trailer through the soft sand back to the road.

Ron reported: 'Our people grew overnight as they had to put their faith into action, like Moses and the children of Israel going throughout the desert. We were short of water like them, too.'

As they entered the desert area from the west, the group erected a two metre high timber cross they had made, high on a rocky hill above an Aboriginal site of significance. One man saw three lights, one on each point of the cross, recognised as the light of the Father, the Son and the Holy Spirit. Another saw two crossed swords over it, recognised as the sword of the word of God in the Old and New Testaments.

A four-year vision was fulfilled for one man when the whole group marched the ten kilometres around the base of Uluru (Ayers Rock) in prayer. Many Australians (both Aborigines and non-Aborigines) draw a lot of inspiration and spiritual power from this rock.

Ben Mason: photo courtesy of the *Centralian Advocate*, Alice Springs

The desert is *marlu* [kangaroo] country and there is a kangaroo tail formed in one corner of the Rock. However, the group saw that 'tail' as a cross formed in the Rock. As they looked at trees growing out of the Rock, they realised that Jesus is our rock and there is life in him — Uluru is God's rock!

The Lord showed them that as they had erected a cross on the other side of the desert, so here, in the centre of the desert and the nation, God had formed a cross in the Rock back there in the Dreamtime.

Such warfare is not without its cost. On their return after re-crossing the desert and holding a final meeting at Cosmo Newberry, people went their separate ways. God allowed the enemy to counter-attack.

A *marlu* appeared in front of Ron and Diana Williams, causing $1200 damage to their vehicle. Another vehicle was plagued with tyre troubles. Noel and Olive Blyth were thrown by a patch of bull-dust[30] and seriously injured, their vehicle a write-off.[31]

Dreaming stories of the area involve the *marlu*, the dingo and the Rainbow Serpent. It is 'red ochre' country, which symbolises blood, possibly the *marlu*'s. One *Yolngu* leader said about the blood, 'That is sacred, taboo — even more powerful than "tongues of fire"! But it's the blood of Jesus Christ that is truly sacred — and it's not taboo!'[32]

I believe that prayer is the key in the warfare in which all Jesus' followers are involved. Crusade leader, Terry Robinson said to me a few years ago:

> You go right through the Ngaanyatjarra area and there's a lot of old people and young people still following the Lord. But if they have Bible teachers come to our area, then people will learn. They all know Jesus is coming back to them but, while they're waiting for the coming of the Lord, they need to know about the walk of Christ, walking with our fellow Christian men, how to know about the newness of life.
>
> They want to learn about being a witness to the Lord, not only going to the church. . . These are the things that the Lord said about being a witness for him: 'Go into all the world and preach the gospel.' That's the thing they gotta do.
>
> If you want a revival, you gotta get on your knees and pray, humble yourself, be humble, clothed with humility, be filled with the Holy Spirit and be a Christian. You gotta fight with Jesus, not fight for the land and for your children with it.[33]

Firefighting, struggles with Western ways, paternalism, structures, social change, culture, ceremonies, traditions and spiritual battles. . . It almost seems like a discouraging end for a revival. But it is not the end — there is still real hope and life!

God hasn't finished with Australia yet! So, what is he doing today?

11

The coming of rain

THE LEGACY OF REVIVAL IN TODAY'S ABORIGINAL CHURCH

THE REVIVAL HERITAGE OF THE ABORIGINAL CHURCH is seen in these inspiring terms by Djiniyini Gondarra:

> Spiritual revival amongst the Aboriginal people in Australia is a turning point. We no longer see God as a white man's God or a God that the missionaries brought to us, but he is our God who has lived with us in our history. But not only in history; he is living with us now in the person of the Holy Spirit.
>
> As we look around, we find many signs of hope among the people — growing maturity in Christ, strength against attacks and commitment to bring the whole truth of Jesus Christ into every part of their life and to every part of the world.[1]

When we began this story of Aboriginal revival, I outlined Wirriyi's vision of the fire which burnt everything to ashes. Djiniyini makes these comments about fire:

> The fire is a very sacred symbol to Aboriginal people, because it symbolises wiping out, burning out everything to leave dust. It's also symbol of wrath, punishment, in *Yolngu* thinking.
>
> It gives you confidence when you make a fire in a dance to challenge somebody — a stronghold. When an enemy

comes and you've burnt fire here in an Aboriginal ceremony — that is my fire! In the olden days, when somebody came to challenge me, I made that fire — and that's where I stand and I will not move.

We're interpreting that as the Spirit of God. It will still conquer me, but I have a fire that is stronger and more powerful that is burning in me. I often preach to them and say: 'The Holy Spirit is the powerful fire. That fire is a flame, a tongue.'[2]

But the picture of God's fire also needs his renewing water. In Wirriyi's vision, new life came out of the ashes: a 'Garden of Eden'. It is rain that brings new growth and life after the bushfire.

Ron Williams' 1979 vision of rivers of revival through Australia included the verses:

I am creating something new. There it is! Do you see it? I have put roads in deserts. . . water in deserts — streams in thirsty lands for my chosen people.[3]

Recently, there have been many visions and dreams involving water among Aborigines, all indicating its renewing, life-giving quality. But it is more than just dreams and visions.

The Central Desert area is uniquely beautiful: there are many magnificent ranges, waterholes and sandhills, all with their own special features, plants, animals and birds.

But the area around Warburton Ranges community has been so barren — practically no trees or plants: just rubbish, dry and desolate. But it is changing.

One day, an Aboriginal man pointed out some trees to Herbert Howell and said: 'You know that scripture — "If my people will humble themselves and pray, turn from their sin and seek my face, then I will heal their land"?. . . There are trees out there now that never used to be there!'[4] Between the airstrip and the hills, there were fairly large trees which they had never noticed before.

Herbert commented to me: 'He is healing the land! That area was extremely barren: the cause of so much dust!. . . there never used to be trees out there. They had all been cut down because people camped round there for years.'[5]

In June 1991, very heavy rains flooded Warburton Ranges during a football carnival. Almost every vehicle was bogged, including the graders. As soon as it cleared, Ron Abbott and I flew in for a week and it rained again and we were stuck there for an extra four days.

I believe God was showing us that he was sending rivers of renewal into the desert — that the rain was a symbol of something he was doing spiritually as well as in nature.

Then, it rained again and again and again — especially at Warburton. There has been frequent, very heavy rain in the area since then. The vegetation, wildflowers and new trees are really beautiful.

Many Aboriginal homes at Warburton now have flowers, trees, creepers and lawns growing. People often ask Herbert and Lorraine for cuttings or seeds, or go out into the bush to bring in local native plants for their own gardens. Aboriginal councils in the Ngaanyatjarra area are planting thousands of native trees and plants to control erosion and re-vegetate the area.

There is a principle that things happen in the natural like this to prepare for corresponding events in the spiritual realm. God really is renewing the land and its people! There are signs of another wave of God's renewing in the Spirit about to burst forth.

✦ The renewal in Aboriginal life

The revival was a time for many Aborigines to discover their personal ministry. Djiniyini Gondarra named some of today's leaders and said:

The results of the revival are seen in the leaders today.

They are a product of that — who come out of it. That is where people started to discern what God has for them. Many Christians were beginning to discover what their ministry is and a few others had a strong sense of call to the ministry to become ministers of the Word.[6]

A number of these people have trained through Nungalinya College in Darwin and the church has ordained them. Others are in college or in various forms of lay ministry. There is leadership in the church in Arnhem Land as a result of the revival.

This has not happened in most of Central Australia and so the church has been struggling. But God is raising up new leaders with a hunger and expectancy of a new and different move of the Holy Spirit. Some people are still standing strong and others are starting to come back to God slowly, but in a different way.

❏ The growth of a corporate identity

But it is not an individual thing. Aborigines are not individualistic and God's renewal involves a new sense of Aboriginal identity. It can be seen in many new Aboriginal organisations and services, such as the Aboriginal health services. In the church, it is expressed through their own church, the Aboriginal Evangelical Fellowship (now a church), formed in 1970. It's seen in conventions and in Aboriginal groups formed within denominational churches.

The Uniting Aboriginal and Islander Christian Congress (UAICC) was formed in 1983 in the Uniting Church after Aboriginal pastor, Charles Harris, visited Elcho Island and saw the revival life. Djiniyini says:

[The UAICC helps the church] start to understand about unity and diversity — how to build a fellowship of God's people with respect, honour and caring for each other. . . God has given the vision to the congress — to challenge the Uniting Church to enter into covenanting with oppressed people when we are being hurt — to say, 'Now we are asking you to enter into covenant with us.' That leads to unity.[7]

Ron Williams spoke of this struggle:

God is breaking down barriers now. I sense a new coming together so the emphasis is not so much on denominations, but on the church of Jesus Christ. There was a real awareness that when the Holy Spirit moved in revival, it showed that we didn't have to be under mission control or even government control. The Holy Spirit is well able to control the Aboriginal church, as Paul wrote to some of the believers in Philippi: 'God is the One who began this good work in you and I am certain that he won't stop before it is complete on the day that Christ Jesus returns.'[8]

❏ *The development of distinctly Aboriginal worship*

The new Christian Aboriginal identity which is developing can be seen in their unique style of worship. Many of the songs are the same ones that Christians sing all over the

Ron and Diana Williams singing at the Central Australian Christian Convention

world, but with their own style. Others are their own songs, written in their own languages.

Some Christian corroborees are still being developed and danced, like the Easter *pulapa* from Yuendumu which we heard about in the 1979 Central Australian Christian Convention. In Central Australia, boomerangs are tapped together as dancers stamp their feet and the stories are sung in traditional melodies. In the north, didgeridoo and rhythm sticks are used in some Christian corroborees, as well as in songs using guitars and other instruments. Their worship also involves a unique style of interpretative dance using both their own songs and tapes of singers like Amy Grant and Bob Fitts.

At the Elcho Island Jubilee in August 1992, Aboriginal Christians looked for a way of worshipping God and found a cassette tape of an up-beat version of Handel's 'Hallelujah Chorus'.

George Dayngumbu looks over the bay from Dharrwar, his homeland centre on Elcho Island

About thirty of the women and teenage girls dressed in long white robes with blue sashes and aprons and danced to this using timbrels. They hadn't joined the Salvation Army: timbrels were used by Jews 3 000 years ago! They were taking the best music and instruments of all worlds to praise the best of all gods. Everyone present at the Jubilee was drawn into a crescendo of praise and worship, climaxing in a standing ovation to God!

Women and girls dancing to Handel's 'Hallelujah Chorus'
at Elcho Island Jubilee: 1992

Some Aboriginal Christians are concerned about syncretism — idolatry combined with the sacred. George Dayngumbu believes that they can't mix traditional music with worship to God. Musicians have to live and play music as God wants it. He talked to me about worship and their clan group which has recorded a number of worship albums:

> Because I'm a good musician, I'm not going to play in the ceremony and then go and play in the church! That's not the way! As a group, we sing to bring healing, to bless people, to give people strength through praising God — and the people can *feel* the singing. That's why we formed the group Dhurrkay Praise. We sing praise [to God] for the sick people and a lot of people have been healed — without touching them. . . the children *know* by singing. We read the Bible in our mind — but the *Yolngu* way is to worship God. . . and sing to the Lord himself.[9]

In January 1992, a *Balanda* worker at Galiwin'ku had a vision about a pure, shining didjeridoo and a pair of clapsticks being approved by God for his worship. He told some of the church leaders about this. They were excited about God's *yidaki* and *bilma* [didgeridoo and rhythm-sticks], which had no traditional designs painted on them. They were concerned that they should be made and dedicated in the right time and way. Once dedicated, no-one could ever use them in any traditional ceremonies.

The first *yidaki* made wasn't good enough — its mouthpiece was too big. Church elder, Maratja declared: 'We want the best for God — God is *yindi mirrthir* [so great and awesome] and we must give him the best.'[10] Wirriyi got an old man to help him make them from the right wood — no traditional markings, smooth. When it was finished, Wirriyi tested it out at his outstation fellowship time to see what the sound was like. They were singing 'In the name of Jesus' and he found it fitted in beautifully at the right pitch. Wirriyi has sometimes had breathing problems when playing for traditional songs, but this time he didn't have breathing problems!

A few days later at the Easter Sunday morning service in 1993, Jesus' resurrection was celebrated with the dedication of these new *yidaki* and *bilma* to lead praise and worship to God alone and they were anointed with oil.

Over twenty of the Ban'thula outstation young people developed a new dance for the dedication. It is based on Psalm 68, verses 24 to 29 and used the *yidaki* and *bilma*, autoharp, flute, guitar and tambourines. During the rest of the service, worship was led by musicians using all these instruments. There was a wonderful harmony in them, with a beautiful tone in the didgeridoo.

God is opening the way for new dimensions of praise and worship from the roots of this land — praise and worship where we will all joyfully participate as never before and that will greatly please the Father!

Both photographs show the dedication of a didgeridoo and rhythm sticks to God:
Elcho Island, Easter, 1993

❐ *The development of a new identity in the outstations*

There's also a new maturity and sense of identity developing in the outstations. Many are finding the communities and towns are too crowded by the Western world, church structures and other clan groups. Galiwin'ku literacy worker, Margaret Miller, told me about one man:

> He has gone to his outstation, so he can be just for God — number one. He knows all about *bungul djama* [ceremonial work] from start to finish and he learnt to do that for his ancestors, but then he came to realise that it has to be God's way — not to throw all those things away, but number one is to be for God, above family and everything else.
>
> At his outstation, he can feel God — in fact, he can't escape from God and he is able to teach his family and clan in God's way. But he's also finding many people from other clans and tribes come to visit for a weekend. They want to be there [where they can't escape from God either], so he's started to have church services while the people are there and they can all share together of God and his presence in a very real way.
>
> A lot of people come and he doesn't have food to give them, but there's fish in the sea and other food in the bush. He's starting a garden of sweet potatoes, bananas, pawpaws — and he's going to build a large shelter so the people can meet together, so they can know God.[11]

George Dayngumbu warned his people that this isn't an escape hatch:

> We're not escaping from the problems by escaping the city — we're escaping the problems by choosing Christ in our hearts. If we are escaping because of the problem, we'll find another problem there, too, if we know nothing about the Lord — because the problem is here [inside us]. If we have a problem here, how can we live peacefully there if we don't get rid of the problem from our heart? So we start life new and fresh and carry Jesus with us to establish there instead of taking the problem to start again somewhere else.[12]

It has been quite awesome to see the Holy Spirit at work among some of the teenagers and children from these outstations. Their commitment to Jesus, their relationship with God and his responses to their prayers shows a maturity beyond many adult Christians. They were very young children or unborn at the time of the excitement of the revival, yet their faith and life is a product of it and they are the church of today.

❑ The emergence of an Aboriginal theology
Djiniyini asserts very strongly that Aboriginal leaders must develop an Aboriginal theology to express their identity. In 1986, he wrote:

> Aboriginal theologians are beginning to understand that Western theology is moulded by Western philosophies. . . preoccupied with intellectual concerns, especially those having to do with the relationship between faith and reason. . . abstract concepts which might have answered the questions of the past, but which fail to grapple with the issues of today (e.g. land rights, racism, prejudice, alcoholism, marriage). . . If holistic evangelism or an evangelistic theology is to fulfil its task in the Aboriginal church, we must be released from individualism and rationalism of Western theology in order to allow the word of God to work with full power.[13]

He refers to Jesus' Great Commission of the church in Matthew 28, verses 19 and 20 and says it 'is to include every aspect of the work which the church is sent into the world to do. . . I understand evangelism in a different sense, which is called "holistic evangelism".'[14]

Holistic evangelism is one of the strong emphases in the charter of the Uniting Aboriginal and Islander Christian Congress. It tries to avoid separating life into spirit, body and society. Evangelism must involve all of a person's needs and life — their sin and despair, hunger and oppression, family and culture, health and material needs of food, housing and clothing:

We urgently need an holistic evangelical theology, which is faithful to scripture and relevant to our varied situation in the Australian Aboriginal world. . . we strongly reject any ideology which is under the curse of science and technology and which is used as an historical mediation of the Christian faith. We strongly uphold the authority of the scriptures. We believe strongly, as Aboriginal theologians, that evangelical or holistic-evangelical theology must root itself in the life of obedience to the word of God and submission to the Lordship of Jesus Christ and that the theological task must be done under the constant operation of the Holy Spirit. . .

We Aboriginal people and Christian leaders will have to address ourselves to such issues as traditional world views, the reality of spiritual powers and denominationalism within the churches. We will have to grapple with the tension between traditional values and the values being introduced by the process of Westernisation, the problem produced by economic dependence and the presence of world powers. . .

We are called to plant Christ in this Aboriginal Australian 'fertile soil', rather than transplant our Western forms of Christianity. . . We must promote Christ as the living and acceptable part of their own ceremony and culture, but our confidence is that Christ has won the victory over all the principalities and powers and that this victory will certainly become manifest if he is given the chance to do the battle.[15]

Many in the traditional church will feel threatened by this process. Western culture and spirits will be challenged by Aboriginal Christians, especially where the church is blind or refuses to listen to God. But we who are not Aboriginal can expect to receive much more love than we have given to Aborigines and it is a vital part of God's purposes today.

Jesus said, 'I did not come to do away with the Law and the Prophets, but to give them their full meaning.'[16] In the process of finding the full meaning of their law and identity, Aborigines will need to get a new understanding of their

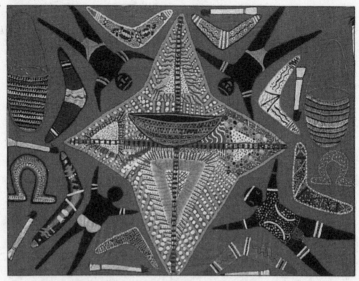

The Christmas banner at Nungalinya College chapel, Darwin

'dreaming' in the light of Jesus Christ.

Djiniyini compares Aboriginal sacred sites and 'dreaming' stories with Jewish places of deep religious significance, such as Bethel, Mt Sinai and Shiloh, where the people focus on God and his law. He says, 'Israel did not worship the ark. It was not an idol: rather, it was a sacred object in a sacred place to remind Israel of the law and of the mighty deeds of Yahweh in history.'[17]

He compares Aboriginal feelings over mining sacred sites to the feelings that Jews would have at the destruction of the ark by bulldozers or drilling for oil in the Temple in Jerusalem:

> In the spirituality of Aborigines, what happens at sacred sites is more like a recognition of ancient moral imperatives than a kind of worship. . . This is not a call to uncritically accept magic and idolatry but. . . to recognise in an ancient culture gifts that may have been given by God himself.[18]

Djiniyini talks of sacred knowledge from the Spirit of the Creator, where Aboriginality is God's gift to this land and its people. He admits that while some of their rituals are not given by God, Aborigines will throw those ones away when that is revealed.

In Central Australia, a whitefella missionary went with some of the old men to a shed used to store some of the implements of the ceremonies. The old men, who had become Christians as adults, said in their language:

> All these things are really important to us, you know. . . but these aren't the most important things. These things don't make any sense unless we've got the whole story as it occurs in the Bible. These are like signposts: just pointing towards the way we should go. But the gospel gives us the real message.[19]

The missionary added that they expressed the hope that the younger generation would come to see this one day.

Aboriginal Christians are in a time of discovery, where Holy Spirit discernment and the truth of God revealed in Jesus, the Word of God, are essential. Many people have become confused, especially those whose knowledge of the word is weak or whose relationship with God is not strongly directed by the Holy Spirit.

☐ *The formation of a Christian identity as Aboriginals*
One of the most significant signs of hope today is the discovery of their identity as *Aboriginal* Christians. Galikali said, 'God's action in that first wave of 1979 to 1985 was to reveal himself as a God who really was God of the *Yolngu* — as their God. The revelation of his holiness and all that goes with it in terms of forgiveness will gradually follow.'[20]

'*Their*' God means the God who speaks their language, in their thought patterns and ways, in their social framework and culture. Aborigines are gradually discovering that God is the Father of Jesus Christ who created every language at the Tower of Babel and made each culture at that time. They are discovering that Jesus did not speak English and live with a Western world view — and God is not even just the God of the Jews.

Many of them have said God gave them their 'law'. What has been happening — and will continue until Christ returns — is their discovery of what this really means. Like the Jews, the Aborigines and people of all cultures have to see that Jesus didn't come to destroy their law, but to reveal what that law really is and what is the garbage that has been dumped on top of God's law to hide it. Djiniyini continues, '. . . God is not somewhere floating over Australia; rather, God is revealed in the life of the people. God in Christ is with all human beings, especially those who are poor, outcast and threatened.'[21]

He quotes Jesus' mission to bring good news to the poor, release for prisoners, sight for the blind, freedom for the broken, proclaiming the year of the Lord's favour[22] and says that Christ is already there in these struggles:

> The prayer of Aboriginal people for Australia is: 'Father, make us one.' It is a prayer that is being realised as justice is being realised in our land. It is a prayer that is being realised as the people of God learn to act together responsively.[23]

✦ The emergence of a heart for others

One aspect of the Aboriginal concept of holistic evangelism means love for others: acting together responsively — seeing, hearing, feeling and responding to what is happening to each other. That is real love — something that God has for each one of us. It is something that is missing too often in race relations.

❐ *Aborigines' and whitefellas' love for each other*

What love do Aboriginal Christians and whitefellas have for each other? Ron Williams' attitude, written in 1984, is shared by a growing group of Aborigines:

I have found myself praying and crying for the nations of East and West Germany and desiring to share with them the reconciling love of Jesus [before the wall was broken down]. . . Indeed, my heart started to cry out for the whole of Europe. The European white man brought the gospel to the black man; now, the black man feels the tug in his heart to be like a boomerang and take the gospel to the white man. . .

Someone once said, 'If it weren't for the Christian missionaries, there would quite possibly be no Aborigines left in Australia today.'

I would have easily become bitter, as I read the history books and heard the stories and saw for myself the atrocities that were committed against the Australian Aborigines in the name of civilisation and Christianity. However, I thank God for the gospel of Jesus Christ, his forgiveness and redeeming love. It is for all mankind. My white brothers have lost themselves through greed and selfishness, materialism and vice, seemingly made justifiable by clever phraseology which still leaves our soul empty. I have cried for my white brothers so many times. In the early days, the black man showed the white man the water holes; now, we can show him his lostness and where to find the living water of life.

My prayer is that my white brothers might swallow their pride and repent before it's too late. I believe the only way that we Australians, black or white, can really find our true identity and destiny is that we put the Lord back into his rightful place as the Lord and Saviour of the world. I believe we need each other. You need both black and white keys on a piano to play harmonious music. We are made to be interdependent as brothers and sisters.

I have an anchor in Aboriginal heritage going back thousands of years before the white man came to Australia. This heritage is that 'people are more important than things' and that 'we need to share and care in order to survive' — in peace and harmony with each other, the land and our environment.

. . .My Aboriginal people are a spiritual people and they have a lot to share with the world.[24]

☐ *A desire to forgive and be reconciled*

There is a developing desire amongst Aborigines for reconciliation and working together with others in the land. Some have travelled overseas to visit American Indians, to Israel, United Kingdom, Germany, Africa, India, Asia and the Pacific. They have sensed that God has been good to them as Aborigines in Australia, despite all the hardship and oppression. There is a desire to deal with the past and put it behind them and go on together. Aboriginal pastor, Bill Bird, is one of the leaders in this.

In 1990, Bill admitted that it wasn't just whitefellas who were wrong in their attitude: his hatred and resentment to whites was bondage to himself and also to whites and was sin. He was on an Emmaus Walk — a spiritual retreat where groups of people let God speak to them and their situation. He cried out to God and to the sixty white men present, asking for forgiveness, and he suddenly found the real Bill Bird, after thirty-eight years as a Christian and thirty-five as a pastor.

He believes that reconciliation comes before justice and brings healing of the hurts of the past. He has taken groups of Aboriginal Christians into schools and various churches. They have stayed in homes of whitefellas and eaten at their tables, even though they had always felt they would prefer to go for takeaways and camp out.

In schools, they shared as part of the social studies program on Aboriginal history and culture and told some of the stories of racial prejudice and massacres without malice or anger, admitting their sin of resentment and hatred and asking forgiveness. They tell whites they love them now. Then, God's Holy Spirit is released to do his work of bringing people to repentance.[25]

Glenn Johnson joined Bill in one of these trips, telling how his hatred drove him to alcoholism when he was fourteen years old, but Jesus had changed his whole life. He said that his people put curses on the land after whites came to Australia, curses that still affect the land today, but are broken through reconciliation.[26] Bill says:

> The response has been tremendous. I've had white people say they want to sell their house and come and live in Redfern to help us! My advice to people who want to help is make friends with some Aboriginal families. Don't just give money — that's an easy way to shed your responsibility. Aborigines want to see your face; they want to look at you; they want you to come and touch them.
>
> The cry for justice in this country still has to be met. But I believe that reconciliation will create a situation where we can discuss the more controversial issues with mutual respect. It is the same with God. God wanted to be friends with us, but there was a problem — sin. God was the offended one, so God took the initiative and clearly forgave us.
>
> That's the message for Aboriginal people. They've been offended, so they take the initiative. They'll be a lot richer for it. If we can only come to the place of forgiving, God will bless our race beyond measure.[27]

But not everyone agrees with Bill or responds like that. Even some of the Western missionaries who have worked together with Bill and other Aboriginal pastors closely have not realised the depth of hatred and resentment the Aborigines felt towards them caused by the missionaries' paternalism. So it was a long time before some of them responded to requests from Aborigines for forgiveness to be given to them — and some still don't see any need for action.

In November 1996, Bill led the launch of a reconciliation movement in Melbourne's city square. He stood on behalf of Australia's indigenous people, asking forgiveness for their hatred of Europeans. It was a very significant step, but church leaders could not respond by asking Aborigines for forgiveness for the things Europeans have done to produce that hatred. There is a long way to go before that happens.

Ron Williams sees God at work in reconciliation so that we can work together:

> . . .the story of the Aboriginal church is God moving among them and sanctifying and purifying them and calling out a people for his name. I also see him working in the white churches and denominations, purifying, so that we might be knit together in love as the fire of the Holy Spirit burns and welds two pieces of metal together.[28]

✦ The conviction that God is renewing the land

Rod Minniecon, Aboriginal pastor from northern New South Wales, knows the importance of this purifying process. He has seen the spiritual impact on the land of untimely deaths, massacres, violence and even abortions. He feels the spirit of death and destruction on the land.

Rod Minniecon preaching on the banks of the Todd River during the Central Australian Christian Convention in 1995

Rod has felt God's leading to go to a number of places, being joined by Aborigines and Westerners in worshipping God together, celebrating Jesus' victory over sin by sharing the body and blood of the 'Lord's supper' together, and bringing cleansing to those places with the blood of Jesus Christ. He also follows the Holy Spirit's leading to bring cleansing in other ways, such as throwing salt on water and releasing spirits of the dead, telling them to go to

God their Maker.

But he firmly believes that this cleansing must be done in the unity of black and white working together. They have seen tremendous release: drought broken, relationships restored, curses broken which had caused sickness and poverty.

This cleansing and renewing process is *God's* work in which we join him. God's word to me in January 1979 was, 'I will renew the land.' Someone asked Dan Armstrong what he had done differently at Galiwin'ku from everywhere else and his answer was simply, 'Nothing!' He went on to say, 'It was a beautiful sovereign work of God.'[29]

This is the story of God renewing the land of Australia. It was not started by Dan Armstrong or Djiniyini, Kevin Dhurrkay or their fathers — or any missionaries. The story is not even the acts of Aboriginal apostles, evangelists or of any people, so much as the acts of God. I believe he uses people, but it is his plan, his power and ability, his timing.

I am convinced it is God's purpose to renew the land of Australia — and that is happening. He has spoken to people today about his plans to renew the land. This book is about some of the ways he is doing this.

The work of the Holy Spirit amongst the Aborigines is pointing out God's revelation of himself in specific ways that are not just for them, but for the whole of the land and all the people in it. Through the experiences of Aborigines seen in the light of God's word, he speaks to us clearly of things we need to know, understand and respond to. One of these responses may be to say 'yes' in words and actions to the following prophetic creed for the land of Australia.

✦ A prophetic creed for the land of Australia
This creed is based partly on Jeremiah 30, especially verses 3, 8 to 11 and 16 to 22.

1. There are many spirits in the land of Australia, some of which have Aboriginal roots.

2. The spirits in the land affect all people living in it, including Westerners.

3. There is a spiritual battle for sovereignty over Australia which requires action on every front, using many different tactics.

4. Jesus Christ is the answer to the needs and struggles of this land and of every Australian, and his forces will be victorious over every evil spirit when he is their commander-in-chief in every action.

5. In the battle, God is purging Aboriginal and all cultures in the land, training Aborigines and others in his forces.

6. God's strategy includes the liberation of Aborigines and all people in the land from every bondage and oppression.

7. God has revealed himself to Aborigines over thousands of years, but the revelation has been corrupted.

8. This revelation is fulfilled in Jesus Christ and his way, revealed in the Bible.

9. God has revealed himself to Aborigines recently through a Christian revival amongst them.

10. This revival gave them a taste of the true nature and power of God, so that they would allow themselves to be refined in God's Holy Spirit fire, allow him to complete all that he has revealed to them and to make Jesus Christ the legitimate leader of the land of Australia.

11. God lifts up and uses the social outcasts, downtrodden and oppressed: he did so repeatedly in the Bible and still does so today. God has chosen to lift up and use Australian Aborigines in his purposes for this land.

12. God gave the land of Australia to Aborigines before Westerners came here and is restoring them to their leadership in this country as they acknowledge Jesus Christ as true leader in the land.

13. God chose the British to bring the good news of Jesus Christ to Australia. Their Western culture has much in it that has been corrupted and has evil roots, as well as much that is good and of benefit to Australia and to Aborigines.

14. There is a huge gap between the Aboriginal and Western world view; both groups need to value and consult each other and to work together.

15. The bondage and suffering of Aborigines through sickness, alcohol, drugs, unemployment, failure, social disintegration and death have spiritual roots, many of which are related to their relationship with Westerners in Australia.

16. Westerners and others in Australia must recognise their ethnocentric attitudes and lay aside superiority towards Aborigines, accepting Aboriginal leadership, guidance, abilities, help and working together with them. Aborigines must also accept leadership, guidance and help from others living in Australia and work together with them.

17. Aborigines and Westerners must forgive each other for their acts and attitudes of injustice, prejudice, hatred and bitterness towards each other and live in true love for each other, working together with each other and God in God's purposes for the land.

18. God desires to give health, justice, prosperity, joy, fulfilment and all his blessings to every person living in Australia, so that they may be a blessing to others.

19. Australia will only experience health, justice, prosperity, joy, fulfilment, renewal of the land, God's blessing and spiritual revival when Aborigines humbly fulfil their God-given role, reconciled justly with Westerners.

20. God plans to use Aborigines and other Australians working in harmony as a prophetic nation to bring total renewal and spiritual revival to other lands.

✦ Aborigines as the feet of the church

In 1 Corinthians 12, verses 12 to 31, Paul wrote:

> The body of Christ has many different parts. . . Some of us
> are Jews, and some are Gentiles. . . Our bodies don't just
> have one part. They have many parts. Suppose a foot says,
> 'I'm not a hand, and so I'm not part of the body.' Wouldn't
> the foot still belong to the body?. . .
>
> God put our bodies together in such a way that even the
> parts that seem the least important are valuable. He did
> this to make all parts of the body work together smoothly,
> with each part caring about the others.

I have often described Aborigines as the feet of the church
in Australia and Westerners as the hands. The feet are much
more ready to go with the gospel than the hands who have
to think, plan and organise for ages. But the hands have tried
to get the feet to walk, dance and run like hands.

One day, I asked Ron Williams if he felt I was putting
Aborigines down by calling them the feet of the church and
he said something like this:

> Whitefellas look at a fingerprint and say, 'That's June Black-
> et.' They talk about the work of your hands and say, 'You
> have beautiful hands!'
>
> Aborigines think about dancing and running, walking
> and standing and say, 'You've got beautiful feet!' They look
> at a footprint and say, 'That's Ron Williams and he's carry-
> ing a kangaroo he's caught!'

The hands and the feet need to thank God for each other
and for what he does through the other parts of the body, also
asking forgiveness for past attitudes. At the final meeting of
the revival mission at Galiwin'ku in May 1979, Dan Armstrong had a vision:

> I saw the young men going out in groups and landing in
> other spots. Everywhere they went, a fire came up. I
> shared this with them — and the Lord gave us the word
> from 1 Corinthians 1, verses 26 to 28: 'those whom the

world thinks common and contemptible are the ones that God has chosen.'[30]

Ron Williams said recently:

As I look upon our Aboriginal people, my prayer used to be, 'Lord Jesus, come quickly: this is a terrible old world.' But I have changed my prayers to be bold enough to ask: 'Lord, let not the sun go down or let not the Son come down yet. We haven't finished the job. Do not hasten the return of the Lord Jesus Christ: we've got a nation to clean up. People don't respect you any more.

'And Lord, we've been so slack as Aboriginal people. We've been so used to handouts and a "give me" philosophy. Lord, if you came back now and you hand over heaven to us on a plate, we won't enjoy it because we'd say, "Lord, we've been having a handout system from the government and our missions the last 200 years and we cannot appreciate heaven because here we have another handout system."

'We know you are God and you're full of goodness and mercy, but give us a chance to also be involved in the Great Commission so we can share by word and, if we have to lay our life down, that we might do that because we have been warriors.

'You gave us a job to do after the Tower of Babel when we sped across the country and we went through the Ice Age, we met with prehistoric animals and we faced Satan and demonic characters. It's all in our dreamtime stories.

'But now you have spared us as a country and you have brought the gospel to us. Give us another chance, Lord, that we might do our part to take the glorious gospel of the Lord Jesus Christ, even as the apostle Paul said in 2 Corinthians 4:

We are like clay jars in which this treasure is stored. The real power comes from God and not from us. We often suffer, but we are never crushed. Even when we don't know what to do, we never give up. In times of trouble God is with us, and when we are knocked down, we get up again. We face death every day because of Jesus. Our bodies show what his death was like, so that his life can also be seen in us. This means that death is working in us, but life is working in you.

'And so, as you see the Aboriginal church struggling in Australia, may it show the life of Jesus also being made manifest in our mortal flesh.'

That's my prayer and aim for an ongoing saga from the great revival that swept across parts of Australia from Elcho and through the desert in the late 1970s and into the 1980s.[31]

God uses both the image of fire and the image of rivers of living water in the Bible to tell of the renewing power of his Holy Spirit. He has used both images in telling his purposes which he is bringing to pass with and through Australia's Aborigines.

I believe that today there are still some of the evil spirits needing to be swept out — but God is at work in renewing the land! And God is starting to use Aborigines to remove some of the blockages and evil spirits from the rest of the world, especially the Western world — and to bring a wonderful deep release of his Holy Spirit!

Australia *is* an island on fire, with the river of life renewing the land. The bushfire is being fanned by Holy Spirit wind and carried by sparks and firesticks as the river flows out, across the seas.

Appendix A:

Sources used

Abbott, Ron and Del:		Transcript of a taped interview with the author, August 1992
Allen, Margaret:		Duplicated newsletter, 22 May 1979
		Letter to the author, 22 May 1979
Armstrong, Dan:	1979	Transcript of a taped meeting on 5 August, 1979, printed in *FFR Prayer Circular*, August 1979
	1981	Transcript of a taped report to O'Conner Uniting Church, 29 March 1981
	1984	'Dan Armstrong's Story of the Elcho Island Revival', in *Australia's New Day* #42, November 1984
Armstrong, Dan and Sue:		'The Revival Today', report written for the author, March 1995
Babbage, Adele:		Report written for the author, March 1995
Balfe, Jeanette:		Letter to the author, 4 April 1992
Barnes, Cyril:		Transcript of a taped interview with the author, April 1991
Bates, Alwyn:		Transcript of a taped interview with the author, 12 March 1992
Berndt, Ronald M:		*An Adjustment Movement in Arnhemland, N.T. of Australia,* University of Western Australia, 1962
Bibuka:		Transcript of a taped interview with the author, April 1993

Bird, Bill:
'Reconciliation', *On Being* Magazine; December 1993–January 1994

Blacket, John:
1975-88 Unpublished personal prayernotes

1991 'It's War', *Khesed News* #10; February 1991

1994 Hearts on Fire, unpublished manuscript, 1994

Blacket, John;
Buchanan, Dianne;
Edwards, Anna
and Ross, Joyce:
Transcript of a taped discussion, Darwin; 4 June 1979

Blackman, Shane:
Transcript of a taped address, in 'Fellowship For Revival Prayer Circular', # 24, November-December 1986

Blyth, Noel:
Personal discussion with the author, 1990

Bodeker, Phil
(Christian, A):
Prayers for Meekatharra: the Good News Column, *The West Australian*, 10 April 1982

The Good News Column, *The West Australian*, 30 April 1982

Bos, Robert:
'Jesus and the Dreaming: Religion and Social Change in Arnhem Land', unpublished

Ph.D. thesis, Brisbane, University of Queensland

Buchanan, Dianne:
1975-85 Unpublished personal diary, 1975–1985

1978 (a) Letter to friends at Yirrkala,
27 November 1978

(b) Duplicated newsletter, December 1978

1979 (a) Letter to Rudders, 8 April 1979

(b) Letter to Rudders, 16 April 1979

(c) Letter to Rudders, May 1979

(d) Duplicated newslettern, 28 June 1979

(e) Letter to a friend at Yirrkala, July 1979

(f) Letter to friends at Yirrkala, August 1979

(g) Duplicated newsletter, September 1979

(h) Duplicated newsletter, 12 December 1979

(i) Note to the author, 12 December 1979

1980 (a) 'Renewal in the Galiwinku (Elcho Island) Church', duplicated paper

(b) Duplicated Newsletter, 12 March 1980

(c) Duplicated Newsletter; November 1980

1990 (a) Duplicated Newsletter; January 1990

(b) Transcript of a taped interview with the author, 8 August 1990

1992 Transcript of a taped interview with the author, August 1992

Buchanan, Dianne, Loechel, Don & Rhonda, and Rudder, John: 1990   (c) Transcript of a taped report to staff at Galiwin'ku, July 1990

Buthimang: Transcript of a taped interview with the author, 16 August 1992

Buthimang and George Dayngumbu: Transcript of a taped interview with the author, March 22, 1990

Butler, Maimie: Transcript of a taped interview with the author, 10 March 1992

Capp, Robert: 1992   Transcript of a taped interview with the author, 14 March 1992

1995   'Church Planting and Nurture in Central Australia', photocopied paper, 17 January 1995

Cotterell, Claude: Transcript of a taped interview with the author, April 1991

Dangatanga: Transcript of a taped interview with the author, 17 August 1990

Dayngumbu, George: Transcript of a taped interview with the author, April 1993

Dean, Margaret: Letter to the author 16 May 1991

Djawungdjawung: Transcript of a taped interview with the author, April 1993

Djilipa: Transcript of a taped interview with the author, 22 March 1990

Djiniyini: see Gondarra

Djorrpum: untitled statement, in *My Mother the Land*, Ian Yule (ed.), Galiwin'ku Action Group, 1980

Douglas, Wilfrid H:	1983	Letter to Rev. David Morley, 1 October 1983
	1992	Phone conversation with the author, 4 March 1992
Edwards, Anna, et al:		see Blacket et al
Edwards, Lawrie:		Personal conversation, 2 September 1995
		'Elcho Island Revisited', interview printed in *Indigenous Leadership*, # 3, May 1995
Flentje, Wendell and Mary:		Letter to the author, 8 April 1991
Forbes, Fred:		Transcript of a taped interview with the author, interpreted by Herbert Howell, 10 March 1992
Galikali:		see Buchanan
Galiwin'ku Church News:		Galiwin'ku, Uniting Church in Australia, 20 August 1972
Glass, Amee:		'Christian Teaching and Response among the Ngaanyatjarra', duplicated paper
Glass, Amee and Hackett, Dorothy:	1981	Duplicated prayer letter, 23 December 1981
	1985	Duplicated prayer letter, June 1985
	1986	Duplicated prayer letter, 1 January 1986
Gondarra, Djiniyini and Dangatanga:	1990	Transcript of a taped interview with the author, March 22
Gondarra, Djiniyini and Gelung:	1990	(a) Notes from an interview with the author, 27 March 1990
		(b) Transcript of taped interview with the author, August, 1990
	1996	Notes from an interview with the author, 18 March 1996
Gondarra, Djiniyini:		untitled statement, in *My Mother the Land*, Yule, Ian (ed.), Galiwin'ku Action Group, 1980
Galiwin'ku Action Group:	1986	Let My People Go, series of reflections of Aboriginal Theology, Bethel Presbytery, Uniting Church in Australia, Darwin
	1990	Author's notes from an interview, 20 March, 1990

	1992	Transcript of a taped interview with the author, 17 August 1992
	1995	Phone conversation with the author, 19 September 1995
Gullick, Barbara and Barry:		Letter to the author, 14 April 1979
Howell, Herbert and Lorraine:	1991	Transcript of a taped interview with the author, October 1991
Howell, Herbert:	1981	Warburton Ranges Mission diary, September 1981
	1991	Transcript of a taped interview with the author, August 1991
	1992	(a) Author's notes from an interview, 10 March 1992
		(b) Transcript of a taped interview with the author, 12 March 1992
		(c) Letter to the author, 14 May 1992
Lindsay, Ian:		*Fire in the Spinifex*, United Aborigines Mission, 1986
Loechel Rhonda:		Letter to Rudders, mid-1979
Loechel, Don and Rhonda, et al:		see Buchanan et al
Magnus, Jim:		'Religious drive eases N-W trouble', *Daily News*, Perth, 26 March 1982
Makarrwala, Harry and Webb, T. Theodor:		'The Old, Bad: The New, Very Good', *The Missionary Review*; Sydney, 5 December 1942
Maratja, Alan:		Transcript of a taped interview with the author, 5 April 1993
McKenzie, Maisie:		*Mission to Arnhemland*, Rigby, 1976
Medway, Kerry:		'Is God raising up Aboriginals to save Australia?', transcript of a taped address at St Thomas Church, Port Macquarie, September 1984
Miller, Margaret:		Transcript of a taped interview with the author, 1993
Morgan, Margaret:		*A Drop in the Bucket*, United Aborigines Mission, 1956
Munroe, Elaine:		Transcript of a taped interview with the author, 10 March 1992
Nance, Carol:		Letter to the author, 26 March 1991

Nance, Rob: Letter the author, 9 April 1991

Newbery, Bernard: Transcript of a taped interview with the author, 10 March 1992

Nyiwula: Report written for the author, January 1993

Richards, Sylvia: 1984   Letter to Bible translators, 1984

   1994   'Road to Reconciliation', *Blue Mountains Gazette*, 25 May 1994

Roberts, Thelma: 1992   Letter and report to the author, March, 1992

   1993   Note to the author, July 1993

Robinson, Terry: Transcript of a taped interview with the author, 17 March 1992

Ross, Joyce, et al: see Blacket et al

Rronang: Transcript of a taped interview with the author, August 1992

Rrurrambu, Kevin and Blacket, John: Transcript of a taped report to missionaries in Alice Springs, 1 September 1981

Rudder, John: Transcript of a taped interview with the author, 24 February 1990

Rudder, John et al: see Buchanan et al

Rudder, Trixie: Transcript of taped testimony at O'Conner Uniting Church, 29 March 1981

Scott, Bobby: Transcript of a taped interview with the author, 11 October 1990

Shepherdson, Ella: *Half a Century in Arnhemland*, PanPrint; 1981

Smythe, Robin: Transcript of a taped interview with the author, 13 March 1992

     The Bible For Today, Contemporary English Version.

Trudgen, Richard: Transcript of a taped interview with the author, 13 August 1992

Tucker, Les: Transcript of a taped interview with the author, 5 March 1992

Webb, T. Theodor: 1931   (a) 'Aboriginal Heroes of Faith', *The Missionary Review*, Methodist Church, Sydney, 5 August 1931

     (b) 'North Australia District, 1931', *The Missionary Review*, Methodist Church, Sydney, 5 November 1931

	1940	'Our Aboriginal Work', in *The Missionary Review*, Methodist Church, Sydney, 5 March 1940
Williams, Alan:	1985	'On the Crest of a Wave', *On Being*; # 43, December 1984/January 1985
	1990	Letter to the author, 20 July 1990
Williams, Louise:		'Australia, the Secret History', 'Good Weekend', *Sydney Morning Herald*, 2 October 1993
Williams, Ron:	1984	*Nuggets from the Goldfields*, Centre Press
	1995	(a) 'Aboriginal Christianity Today', transcript of a message tape to the author, March 1995 (b) Transcript of a taped interview with the author, 24 May 1995
Wirriyi:		Transcript of a taped interview with the author, August 1990, with added details from a version he gave to Margaret Miller in 1992
Yates, Bonnie:		Transcript of a taped interview with the author, 10 March 1992
Yule, Ro:		Letter to the author, 29 May 1979

Appendix B:

List of words and people

Pronunciation of Aboriginal words in this book

1. Djam. = Djambarrpuyngu language

2. Ng. = Ngaanyatjarra language — language of the Central Desert around Warburton Ranges in Western Australia

ng

Many Aboriginal languages use the sound 'ng' [as in sing], even to begin a word. It is generally written in a special way to distinguish between this sound and an 'n' followed by a 'g'. Because of technical difficulties and readers' unfamiliarity with this practice, it is not followed in this book.

'ng' is mostly the single sound as in 'sing'. Only occasionally is it the double sound found in 'congratulate'. 'ng' can also be followed by 'g', as in *'bunggul'*.

Other sounds:

'a' sounds like 'but' or 'ado'

'u' sounds like 'put'

'ä' and 'aa' sound like 'father'

'uy' is like 'poison'

'ny' is like 'new' [but not as Americans pronounce it, 'noo']

'l', 'n' and 'd' are retroflex sounds made with the tongue curled back at the roof of the mouth.

'rr' is trilled as in Scottish pronunciation.

Thus, Djambarrpuyngu is pronounced as 'Djam-barr-poi-ngoo' and Batangga as 'But-ung-gu' [but not 'But-ung-goo']

List:

AEF	Aboriginal Evangelical Fellowship
Anangu	Aboriginal person from the Pitjantjatjara group of tribes around the north of South Australia
Arnhem Land	North-east section of the Northern Territory which is mainly Aboriginal reserve land
Balanda	Non-Aboriginal person
	A term used in north-eastern Arnhem Land, mainly applied to Europeans. It is derived from Macassan villagers' contact with 'Hollanders' (Dutch) in Indonesia
bäpa	Father — Djam.
Batangga	Wangurri clan leader at Galiwin'ku, younger brother of Makarrwala; *yirritja*.
Bibuka	*Yolngu* woman
Bill Bird	Aboriginal pastor, Sydney
bilma	Rhythm-sticks — Djam.
Birrinydjawuy	Gupapuyngu clan leader at Milingimbi; first Christian in the area.
Blackstone	Central Australian Aboriginal community
bull-dust	Australian term for a large, deep patch of very fine, soft dirt, often found in a firm, gravel road
bunggul	Traditional ceremonial dances. Djam.
bunggul djama	Ceremonial work
Burrumarra	Warramirri clan leader at Galiwin'ku; *yirritja*
Buthimang	Wangurri elder at Elcho Island
Butler, Maimie	Ngaanyatjarra woman
CACC	Central Australian Christian Convention
Coterill, Claude	Retired UAM Goldfields missionary
crow	Totem for Golamala clan, Arnhem Land
crusades	Term used for the series of meetings held by the revival teams from the Warburton Ranges and Goldfields areas
Dhurrkay	Wongurri clan surname
	1. Kevin — Clan leader at Galiwin'ku; son of Batangga; *yirritja*; assistant school principal; church elder; evangelist of the revival. Since his death in 1991, his *Yolngu* name is not used, but only his English Christian name and clan surname.

2. George Dayngumbu — Wangurri clan leader and church elder at Galiwin'ku; son of Batangga; *yirritja*.

dhuwa	One of the two moieties or groupings of all life in north-eastern Arnhem Land
Djambarrpuyngu	A tribe/language of the Elcho Island area used as the main communication language for the area
Djang'kawu	Dreaming-sisters involved in naming physical features in Arnhem Land
djäma	Work — Djam.
Djilipa	*Yolngu* man
Djiniyini	[previously also known as 'Terry'] Rev. Dr Djiniyini Gondarra, minister of the Galiwin'ku Uniting Church parish at the time of the revival; theologian, Bible teacher, leader in many areas of Aboriginal church life; son of Wili, Golumala clan leader, *dhuwa*.
Douglas, Wilf	Pioneer missionary linguist in Western Australia
dreaming	[sometimes wrongly called 'dreamtime' and often considered to be untrue myths] A non-Aboriginal word referring to Aboriginal law, sacred stories, songs, paintings and ritual items which are the foundation of Aboriginal identity and their relationship with land.
Dunn, Wally	Pitjantjatjara co-worker with the author in Central Australia
Flentje, Wendell	Missionary agriculturalist at Galiwin'ku
Forbes, Fred	Ngaanyatjarra pioneer Christian
Galikali	1. one of eight sub-section group names used in north-east Arnhem Land. Everyone is born into a particular subsection determined by one of their parent's subsections. Aborigines use these names like many people use relationship terms such as 'uncle' or 'cousin'. They seldom use personal names, preferring to use relationship or sub-section names to identify people. Many non-Aborigines who come to live and work with them are adopted into families and given these names. 2. Dianne Buchanan went to Elcho Island as a schoolteacher, and was adopted by the *Yolngu* as Galikali. Most *Yolngu* call her Galikali and I have used

	this Aboriginal name for her throughout the book.
Galiwin'ku	Aboriginal town or community on Elcho Island. The name is also used for the whole island.
Gelung	Christian leader at Galiwin'ku during the revival; wife of Djiniyini; Wangurri clan; *yirritja*.
George Dayngumbu Dhurrkay	Wangurri clan leader and church elder at Galiwin'ku; son of Batangga; *yirritja*.
Glass, Amee	Ngaanyatjarra Bible translator
Gondarra	[previously also known as 'Terry'] Rev. Dr Djiniyini Gondarra, minister of the Galiwin'ku Uniting Church Parish at the time of the revival; theologian, Bible teacher, leader in many areas of Aboriginal church life; son of Wili, Golumala clan leader, *dhuwa*.
Gunapipi	Ceremony associated with propagation of life
gurtha	Fire, firewood, tongues of fire — Djam. See the beginning of chapter 11 for details of its spiritual and political significance.
Higgins, Ken	UCA minister at Galiwin'ku until 1976
Howell, Herbert and Lorraine	Ngaanyatjarra Missionary linguists
Kevin Dhurrkay	Wangurri clan leader at Galiwin'ku; son of Batangga; *yirritja*; assistant school principal; church elder; evangelist of the revival. His *Yolngu* name has not been used since his death in 1991.
Kraak, Jim	Missionary engineer at Galiwin'ku
Lennon, Albert	Pitjantjatjara elder
Lindsay, Ian	UAM missionary in the Goldfields
Macassan	or Maccasarese: tribal people from central Indonesia who had a very significant influence on *Yolngu*
makarrata	Peacemaking ceremony in which an accused person stands between two groups of offended men who throw spears to injure him. Djam
Makarrwala	Wangurri clan leader at Milingimbi, one of the first Christians in the area; *yirritja*
mala	clan — Djam
Maratja, Alan Dhamarrandji	Djambarrpuyngu church elder at Galiwin'ku, member of the Bible translation team, frequently leads teams to minister in various parts of Australia

mari	trouble Djam
märryulk	Djam. Unbelief
Marshall, Chris	Community Officer, Warburton Ranges
Mason, Ben	Aboriginal evangelist and leader
Mawunydjil	UCA *Yolngu* minister
McKenzie, Kinyin	Pitjantjatjara man who started the Central Australian conventions
Medway, Kerry	Anglican minister in Central Australia
Milingimbi	First mission settlement in north-east Arnhem Land
minydjalpi	sacred dilly bag seen as proof that a clan has authority over their land — Djam.
Mt Margaret	UAM mission settlement in the Goldfields
Mulga, Joe	Goldfields Aboriginal Christian
moiety	Aboriginal life in Arnhem Land is divided into two complementary groups or moieties: *dhuwa* and *yirrit-ja*. All animals and people belong to one of these moieties. A *dhuwa* person can only marry a *yirritja* person.
Newbery, Bernard	Ngaanyatjarra Christian leader
Ngaanyatjarra	tribe/language of the Central Desert around Warburton Ranges
Nungalinya College	Combined church training college in Darwin
Nyiwula	Galpu clan leader at Galiwin'ku, wife of Kevin Dhurrkay; *dhuwa*
Nyoongar	Term used for the Aboriginal people of the tribes of the south-west area of Western Australia.
outstation	Small bush community of Aborigines
petrol sniffing	A form of substance abuse like glue sniffing, smoking or alcohol abuse which is very common among tribal Aboriginal children and young adults, but destroys brain cells and has permanently maimed or killed many of them.
Pitjantjatjara	Tribe/language of the Central Desert around Uluru (Ayers Rock) and across the north of South Australia
prophecy	A term used in the Bible and by Christians for messages spoken from God, as well as foretelling actions and events
pulapa	Warlpiri ceremonial dance

Ragata, Jovilisi	UCA missionary community worker in Arnhem Land
rangga	[see also totem] Poles with sacred designs carved and painted on them. These designs represent Aborigines' personal and clan identities and their affiliation with particular sites ÷ Djam.
Rärrkminy	[previously known as Wanymuli] A matriarch of the Djambarrpuyngu clan who works in the Bible translation program at Galiwin'ku; *dhuwa*
renewal, revival	Renewal and revival are often used interchangeably, referring to God's action in bringing new life to people and society. Revival tends to be a more intense action, but renewal is a more enduring one.
RFDS	Royal Flying Doctor Service: operates in remote parts of Australia.
Roberts, Thelma	UAM missionary at Warburton Ranges
Robertson, Arthur	Ngaanyatjarra Aboriginal pastor
Robinson, Terry	Ngaanyatjarra leader of the crusades
Ross, Joyce	UCA missionary linguist in Arnhem Land
Rronang, Rev. Dhalnganda Garrawarra	*Yolngu* UCA minister and theologian
Rudder, John and Trixie	Missionary teachers in Arnhem Land
Schenk, Rudolphe (Rod)	Pioneer UAM missionary in the Goldfields
Scott, Bobby	Mt Margaret *Wangkayi* pastor and leader of the crusades
Sheppies	Rev. Harold and Mrs Ella Shepherdson: pioneer missionaries of Elcho Island mission and community; engineer and pilot, teacher and nurse
Smythe, Robin	Ngaanyatjarra Christian man
tongues	The supernatural ability to pray or speak in languages which the speaker has not learned. See Acts 2: 4, 1 Corinthians 12–14, especially 14: 26-28.
totem	[see also *rangga*] Animal, bird, fish, creature or object of spiritual significance to a group, often represented in ceremonies and songs. Carvings or paintings of them are sometimes referred to as totems also.
Tucker, Les	Goldfields Aboriginal Christian leader

UAICC	Uniting Aboriginal and Islander Christian Congress, part of the Uniting Church in Australia
UAM	United Aborigines Mission
UCA	Uniting Church in Australia, formed from the union of the Methodist, Presbyterian and Congregational churches in 1977
Wade, Will	Pioneer UAM missionary in the Central Desert
Wangkayi	[also spelt *'wongai'* or *'wongayi'*] Term used for Aborigines from the Goldfields and Central Desert
Warakurna	Ngaanyatjarra Aboriginal community
Warburton Ranges	Aboriginal mission/community (often called Ranges or Warburton) in the middle of the Central Desert, about halfway between Kalgoorlie and Alice Springs
Webb, Rev. T. Theodor	Pioneering missionary anthropologist in north-east Arnhem Land
Wili Golumala	Clan leader at Galiwin'ku; mission boat captain; father of Djiniyini; *dhuwa* moiety.
Williams, Bob	Aboriginal Christian pioneer in Western Australia
Williams, Ron and Diana	Aboriginal evangelist, elder and minister married to an American missionary teacher
Wirriyi	*Yolngu* elder
woomera	Spear thrower
yidaki	Didgeridoo — Djam.
yirritja	One of the two moieties or groupings of all life in north-eastern Arnhem Land
Yirrkala	Aboriginal community in Arnhem Land
Yolngu	Aborigine. Term used in north-eastern Arnhem Land for local Aborigines, but often used by them to refer to all Aborigines, in contrast to non-Aborigines.
Yolngu matha	Aboriginal words/tongue, i.e. language — Djam.

Endnotes

Introduction

1. Gelung Gondarra described the painting to the author in 1996 in this way:

God the Father is surrounded by his glory. From his mouth come the words he speaks which create and renew the world. He speaks a message through the wind, cloud, fire and all creation. The fire always symbolises the tongues of Holy Spirit fire which consume and refine our lives. In Aboriginal ceremonies, the tongues of fire are very significant, and symbolise purifying.

The Psalm talks of how God rides on the winds, and the clouds are his chariot. The wind is his messenger. We can feel and see and smell his message in the created world around us through the changing seasons, represented by the four winds. The flashes of lightning *[omitted from the painting]* are also his servants. Lightning has a similar message to the fire. It speaks God's word of judgement of sin.

Everything in creation lies on the foundation which is still to be fully discovered in every culture. God speaks, calling us to discover him through my *luku ngurrnggitj* [black roots/ashes]. In the ancient time, Aborigines lived there and we still see their ashes and lives for us to live by. Few people discover this truth and live by it. It is the pure culture.

God speaks to me through my *ngurrnggitjkurru* [blackness] so I can see God through an Aboriginal perspective. We can only take the things of God from our culture and leave all the rest to God's work. The Psalm talks about faith like a rock or foundation. The fire of the Holy Spirit surrounds the foundation rock

297

of God's word. It is shaped like the *bamurunggu* — the Golumala clan rock which represents wild honey and also fire.

2. Wirriyi, in discussion with the author, 1990 and with Margaret Miller, 1992
3. Buthimang, in discussion with the author, 1992
4. 1 Kings chapters 18 and 19

Chapter 1

1. Djiniyini Gondarra, in discussion with the author, 1995
2. Djiniyini Gondarra, in *Let My People Go*, 1986, p.iv
3. Djilipa, in discussion with the author, 1990, p.6
4. Rronang to the author, 1992
5. *Ibid*
6. Ron Williams, in correspondence with the author, March 1995
7. *Ibid*
8. *Ibid*
9. Ron Williams, in discussion the author, 24 May 1995
10. Dangatanga, in discussion the author, 1990
11. Noel Blyth, in a letter to the author, 1990
12. Ron Williams, in discussion with the author, March 1995
13. *Ibid*
14. L. Williams, in the *Sydney Morning Herald*, October 2, 1993, p.14
15. *Ibid*, p.14
16. *Ibid*, p.14
17. Ron Williams, in discussion with the author, 24 May 1995, p.2

Chapter 2

1. Kerry Medway, transcript address, September 1984
2. Ron Williams, in discussion with the author, 24 May 1995, p.2
3. T. Theodore Webb, 'Our Aboriginal Work', in the *Missionary Review*, Methodist Church, Sydney, 1940, pp.14-15
4. Djiniyini Gondarra, *Let My People Go*, Bethel Presytery, Darwin, 1986, p.2
5. Maisie McKenzie, *Mission to Arnhemland*, Rigby, 1976, p.216
6. Royal award: Member of the British Empire
7. Djiniyini Gondarra, in discussion with the author, 1995

8. Harry Makarrwala and T. Theodor Webb, *The Missionary Review*, Methodist Church, Sydney, 5 December 1942, pp.4-5
9. T. Theodor Webb, *op.cit.*, 5 August 1931, pp.4-7
10. *Ibid*
11. *Ibid*
12. *Ibid*, pp.4-7
13. *Op.cit*, 5 November 1931, p.5
14. Richard Trudgen, in discussion with the author, 13 August 1992
15. Ella Shepherdson, *Half a Century in Arnhemland*, 1981, p.23
16. *Ibid*
17. George Dayngumbu, in discussion with the author, April 1993
18. *Ibid*
19. *Ibid*; see also Ronald M. Berndt, *An Adjustment Movement in Arnhemland*, thesis, University of Western Australia, Mouton, 1962
20. George Dayngumbu, *op. cit.*, April 1993
21. *Ibid*
22. Djorrpum in *My Mother the Land*, 1980, pp.18-19
23. *Galiwin'ku Church News*, Uniting Church in Australia, 20 August 1972
24. *Ibid*

Chapter 3

1. Zechariah 13: 8-9
2. Ron Williams, in discussion with the author, 24 May 1995, p.2
3. Dianne Buchanan, 'Renewal in the Galiwinku (Elcho Island) Church', duplicated paper, 1980, p.1
4. John Rudder, in discussion with the the author, 24 February 1990
5. Dianne Buchanan, *op. cit.*, p.2
6. John Rudder, in Dianne Buchanan et al: Report to staff at Galiwin'ku, July 1990, p.14
7. Rhonda Loechel, in Dianne Buchanan, et al, *ibid*, p.18
8. John Rudder to the author, 24 February 1990, p.5. [The 'things described in the Bible' referred to are in 1 Corinthians 12: 8 and 14: 6 and other places.]
9. *Ibid*
10. Dianne Buchanan, *op. cit.*, p.2

11. John Rudder, *op. cit.*, p.5
12. Djiniyini Gondarra, *Let My People Go*, UCA, 1986, p.4
13. Richard Trudgeon, in discussion with the author, 13 August 1992
14. Djiniyini Gondarra, *op. cit.*
15. in Dianne Buchanan, et al, *ibid*
16. in Dianne Buchanan, et al, *ibid*, p.14
17. Dianne Buchanan, *ibid*
18. *Ibid*
19. in John Blacket et al, taped discussion, 4 June 1979, p.24
20. Djiniyini Gondarra, in discussion with the author, 17 August 1992
21. Djiniyini and Gelung Gondarra to the author, 20 March 1990 pp.6-10.
22. *Ibid*, pp.16-17
23. Dianne Buchanan, letter to friends at Yirrkala, 27 November 1978
24. Dianne Buchanan, newsletter, December 1978
25. James 5: 14-15
26. Joel 2: 20, RSV
27. Djilipa, in discussion with the author, 22 March 1990, pp.4-5
28. Bibuka to the author, April 1993
29. Nyiwula, in a written report to the author, January 1993, pp.1-2
30. *Ibid*, pp.2-3

Chapter 4

1. Djiniyini Gondarra, *Let My People Go*, UCA, 1986, pp.6-8
2. *Ibid*,p.5
3. *Ibid*,pp.8-9
4. Djawungdjawung, in discussion with the author, April 1993
5. Djiniyini Gondarra, *ibid*
6. John Blacket et al, taped discussion, 4 June 1979, p.14
7. Dianne Buchanan, diary, 1979
8. Dianne Buchanan, in a letter to John and Trixie Rudder, May 1979
9. Dianne Buchanan, in a letter to John and Trixie Rudder, 16 April 1979
10. Barbara and Barry Gullick, in a letter to John and June Blackett, 14 April 1979
11. John Blacket et al, *ibid*, p. 21

12. Dianne Buchanan, 'Renewal in the Galiwinku (Elcho Island) Church', 1980
13. Wendell and Mary Flentje, letter to the author, 1991
14. Dianne Buchanan, diary, 22 April, 1979
15. John Blacket et al, *ibid*, p. 18
16. Dianne Buchanan, diary, 1979
17. *Ibid*
18. Dianne Buchanan in letter to John and Trixie Rudder, May 1979
19. Rronang in taped interview with the author, August 1992, pp.1-8
20.
21. Dangatanga in taped interview with the author, 17 August 1990 pp.1-3
22. Dianne Buchanan, *ibid*
23. Djiniyini Gondarra, in taped interview with the author, p.14
24. Dianne Buchanan, diary, 5 May 1979
25. Dianne Buchanan, diary, 6 May 1979
26. Margaret Allen, in letter to the author, 22 May 1979
27. Dianne Buchanan, diary, 7 May 1979
28. Dianne Buchanan, in letter to John and Trixie Rudder, 16 April 1979
29. Dianne Buchanan, in letter to John and Trixie Rudder, May 1979
30. *Ibid*
31. Dan Armstrong, in *FFR Prayer Circular*, August 1979
32. Dianne Buchanan, *op. cit.*
33. Dan Armstrong, *op. cit.*
34. *Ibid*
35. Margaret Allen, in a letter to the author, 22 May 1979
36. Ro Yule, in a letter to the author, 29 May 1979
37. Dianne Buchanan, in a newsletter, 28 June 1979
38. Djiniyini Gondarra, in taped interview with the author, August 1990, p.16
39. Wendell and Mary Flentje, in a letter to the author, 8 April 1991
40. Rronang, in a taped interview with the author, August 1992
41. Dianne Buchanan, in her newsletter, 28 June 1979

Chapter 5

1. Djilipa, in a taped interview with the author, 22 March 1990, p.4
2. Wendell Flentje, in a letter to the author, 8 April 1991

3. Dianne Buchanan, in a newsletter, 12 December 1979
4. Djilipa, *op. cit.*, p.6
5. Dianne Buchanan, *op. cit.*, p.3
6. Dianne Buchanan, in a note to John and June Blacket, 12 December 1979
7. Rob Nance, in a letter to the author, 9 April 1991
8. Anna Edwards, in John Blacket et al, taped discussion, 4 June 1979, p.21
9. Djiniyini Gondarra, in a taped interview with the author, August 1990, p.12
10. Dangatanga, in a taped interview with the auther, 17 August 1990, pp.3-4
11. Dianne Buchanan, in her newsletter, September 1979
12. George Dangumbu, in a taped interview with the author, April 1993
13. Shane Blackman, in a taped address, November-December 1986
14. Djiniyini and Gelung Gondarra, in a taped interview with the author, August 1990, p.12.
15. *op. cit.*, p.13
16. Djiniyini and Gelung Gondarra, in an interview with the author, 18 March 1996
17. Margaret Dean to the author, 16 May 1991 and Dianne Buchanan, diary, 26 May 1979
18. Dangatanga in a taped interview with the author, 16 May 1990
19. Djiniyini and Gelung Gondarra, *op. cit.*
20. Carol Nance to the author, 26 March 1991
21. Dianne Buchanan, in her newsletter, 12 December 1979
22. Dianne Buchanan et al, taped report to staff, p.22
23. Dianne Buchanan, in her newsletter, November 1980
24. Dianne Buchanan, in her newsletter, 18 March 1980
25. *Ibid*
26. Joyce Ross in John Blacket et al, taped discussion, 4 June 1979, pp.8-9
27. Buthiman in a taped interview with the author, July 1990, pp.1-2
28. *Ibid*
29. Dianne Buchanan, in her newsletter, 12 December 1979
30. *Ibid*
31. *Ibid*
32. Dianne Buchanan, in her newsletter, November 1980

33. Carol Nance, in a letter to the author, 26 March 1991
34. Dan Armstrong, in a taped report to O'Connor Uniting Church, 29 March 1981
35. *Ibid*
36. *Ibid*
37. *Ibid*
38. Trixie Rudder, in a taped testimony to O'Connor Uniting Church, 29 March 1981, pp.2,4
39. *Op. cit.*, p.3
40. *Op. cit.*, pp.4-6
41. *Ibid*
42. *Op. cit.*, p.3
43. *Op. cit.*, p.6
44. Dan Armstrong, *op. cit.*

Chapter 6

1. Dianne Buchanan, in a letter to friends at Yirrkala, August 1979
2. Fred Forbes, in a taped interview with the author, 10 March 1992, pp.2-3
3. Amee Glass, in 'Christian Teaching and Response among the Ngaanyatjarra', duplicated paper, 1991. Details of the background on Warburton are taken from this paper.
4. Thelma Roberts, in a letter and report to the author, March 1992
5. Maimie Butler, in a taped iterview with the author, 10 March 1992
6. Thelma Roberts, *op. cit.*
7. In Alan Williams, 'On the Crest of a Wave', *On Being*, December 1984-January 1985, pp.9-10
8. 'Nyoongar' is the term used for the Aboriginal tribes people of the south-west area of Western Australia
9. 'Wangkayi' is a term used for Aborigines from the Goldfields and Central Desert, Western Australia
10. Ron Williams, *Nuggets from the Goldfields*, Centre Press, 1984, p.27
11. Wilfrid Douglas, in a letter to the Rev. David Morley, 1 October 1983
12. Herbert and Lorraine Howell, in a taped interview with the author, October 1991
13. *Ibid*

14. *Ibid*
15. Kevin Rrurrambu and John Blacket, in a taped report to missionaries, 1 September 1981
16. Herbert and Lorraine Howell, in a taped interview with the author, August 1991
17. Herbert Howell, Warburton Ranges Mission diary, September 1981
18. Herbert and Lorraine Howell, in a taped interview with the author, October 1991
19. Kevin Rrurrambu and John Blacket, *op. cit.*
20. Herbert and Lorraine Howell, *op. cit.*
21. Kevin Rrurrambu and John Blacket, *op. cit.*
22. Amee Glass, in Kevin Dhurrkay and John Blacket, *op. cit.*
23. Herbert Howell, in the Warburton Ranges Mission diary, September 1981
24. Alwyn Bates, in a taped interview with the author, 12 March 1992
25. Maimie Butler, *op. cit.*
26. In Thelma Roberts, in a note to the author, July 1993
27. Herbert Howell, *op. cit.*
28. Herbert and Lorraine Howell, *op. cit.*

Chapter 7

1. Mamie Butler, in a taped interview with the author, 10 March 1992
2. Thelma Roberts, in a letter and report to the author, March 1992
3. Ian Lindsay, *Fire in the Spinifex*, UAM, 1986, p. 15
4. Jeanette Balfe, in a letter to the author, 4 April 1992
5. Herbert Howell, author's notes from an interview, 10 March 1992
6. *Ibid*
7. Amee Glass and Dorothy Hackett, in a prayer letter, 23 December 1981
8. Amee Glass, 'Christian Teaching and Response among the Ngaanyatjarra', duplicated paper, 1991
9. Terry Robinson, taped interview wiith the author, 17 March 1992
10. Herbert and Lorraine Howell, in a taped interview with the author, October 1991
11. Robin Smythe, in a taped interview with the author, 13

March 1992
12. John Blacket, prayer notes, 18 November 1981
13. Thelma Roberts, in a letter and report to the author, March 1992
14. Galatians 5: 22
15. Djiniyini and Gelung Gondarra, in a taped interview with the author, August 1990, pp.10-11
16. *Ibid*
17. In Herbert Howell, in a taped interview with the author, August 1991, p.11
18. Djiniyini Gondarra, in a taped interview with the author, 12 March 1992, p.11
19. Thelma Roberts, *op. cit.*
20. *Ibid*
21. In Herbert Howell, in a taped interview with the author, August 1991, p.10
22. Isaiah 61: 3
23. Thelma Roberts in a letter and report to the author, March 1992
24. Robin Smythe, *op. cit.*
25. The passage is 2 Corinthians 5: 17: 'Anyone who belongs to Christ is a new person. The past is forgotten, and everything is new.'
26. Bernard Newbery, in a taped interview with the author, 10 March 1992, pp.1-2
27. Terry Robinson, in a taped interview with the author, 17 March 1992
28. *Op. cit.*, p.4
29. Bonnie Yates, in a taped interview with the author, 10 March 1992
30. Bernard Newbury, *op. cit.*, pp.2 and 32
31. Herbert Howell, *op. cit.*, pp.1-2
32. *Ibid*

Chapter 8

1. Ron Williams, *Nuggets from the Goldfields*, Centre Press, 1984, pp.1-2
2. *Op. cit.*, p.2
3. *Op. cit.*, pp.2, 8-12
4. *Op. cit.*, p.6
5. *Op. cit.*, pp.6-7

6. Information on Bob Williams is from Alan Williams, in a letter to the author, 20 July 1990

7. Matthew 5: 12

8. Bobby Scott, in a taped interview with the author, 11 October 1990, pp.1-2

9. *op. cit.*, pp.2-3

10. Claude Cotterill, in a taped interview with the author, April 1991

11. Ron Williams, *op. cit.*, p.27

12. Bobby Scott, *op. cit.*

13. Isaiah 54: 2

14. Bobby Scott, *op. cit.*, p.2

15. *op. cit.*, pp.2-3

16. Ian Lindsay, *Fire in the Spinifex*, UAM, 1986, p.18

17. Terry Robinson, in a taped interview with the author, 17 March 1992, pp.5-6

18. Bobby Scott, *op. cit.*, p.3

19. Alwyn Bates, in a taped interview with the author, 12 March 1992, p.2

20. Terry Robinson, *op. cit.*, pp.6-7

21. Ian Lindsay, *op. cit.*, p.20

22. *Ibid*, p.29

23. Les and Kathy Tucker, in a taped interview with the author, 5 March 1992

24. Ron Williams, *op. cit.*, p.28

25. Wilfred Douglas, in a conversation with the author, 4 March 1992

26. Phil Bodeker, *West Australian*, 10 April 1982

27. Jim Magnus, *Daily News*, 26 March 1982

28. Les Tucker, *op. cit.*, 1992

29. Cyril Barnes, in a taped interview with the author, April 1991

30. Bobby Scott, *op. cit.*, pp.3-4

31. Ian Lindsay, *op. cit.*, p.29

32. Bobby Scott, *op. cit.*, p.4

33. Ian Lindsay, *op. cit.*, p.30

34. Phil Bodeker, *West Australian*, 30 April 1982

35. Bobby Scott, *op. cit.*

36. Ron and Del Abbott, in a taped interview with the author, August 1992

37. *Ibid*

38. *Ibid*

39. *Ibid*
40. Terry Robinson, *op. cit.*
41. Bobby Scott, *op. cit.*
42. *Op. cit.*, p.3
43. *Op. cit.*, pp.3-4
44. Ron Williams, *op. cit.*, p.28
45. Les and Kathy Tucker, *op. cit.*, p.2
46. Terry Robinson, *op. cit*, pp.5-6
47. Bobby Scott, *op. cit.*, p.4
48. Ian Lindsay, *op. cit.*, p.31
49. Terry Robinson, *op. cit.*, pp.5-6
50. Alwyn Bates, *op. cit.*
51. Bernard Newbery, in a taped interview with the author, 10 March 1992, p.3
52. Terry Robinson, *op. cit.*, pp.5-6
53. Philippians 3: 5
54. Bobby Scott, *op. cit.*, p.10
55. Ron and Del Abbott, *op. cit.*
56. Bobby Scott, *op. cit.*, p.8
57. Ron and Del Abbott, *op. cit.*
58. *Op. cit.*
59. Terry Robinson, *op. cit.*, p.4
60. Bobby Scott, *op. cit.*, pp.12-13
61. Terry Robinson, *op. cit.*, pp.3-4
62. Donny Robinson, in discussion with the author, 1992
63. Terry Robinson,*op. cit.*, pp.2-3
64. Elaine Munroe, *op. cit.*, pp.1-2
65. Les and Kathy Tucker, *op. cit.*, p.2
66. Ron and Del Abbott, *op. cit.*
67. Matthew 28: 19
68. Bobby Scott, *op. cit.*, p.2

Chapter 9

1. Djiniyini Gondarra, *Let My People Go*, UCA, 1986, pp.10-11
2. Amee Glass, 'Christian Teaching and Response among the Ngaanyatjarra', duplicated paper, 1991
3. Dianne Buchanan, in a taped interview with the author, 8 August 1990, p.4
4. Lawrie Edwards, in a conversation with the author, 2 September 1995
5. Dianne Buchanan, in a letter to a friend in Yirrkala, July 1979

6. Robert Capp, 'Church Planting and Nurture in Central Australia', photocopied paper, 17 January 1995, p.9

7. Richard Trudgen, in a taped interview with the author, 13 August 1992

8. *op. cit.*

9. *op. cit.*

10. Herbert Howell, personal conversation, 1995

11. Dan and Sue Armstrong, in 'The Revival Today', a report written to the author in March 1995, p.3

12. Acts 5: 38-39

13. In Ron Abbott, in an interview with the author, August 1992

14. *Ibid*

15. *Ibid*

16. *Ibid*

17. 1 Corinthians 7: 20, CEV

18. Bernard Newbery, in Herbert Howell's taped interview with the author, August 1991, p.11

19. Bernard Newbery, in a taped interview with the author, 10 March 1992, p.3

20. Herbert Howell, in a discussion with the author, March 1992, p.4

21. Ron and Del Abbott, *op. cit.*

Chapter 10

1. Ron Williams, in a transcript to the author, March 1995, p.2

2. Djiniyini Gondarra, in a taped interview with the author, 17 August 1992

3. Ian Lindsay, *Fire in the Spinifex*, UAM, 1986, p.34

4. Ron Williams, *op. cit.*, pp.1-2

5. Dan and Sue Armstrong, 'The Revival Today', a report written to the author, March 1995, p.5

6. Djiniyini Gondarra, *My Mother the Land*, UCA, 1980, pp.8-9

7. Robin Nance, in a letter to the author, 9 April 1991

8. Richard Trudgeon, in a taped interview with the author, 13 August 1992

9. 1 Samuel 4: 21

10. Terry Robinson, in a taped interview with the author, 17 March 1992

11. Ian Lindsay, *op. cit.*, p.41

12. *Op. cit.*, pp.41-43

13. *Op. cit.*, p.36

14. Robin Nance, *op. cit.*
15. Herbert Howell, in a taped interview with the author, 12 March 1992, p.2
16. Amee Glass and Dorothy Hackett, prayer letter, June 1985
17. Amee Glass and Dorothy Hackett, prayer letter, 1 January 1986
18. Dianne Buchanan, newsletter, 12 December 1979
19. Dianne Buchanan, in a taped interview with the author, 8 August 1990
20. Dangatanga, in a taped interview with the author, 17 August 1990
21. Sylvia Richards, in a letter to Bible translators, 1984
22. 1 Kings 16–21
23. Djiniyini and Gelung Gondarra, in an interview with the author, 27 March 1990
24. George Dayngumbu, in a taped interview with the author, April 1993
25. Djiniyini Gondarra and Dangatanga, in a taped interview with the author, 22 March 1990
26. Djiniyini and Gelung Gondarra, 1996
27. Djiniyini and Gelung Gondarra, in an interview with the author, 22 March 1990
28. Dianne Buchanan, newsletter, January 1990
29. Dianne Buchanan, in a taped interview with the author, August 1992
30. Australian term for a large, deep patch of very fine, soft dirt, often found in a firm gravel road.
31. John Blacket, 'It's War', *Khesed News*, February 1991
32. Djiniyini Gondarra and Dangatanga, in a taped interview with the author, 22 March 1990
33. Terry Robinson, in a taped interview with the author, 17 March 1992

Chapter 11

1. Djiniyini Gondarra, *Let My People Go*, UCA, 1986, p.14
2. Djiniyini Gondarra, in a taped interview with the author, 17 August 1992
3. Isaiah 43: 19-21
4. 2 Chronicles 7: 14
5. Herbert and Lorraine Howell, in a taped interview with the author, October 1991, pp.5-6

6. Djiniyini Gondarra, *Let My People Go,*UCA, 1986, p.10
7. Djiniyini Gondarra, in a taped interview with the author, 17 August 1992
8. Ron Williams, in a tape message to the author, March 1995, p.2
9. George Dayngumbu, in a taped interview with the author, April 1993
10. Alan Maratja, in a taped interview with the author, 5 April 1993
11. Margaret Miller, in a taped interview with the author, 1993
12. George Dayngumbu, *op. cit.*
13. Djiniyini Gondarra, *Let My People Go*, UCA, 1986, p.22
14. *Op. cit.*, p.5
15. *Op. cit.*, pp.20-21
16. Matthew 5: 17
17. Djiniyini Gondarra, *op. cit.*, p.31
18. *Op. cit.*, p.33
19. Robert Capp, in a taped interview with the author, 14 March 1992, p.1
20. Dianne Buchanan, in a taped interview with the author, 8 August 1990, p.15
21. Djiniyini Gondarra, *op. cit.*, p.34
22. Luke 4: 18-19
23. Djiniyini Gondarra, *op. cit.*, p.35
24. Ron Williams, *Nuggets from the Goldfields*, Centre Press, 1984, pp.16-18, 34-36
25. Adele Babbage, in a report written to the author, March 1995
26. Bill Bird, 'Road to Reconciliation', *On Being*, December 1993–January 1994, p.28
27. Bill Bird, *op. cit.*, pp.22-24
28. Ron Williams, in a taped message to the author, March 1995, p.5
29. In Alan Williams, 'On the Crest of a Wave', *Australia's New Day*, December 1984/January 1985, p.8
30. Dan Armstrong, in 'Dan Armstrong's Story of the Elcho Island Revival', *Australia's New Day*, November 1984, p.15
31. Ron Williams, in a taped message to the author, 24 May 1995

Acknowledgements of photographs

Sue Armstrong, p.107

The Berndt Museum of Anthropology,
    University of Western Australia, pp.62–63

The Bible Society, p.218

The *Centralian Advocate*, p.254

Dianne Buchanan, p.129

Gelung Gondarra, p.21

Ian Lindsay, p.182

Margaret Miller, pp.114

Khesed Ministries/Michael Chambers, pp.172, 239, 264

Ian Morris, p.219

Dorothy Nyiwula, p.83

Thelma Roberts, pp.178

John Rudder, Elcho Island map

John and Trixie Rudder, p.68

Rev. Harold Shepherdson, pp.35, 39, 42, 45, 49, 50, 52, 59, 60

Peter Soet, p.148

Michael Tayler, p.143

Nungalinya College, p.268

John Waterhouse, back cover

The West Australian, p.197

All other photos, including front cover photograph, and maps are copyright: John Blacket/Khesed Ministries Inc., WA.

Index

References in bold are key references

12

Reflections

Many people have described this movement as the first revival ever seen in Australia. But there was a real heritage of the Holy Spirit's presence in this land before 1979. Holy Spirit was here before white man came, even if the Aboriginal people didn't know and respect Him or even know His name.

Back in 1606 there was a prophetic declaration over the islands of the South Pacific – including the undiscovered land of Australia. 14th May 1606 was Pentecost Sunday - the day when we celebrate the first outpouring of the Holy Spirit on the early church – and De Quiros had arrived at Vanuatu. He and his crew declared these islands to be 'Terra Australis del Espirtu Santo' – 'The Southern Land of the Holy Spirit'. Muskets were fired and the men shouted with joy 'Long live the faith of Christ'.

The historic Holy Spirit 'outpouring' at Asuza Street in USA is regarded as the birth of the modern Pentecostal movement, but there were similar events in Australia even before that. Barry Chant, Australian Pentecostal historian wrote,* 'The earliest pioneer of aggressive belief in the supernatural power of God in this country was John Alexander Dowie. He was a man †of faith and vision who dared to attempt great things for God. He built big churches here in Australia and managed to establish a whole city in the United States.' In 1888 Dowie moved from Australia to USA and later attracted 10,000 to move to his Christian city, just north of Chicago.

Chant also records remarkable outpouring of the Holy Spirit back in 1862 at the Pirie Street Methodist Church in Adelaide with John Watsford, the first Australian-born Methodist minister, as well as other early moves of the Holy Spirit.

---

* Dr Barry Chant, 'Building with God' in *Church on Fire*, ed. Geoff Waugh, Joint Board of Christian Education, 1991, p99. See also his chapter in *Reviving Australia*; ed. Mark Hutchinson, Edmund Campion & Stuart Piggin, published by the Centre for the Study of Australian Christianity, 1994, pp 97-122. Barry's books include *Heart of Tire – a history of Pentecostalism in Australia'*.

Possibly indigenous Australians took a keen part in some of this, but I have also become aware recently of a powerful move of God among indigenous Australians around 1930 at Pinnacle Pocket on the Atherton Tablelands in north Queensland. We are just beginning to piece together reports of this move, which is still having an impact today, sending out many of the indigenous Christian leaders of the last fifty years into the nation. They have been people of real faith and power, like Ps. Peter Morgan in Darwin, Ps. Tim Edward's father, and Ps Norm Miller's mother. Ps Peter Walker's father was also involved in a similar movement in northern New South Wales in the early-mid 20th century.

During the 1990s there have been a number of significant moves of God's Spirit among indigenous people: Mornington Island, Queensland, the Pilbara and Kimberley regions in Western Australia, and, more recently, in Cairns. In some towns the police and hotels suddenly found themselves with little work because of attitude changes. One publican was complaining to the media that his livelihood had been destroyed. In one town a new million-dollar police station suddenly seemed to be a white elephant.

In the Introduction (p23), I mentioned the vision of revival in Australia, which I had in January 1979. The revival began as a spark at Elcho Island and lit fires all over the land, going from black to black, and from black to white all over the land, renewing the land and going beyond Australia to other lands.

That fire has gone to many parts of Australia and touched many non-Aborigines. Aboriginal Christians have held regular conventions in parks, showgrounds, churches and even in the Great Hall of Parliament House in the nation's capital. Politicians have told indigenous leaders that the prayer, worship and ministry of their *Praise Corroboree* were vitally important to the nation and must continue in Parliament House. Indigenous Christians are beginning to be heard by the nation's leaders.

In 2002, God brought a vision He gave to Ps Tim Edwards to fulfillment, with the first *World of Worship*, held in the Cairns Convention Centre. It was the first real partnership in ministry between the internationally famous worship team from *Hillsong* with indigenous people, and they were thrilled to be involved and all really learned to appreciate each other. Many thought it would be a second-rate event because indigenous people were leading it, but even the Convention Centre staff praised the leaders and all their group very highly above almost all their events.

Indigenous Christians have been involved beyond Australia in various ways for many years, but it is increasing rapidly. Some have taught at Haggai Institute, which trains indigenous leadership from many nations. Australian Aborigines have spoken, sung, played the didgeridoo, danced and ministered in PNG, Africa, UK, USA, Philippines, Malaysia, Fiji, NZ, Canada, Israel, Germany and many other nations. I have heard that the Pinnacle Pocket church is responsible for planting a church in New Guinea that has been going for many years.

Sometime around 1996, Ps Peter Compton took a tall Yugoslav elder from his church in Perth to minister with him in the PNG highlands. Peter is short and dark-skinned and melted in with the Highlanders, but Victor really stood out, and the people were expecting him to preach and lead. But they could hardly get a word out of Victor in public: he carried Peter's Bible for him and brought him cups of tea while Peter taught and preached his fiery messages! It broke the stereotypes of the mission era, and encouraged the Highlanders to find their place in ministry.

In 1996 in Rotorua, New Zealand, another vision became a reality as a Maori, Monte Ohia, convened the *1st World Christian Gathering on Indigenous People*. Indigenous people and their friends from around the world gathered to explore their faith and practices and encourage each other in each of their unique forms of worship. Two years later, it was time for the North American indigenous people to host the 2nd WCGIP in Dakota, USA, and then in January 2000 the third Gathering was held in Sydney, hosted by Aborigines.

These events are continuing every two years, providing a point of real release for indigenous people in their own Christian walk, but also in releasing their ministry to the world. It has been amazing to hear reports of the ministry opportunities which the North American indigenous people have had since that Gathering in Sydney!

It takes a lot of organisation, finance, prayer and effort for these events and ministries to take place, and some are really struggling. Some of the conventions like the Central Australian Christian Convention have run their season and closed down. Many Aboriginal communities are in a total social mess, with youth suicide at an alarming rate [unknown among Aborigines in the past], political fights and court cases, and a sense of hopelessness. The governments are really struggling to find answers to indigenous crime, major health problems, drug taking, poor education, unemployment....

Some years ago, Ps Tim Edwards was asking God, 'Where do we go from here? We have had many government policies like segregation, assimilation, self-management and reconciliation, and they have all failed!' The reply has been affirmed all over the world: 'Partnership'.

It is only when we realise that we need each other and come to really appreciate each other's gifts and abilities, that we can respect and work together as the Body of Jesus Christ, doing His work in His way effectively.

> *Without its feet, the church is crippled in a wheelchair*
> *- needlessly*
> *Without its hands, the church is handicapped - needlessly.*

It's time we realised the gifts God has put in His church are spread around the different people-groups for a purpose, and we got on with the job of sharing God's love and truth around to all people – in partnership together.

Other resources available from bookshops

or direct from *Khesed Publications*

PO Box 448 Cannington Western Australia 6987
admin@khesed.org.au   Website: khesed.org.au

Khesed: God's covenant love poured out on all mankind

Rebuilding nations through partnership in Jesus Christ

God's Story   80 minute DVD of the story in the Bible from Creation and the Fall through to the end of time. An Australian version of this classic that has brought many thousands of Buddhists, Hindus, Muslims, tribal people and non-religious people to accept the Truth of God's Word and trust in Jesus Christ.
Further details from   www.gods-story.org

God's Feet   Booklet and DVD by John Blacket
Limping under the crippling power of shame, sorcery and curses, or dancing in God's blessings and glory.

God's Dirt   A booklet and DVD that comes from a drawing in the sand telling indigenous people how God's dirt is sick, so He can't bless us, and what can be done to bring transformation.
God's blood covenant with mankind through Jesus Christ

Chosen - By God to Redeem Cultures

320 pages with 79 colour photos and a wealth of very timely and significant stories and teaching from indigenous people from around the world on our stewardship of God's land and His ways and protocols for living together and reaching out to the world in His power and effectiveness. From the 3rd World Christian Gathering on Indigenous Peoples in Sydney

One Lord - Different Cultures

- a 52 page simpler-English, shorter version of *Chosen*, with photos.
Also available as a 55 minute DVD.

In Preparation – 2010 releases:

• CD/MP3 book reading of *Fire in the Outback* by the author
• DVD telling this indigenous revival-fire story, including up-to-date details from other parts of the nation.